This book is due on the last date stamped below.
Failure to return books on the date due m~
in assessment of overdue fees

DEC ⁊

American River College Library
4700 College Oak Drive
Sacramento, CA 95841

BLOOM'S
HOW TO WRITE ABOUT

Herman Melville

LAURIE A. STERLING

BLOOM'S
LITERARY CRITICISM
An imprint of Infobase Publishing

Bloom's How to Write about Herman Melville

Copyright © 2009 by Laurie A. Sterling

All rights reserved. No part of this book may be reproduced or utilized in any form or by any means, electronic or mechanical, including photocopying, recording, or by any information storage or retrieval systems, without permission in writing from the publisher. For information contact:

Bloom's Literary Criticism
An imprint of Infobase Publishing
132 West 31st Street
New York NY 10001

Library of Congress Cataloging-in-Publication Data

Sterling, Laurie A.
  Bloom's how to write about Herman Melville / Laurie A. Sterling ; introduction by Harold Bloom.
      p. cm.—(Bloom's how to write about literature)
  Includes bibliographical references and index.
  ISBN 978-0-7910-9744-1 (acid-free paper) 1. Melville, Herman, 1819–1891—Criticism and interpretation. 2. Criticism—Authorship. 3. Report writing. I. Bloom, Harold. II. Title. III. Title: How to write about Herman Melville. IV. Title: Herman Melville. V. Series.
  PS2387.S69 2009
  813'.3—dc22   2008005708

Bloom's Literary Criticism books are available at special discounts when purchased in bulk quantities for businesses, associations, institutions, or sales promotions. Please call our Special Sales Department in New York at (212) 967-8800 or (800) 322-8755.

You can find Bloom's Literary Criticism on the World Wide Web
at http://www.chelseahouse.com

Text design by Annie O'Donnell
Cover design by Ben Peterson

Printed in the United States of America

Bang MSRF 10 9 8 7 6 5 4 3 2 1

This book is printed on acid-free paper.

CONTENTS

SERIES
INTRODUCTION

BLOOM's How to Write about Literature series is designed to inspire students to write fine essays on great writers and their works. Each volume in the series begins with an introduction by Harold Bloom, meditating on the challenges and rewards of writing about the volume's subject author. The first chapter then provides detailed instructions on how to write a good essay, including how to find a thesis; how to develop an outline; how to write a good introduction, body text, and conclusions; how to cite sources; and more. The second chapter provides a brief overview of the issues involved in writing about the subject author and then a number of suggestions for paper topics, with accompanying strategies for addressing each topic. Succeeding chapters cover the author's major works.

The paper topics suggested within this book are open-ended, and the brief strategies provided are designed to give students a push forward on the writing process rather than a road map to success. The aim of the book is to pose questions, not answer them. Many different kinds of papers could result from each topic. As always, the success of each paper will depend completely on the writer's skill and imagination.

HOW TO WRITE ABOUT HERMAN MELVILLE: INTRODUCTION

THE REWARD of writing well about Herman Melville owes a great deal to the rugged challenges. Though Melville is anything but a one-book author, all of us associate him, initially and finally, with his masterpiece, *Moby-Dick*. His genius irradiates that American prose epic, one of our nation's inescapable literary works, together with *Leaves of Grass*, *Huckleberry Finn*, *The Scarlet Letter*, *Walden*, Emerson's *Essays*, and Emily Dickinson's poetry. The 20th century added Faulkner's major novels, the best fictions of Hemingway and Scott Fitzgerald, some plays by O'Neill, and the poetry of Robert Frost, Wallace Stevens, and Hart Crane. Of all these, only Walt Whitman's metamorphic *Leaves* outshines *Moby-Dick*, in my judgment.

Moby-Dick perpetually challenges readers, partly by bold appropriations from Shakespeare and the British High Romantics, Byron and Shelley, but also by its even bolder ambitions to rival the great works of the Western epic tradition: the Bible, Homer, Virgil, Dante, Spenser, Cervantes, and Milton. A citizen of Andrew Jackson's and Lincoln's America, Melville deliberately democratized the epic, making Ahab, his mates, and harpooners, and the rest of his crew, into figures of aesthetic dignity comparable to biblical and Homeric heroes. Captain Ahab fuses aspects of Odysseus, Don Quixote, Macbeth, and Milton's Satan and is clearly an exemplary quester for Melville's own vision, though many misguided

Melville scholars regard the *Pequod*'s commander more as villain than as hero. That has not been my own reading experience from childhood on.

I do not know how many times I have reread *Moby-Dick* in the two-thirds of a century since my first encounter with it, but I have just finished it again and could not avoid identifying both with Ahab and with the narrator, Ishmael, two very different figures. No one wants to sympathize with Macbeth, but, nevertheless, he uniquely captures the anticipatory element in the imagination of each of us. Ahab also ensnares that faculty of spirit, in a vivid imitation of Shakespeare's extraordinary art. To write about Ahab is an adventure in confronting Shakespeare's influence on Melville.

Part of the reward is to understand both Macbeth and Captain Ahab better, once you have explored both their differences and their similarities. Melville found in Shakespeare the true entrance to the labyrinthine enigmas of human nature, subtlest of guides to the exploration of our end and destiny. Ahab, seeking to strike through the mask of appearances, finds in the White Whale the principle of a divinely ordained tyranny, the universe of death. As dispassionate in judging Ahab as Shakespeare was in regard to Macbeth, Melville does not allow his surrogate Ishmael to narrate the final three-day chase of Moby Dick by the *Pequod*. Ishmael returns in a Jobian epilogue to establish himself as the inevitable survivor of the destruction caused by the White Whale's triumph.

To write usefully about *Moby-Dick*, you first must make a provisional pact with yourself. How are *you* to achieve a dispassionate stance toward the darkest of American epics? At different moments, in my own critical career, Ahab has seemed to me a Promethean hero like William Blake's Orc, the spirit of revolt, or a hero-villain in Macbeth's wake. Now I find he is neither or alternately both. From Shakespeare, Melville learned how to distance himself from his own creation, though he realized that the uncanny Shakespearean disinteredness forever was beyond him. To write about *Moby-Dick*, we also need to cultivate a deep reader's passionate disinteredness, even if we never can attain that difficult stance.

HOW TO WRITE A GOOD ESSAY

By Laurie A. Sterling

WHILE THERE are many ways to write about literature, most assignments for high school and college English classes call for analytical papers. In these assignments, you are presenting your interpretation of a text to your reader. Your objective is to interpret the text's meaning in order to enhance your reader's understanding and enjoyment of the work. Without exception, strong papers about the meaning of a literary work are built upon a careful, close reading of the text or texts. Careful, analytical reading should always be the first step in your writing process. This volume provides models of such close, analytical reading, and these should help you develop your own skills as a reader and as a writer.

As the examples throughout this book demonstrate, attentive reading entails thinking about and evaluating the formal (textual) aspects of the author's works: theme, character, form, and language. In addition, when writing about a work, many readers choose to move beyond the text itself to consider the work's cultural context. In these instances, writers might explore the historical circumstances of the time period in which the work was written. Alternatively, they might examine the philosophies and ideas that a work addresses. Even in cases where writers explore a work's cultural context, though, papers must still address the more formal aspects of the work itself. A good interpretative essay that evaluates Charles Dickens's use of the philosophy of utilitarianism in his novel *Hard Times,* for example, cannot adequately address the author's treatment of the philosophy without firmly grounding this discussion in the book itself. In other words, any

1

analytical paper about a text, even one that seeks to evaluate the work's cultural context, must also have a firm handle on the work's themes, characters, and language. You must look for and evaluate these aspects of a work, then, as you read a text and as you prepare to write about it.

WRITING ABOUT THEMES

Literary themes are more than just topics or subjects treated in a work; they are attitudes or points about these topics that often structure other elements in a work. Writing about theme therefore requires that you not just identify a topic that a literary work addresses but also discuss what that work says about that topic. For example, if you were writing about the culture of the American South in William Faulkner's famous story "A Rose for Emily," you would need to discuss what Faulkner says, argues, or implies about that culture and its passing.

When you prepare to write about thematic concerns in a work of literature, you will probably discover that, like most works of literature, your text touches upon other themes in addition to its central theme. These secondary themes also provide rich ground for paper topics. A thematic paper on "A Rose for Emily" might consider gender or race in the story. While neither of these could be said to be the central theme of the story, they are clearly related to the passing of the "Old South" and could provide plenty of good material for papers.

As you prepare to write about themes in literature, you might find a number of strategies helpful. After you identify a theme or themes in the story, you should begin by evaluating how other elements of the story—such as character, point of view, imagery, and symbolism—help develop the theme. You might ask yourself what your own responses are to the author's treatment of the subject matter. Do not neglect the obvious, either: What expectations does the title set up? How does the title help develop thematic concerns? Clearly, the title "A Rose for Emily" says something about the narrator's attitude toward the title character, Emily Grierson, and all she represents.

WRITING ABOUT CHARACTER

Generally, characters are essential components of fiction and drama. (This is not always the case, though; Ray Bradbury's "August 2026: There

Will Come Soft Rains" is technically a story without characters, at least any human characters.) Often, you can discuss character in poetry, as in T. S. Eliot's "The Love Song of J. Alfred Prufrock" or Robert Browning's "My Last Duchess." Many writers find that analyzing character is one of the most interesting and engaging ways to work with a piece of literature and to shape a paper. After all, characters generally are human, and we all know something about being human and living in the world. While it is always important to remember that these figures are not real people but creations of the writer's imagination, it can be fruitful to begin evaluating them as you might evaluate a real person. Often you can start with your own response to a character. Did you like or dislike the character? Did you sympathize with the character? Why or why not?

Keep in mind, though, that emotional responses like these are just starting places. To truly explore and evaluate literary characters, you need to return to the formal aspects of the text and evaluate how the author has drawn these characters. The 20th-century writer E. M. Forster coined the terms *flat* characters and *round* characters. Flat characters are static, one-dimensional characters who frequently represent a particular concept or idea. In contrast, round characters are fully drawn and much more realistic characters who frequently change and develop over the course of a work. Are the characters you are studying flat or round? What elements of the characters lead you to this conclusion? Why might the author have drawn characters like this? How does their development affect the meaning of the work? Similarly, you should explore the techniques the author uses to develop characters. Do we hear a character's own words, or do we hear only other characters' assessments of him or her? Or, does the author use an omniscient or limited omniscient narrator to allow us access to the workings of the characters' minds? If so, how does that help develop the characterization? Often you can even evaluate the narrator as a character. How trustworthy are the opinions and assessments of the narrator? You should also think about characters' names. Do they mean anything? If you encounter a hero named Sophia or Sophie, you should probably think about her wisdom (or lack thereof), since *Sophia* means "wisdom" in Greek. Similarly, since the name *Sylvia* is derived from the word *sylvan,* meaning "of the wood," you might want to evaluate that character's relationship with nature. Once again, you might look to the title of the work. Does Herman Melville's "Bartleby, the Scrivener" signal anything about Bartleby himself? Is Bartleby adequately defined by his job as scrivener? Is this part of Melville's point? Pursuing questions like these can help you develop thorough papers about characters from psychological, sociological, or more formalistic perspectives.

WRITING ABOUT FORM AND GENRE

Genre, a word derived from French, means "type" or "class." Literary genres are distinctive classes or categories of literary composition. On the most general level, literary works can be divided into the genres of drama, poetry, fiction, and essays, yet within those genres there are classifications that are also referred to as genres. Tragedy and comedy, for example, are genres of drama. Epic, lyric, and pastoral are genres of poetry. *Form,* on the other hand, generally refers to the shape or structure of a work. There are many clearly defined forms of poetry that follow specific patterns of meter, rhyme, and stanza. Sonnets, for example, are poems that follow a fixed form of 14 lines. Sonnets generally follow one of two basic sonnet forms, each with its own distinct rhyme scheme. Haiku is another example of poetic form, traditionally consisting of three unrhymed lines of five, seven, and five syllables.

While you might think that writing about form or genre might leave little room for argument, many of these forms and genres are very fluid. Remember that literature is evolving and ever changing, and so are its forms. As you study poetry, you may find that poets, especially more modern poets, play with traditional poetic forms, bringing about new effects. Similarly, dramatic tragedy was once quite narrowly defined, but over the centuries playwrights have broadened and challenged traditional definitions, changing the shape of tragedy. When Arthur Miller wrote *Death of a Salesman,* many critics challenged the idea that tragic drama could encompass a common man like Willy Loman.

Evaluating how a work of literature fits into or challenges the boundaries of its form or genre can provide you with fruitful avenues of investigation. You might find it helpful to ask why the work does or does not fit into traditional categories. Why might Miller have thought it fitting to write a tragedy of the common man? Similarly, you might compare the content or theme of a work with its form. How well do they work together? Many of Emily Dickinson's poems, for instance, follow the meter of traditional hymns. While some of her poems seem to express traditional religious doctrines, many seem to challenge or strain against traditional conceptions of God and theology. What is the effect, then, of her use of traditional hymn meter?

WRITING ABOUT LANGUAGE, SYMBOLS, AND IMAGERY

No matter what the genre, writers use words as their most basic tool. Language is the most fundamental building block of literature. It is essential that you pay careful attention to the author's language and word choice as you read, reread, and analyze a text. Imagery is language that appeals to the senses. Most commonly, imagery appeals to our sense of vision, creating a mental picture, but authors also use language that appeals to our other senses. Images can be literal or figurative. Literal images use sensory language to describe an actual thing. In the broadest terms, figurative language uses one thing to speak about something else. For example, if I call my boss a snake, I am not saying that he is literally a reptile. Instead, I am using figurative language to communicate my opinions about him. Since we think of snakes as sneaky, slimy, and sinister, I am using the concrete image of a snake to communicate these abstract opinions and impressions.

The two most common figures of speech are similes and metaphors. Both are comparisons between two apparently dissimilar things. Similes are explicit comparisons using the words *like* or *as*; metaphors are implicit comparisons. To return to the previous example, if I say, "My boss, Bob, was waiting for me when I showed up to work five minutes late today—the snake!" I have constructed a metaphor. Writing about his experiences fighting in World War I, Wilfred Owen begins his poem "Dulce et decorum est" with a string of similes: "Bent double, like old beggars under sacks, / Knock-kneed, coughing like hags, we cursed through sludge." Owen's goal was to undercut clichéd notions that war and dying in battle were glorious. Certainly, comparing soldiers to coughing hags and to beggars underscores his point.

"Fog," a short poem by Carl Sandburg provides a clear example of a metaphor. Sandburg's poem reads:

The fog comes
on little cat feet.

It sits looking
over harbor and city
on silent haunches
and then moves on.

Notice how effectively Sandburg conveys surprising impressions of the fog by comparing two seemingly disparate things—the fog and a cat.

Symbols, by contrast, are things that stand for, or represent, other things. Often they represent something intangible, such as concepts or ideas. In everyday life we use and understand symbols easily. Babies at christenings and brides at weddings wear white to represent purity. Think, too, of a dollar bill. The paper itself has no value in and of itself. Instead, that paper bill is a symbol of something else, the precious metal in a nation's coffers. Symbols in literature work similarly. Authors use symbols to evoke more than a simple, straightforward, literal meaning. Characters, objects, and places can all function as symbols. Famous literary examples of symbols include Moby Dick, the white whale of Herman Melville's novel, and the scarlet *A* of Nathaniel Hawthorne's *The Scarlet Letter.* As both of these symbols suggest, a literary symbol cannot be adequately defined or explained by any one meaning. Hester Prynne's Puritan community clearly intends her scarlet *A* as a symbol of her adultery, but as the novel progresses, even her own community reads the letter as representing not just *adultery,* but *able, angel,* and a host of other meanings.

Writing about imagery and symbols requires close attention to the author's language. To prepare a paper on symbolism or imagery in a work, identify and trace the images and symbols and then try to draw some conclusions about how they function. Ask yourself how any symbols or images help contribute to the themes or meanings of the work. What connotations do they carry? How do they affect your reception of the work? Do they shed light on characters or settings? A strong paper on imagery or symbolism will thoroughly consider the use of figures in the text and will try to reach some conclusions about how or why the author uses them.

WRITING ABOUT HISTORY AND CONTEXT

As noted above, it is possible to write an analytical paper that also considers the work's context. After all, the text was not created in a vacuum. The author lived and wrote in a specific time period and in a specific cultural context and, like all of us, was shaped by that environment. Learning more about the historical and cultural circumstances that surround the author and the work can help illuminate a text and provide you with productive material for a paper. Remember, though, that when you write analytical papers, you should use the context to illuminate the text. Do not lose sight of your goal—to interpret the meaning of the literary work. Use historical or philosophical research as a tool to develop your textual evaluation.

Thoughtful readers often consider how history and culture affected the author's choice and treatment of his or her subject matter. Investigations into the history and context of a work could examine the work's relation to specific historical events, such as the Salem witch trials in 17th-century Massachusetts or the restoration of Charles to the British throne in 1660. Bear in mind that historical context is not limited to politics and world events. While knowing about the Vietnam War is certainly helpful in interpreting much of Tim O'Brien's fiction, and some knowledge of the French Revolution clearly illuminates the dynamics of Charles Dickens's *A Tale of Two Cities*, historical context also entails the fabric of daily life. Examining a text in light of gender roles, race relations, class boundaries, or working conditions can give rise to thoughtful and compelling papers. Exploring the conditions of the working class in 19th-century England, for example, can provide a particularly effective avenue for writing about Dickens's *Hard Times*.

You can begin thinking about these issues by asking broad questions at first. What do you know about the time period and about the author? What does the editorial apparatus in your text tell you? These might be starting places. Similarly, when specific historical events or dynamics are particularly important to understanding a work but might be somewhat obscure to modern readers, textbooks usually provide notes to explain historical background. These are a good place to start. With this information, ask yourself how these historical facts and circumstances might have affected the author, the presentation of theme, and the presentation of character. How does knowing more about the work's specific historical context illuminate the work? To take a well-known example, understanding the complex attitudes toward slavery during the time Mark Twain wrote *Adventures of Huckleberry Finn* should help you begin to examine issues of race in the text. Additionally, you might compare these attitudes to those of the time in which the novel was set. How might this comparison affect your interpretation of a work written after the abolition of slavery but set before the Civil War?

WRITING ABOUT PHILOSOPHY AND IDEAS

Philosophical concerns are closely related to both historical context and thematic issues. Like historical investigation, philosophical research can provide a useful tool as you analyze a text. For example, an investigation into the working class in Dickens's England might lead you to a topic on the philosophical doctrine of utilitarianism in *Hard Times*. Many other works explore philosophies and ideas quite explicitly. Mary Shelley's famous novel *Frankenstein,* for example, explores John Locke's tabula rasa theory of human knowledge as she portrays the intellectual and emotional development of Victor Frankenstein's creature. As this example indicates, philosophical issues are somewhat more abstract than investigations of theme or historical context. Some other examples of philosophical issues include human free will, the formation of human identity, the nature of sin, or questions of ethics.

Writing about philosophy and ideas might require some outside research, but usually the notes or other material in your text will provide you with basic information and often footnotes and bibliographies suggest places you can go to read further about the subject. If you have identified a philosophical theme that runs through a text, you might ask yourself how the author develops this theme. Look at character development and the interactions of characters, for example. Similarly, you might examine whether the narrative voice in a work of fiction addresses the philosophical concerns of the text.

WRITING COMPARISON AND CONTRAST ESSAYS

Finally, you might find that comparing and contrasting the works or techniques of an author provides a useful tool for literary analysis. A comparison and contrast essay might compare two characters or themes in a single work, or it might compare the author's treatment of a theme in two works. It might also contrast methods of character development or analyze an author's differing treatment of a philosophical concern in two works. Writing comparison and contrast essays, though, requires some special consideration. While they generally provide you with plenty of material to use, they also come with a built-in trap: the laundry list. These papers often become mere lists of connections between the works. As this chapter will discuss, a strong thesis must make an assertion that you want to prove or validate. A strong comparison/contrast thesis, then, needs to comment on the significance of the similarities and differences you observe. It is not enough merely to assert that the works contain similarities and differences. You might, for example, assert why the similarities and differences are important and explain how they illuminate the works' treatment of theme. Remember, too, that a thesis should not be a statement of the obvious. A comparison/contrast paper that focuses only on very obvious similarities or differences does little to illuminate the connections between the works. Often, an effective method of shaping a strong thesis and argument is to begin your paper by noting the similarities between the works but then to develop a thesis that asserts how these apparently similar elements are different. If, for example, you observe that Emily Dickinson wrote a number of poems about spiders, you might analyze how she uses spider imagery differently in two poems. Similarly, many scholars have noted that Hawthorne created many "mad scientist" characters, men who are so devoted to their science or their art that they lose perspective on all else. A good thesis comparing two of these characters—Aylmer of "The Birthmark" and Dr. Rappaccini of "Rappaccini's Daughter," for example—might initially identify both characters as examples of Hawthorne's mad scientist type but then argue that their motivations for scientific experimentation differ. If you strive to analyze the similarities or differences, discuss significances, and move beyond the obvious, your paper should move beyond the laundry list trap.

PREPARING TO WRITE

Armed with a clear sense of your task—illuminating the text—and with an understanding of theme, character, language, history, and philosophy, you are ready to approach the writing process. Remember that good writing is grounded in good reading and that close reading takes time, attention, and more than one reading of your text. Read for comprehension first. As you go back and review the work, mark the text to chart the details of the work as well as your reactions. Highlight important passages, repeated words, and image patterns. "Converse" with the text through marginal notes. Mark turns in the plot, ask questions, and make observations about characters, themes, and language. If you are reading from a book that does not belong to you, keep a record of your reactions in a journal or notebook. If you have read a work of literature carefully, paying attention to both the text and the context of the work, you have a leg up on the writing process. Admittedly, at this point, your ideas are probably very broad and undefined, but you have taken an important first step toward writing a strong paper.

Your next step is to focus, to take a broad, perhaps fuzzy, topic and define it more clearly. Even a topic provided by your instructor will need to be focused appropriately. Remember that good writers make the topic their own. There are a number of strategies—often called "invention"—that you can use to develop your own focus. In one such strategy, called *freewriting*, you spend 10 minutes or so just writing about your topic without referring back to the text or your notes. Write whatever comes to mind; the important thing is that you just keep writing. Often this process allows you to develop fresh ideas or approaches to your subject matter. You could also try *brainstorming*: Write down your topic and then list all the related points or ideas you can think of. Include questions, comments, words, important passages or events, and anything else that comes to mind. Let one idea lead to another. In the related technique of *clustering*, or *mapping*, write your topic on a sheet of paper and write related ideas around it. Then list related subpoints under each of these main ideas. Many people then draw arrows to show connections between points. This technique helps you narrow your topic and can also help you organize your ideas. Similarly, asking journalistic questions—Who? What? Where? When? Why? and How?—can develop ideas for topic development.

Thesis Statements

Once you have developed a focused topic, you can begin to think about your thesis statement, the main point or purpose of your paper. It is imperative that you craft a strong thesis, otherwise, your paper will likely be little more than random, disorganized observations about the text. Think of your thesis statement as a kind of road map for your paper. It tells your reader where you are going and how you are going to get there.

To craft a good thesis, you must keep a number of things in mind. First, as the title of this subsection indicates, your paper's thesis should be a statement, an assertion about the text that you want to prove or validate. Beginning writers often formulate a question that they attempt to use as a thesis. For example, a writer exploring the character of Bartleby in Melville's "Bartleby, the Scrivener" might write, The narrator of "Bartleby, the Scrivener," calls Bartleby "unaccountable" and "inscrutable." If the narrator cannot explain Bartleby, how can readers make sense of him? While a question like this is a good strategy to use in the invention process to help narrow your topic and find your thesis, it cannot serve as the thesis statement because it does not tell your reader what you want to assert about Bartleby. A writer might shape this question into a thesis by instead proposing an answer to that question: Although Bartleby is an "inscrutable" character, he can be productively interpreted as a symbol of poverty and of the biblical reminder that "ye have the poor always with you" (King James Bible Matthew 26:11). Notice that this thesis suggests one possible way to interpret Bartleby and his strange behavior.

Second, remember that a good thesis makes an assertion that you need to support. In other words, a good thesis does not state the obvious. If you tried to formulate a thesis about friendship by simply saying, In "Bartleby, the Scrivener," Melville's title character is an "inscrutable" man who begins the story as a good law copyist but eventually decides not to work at all, you have done nothing but rephrase the obvious. You might try to develop a thesis from that point by asking yourself some further questions: What makes Bartleby a good worker early in the story? Why might Bartleby refuse to work? What do you think about the narrator's response to Bartleby and his refusal? What are the effects of Bartleby's refusal to work? Such a line of questioning might lead you to a more viable thesis.

As the comparison with the road map also suggests, your thesis should appear near the beginning of the paper. In relatively short papers (three to six pages), the thesis almost always appears in the first paragraph. Some writers fall into the trap of saving their thesis for the end, trying to provide a surprise or a big moment of revelation, as if to say, "TA-DA! I've just proved that in 'Bartleby, the Scrivener,' and 'The Paradise of Bachelors and the Tartarus of Maids' Melville demonstrates that human values are destroyed by the values of business." Placing a thesis at the end of an essay can seriously mar the essay's effectiveness. If you fail to define your essay's point and purpose clearly at the beginning, your reader will find it difficult to assess the clarity of your argument and understand the points you are making. When your argument comes as a surprise at the end, you force your reader to reread your essay in order to assess its logic and effectiveness.

Finally, you should avoid using the first person ("I") as you present your thesis. Though it is not strictly wrong to write in the first person, it is difficult to do so gracefully. While writing in the first person, beginning writers often fall into the trap of writing self-reflexive prose (writing *about* their paper *in* their paper). Often this leads to the most dreaded of opening lines: "In this paper I am going to discuss . . ." Not only does this self-reflexive voice make for very awkward prose, it frequently allows writers to boldly announce a topic while completely avoiding a thesis statement. An example might be a paper that begins as follows: In chapter 1, "Loomings," Ishmael claims that his story of Narcissus is "the key to it all." In this paper I am going to explore this statement. The author of this paper has done little more than announce a topic for the paper (Ishamel's statement that the story of Narcissus is "the key to it all"). While she may have intended the last sentence as a thesis, she fails to present her opinion about the significance of the Narcissus myth. To improve this "thesis," the writer would need to back up a couple of steps. A stronger thesis would explain, first of all, just *what* the myth is the key to. (Ishmael's phrasing, "it all," is a bit vague here.) Beyond that, the author should make an assertion about how or why that myth is the key to understanding the text. A stronger and more developed version of this "thesis" might read, Ishmael's version of the Narcissus myth is the "key" to understanding the different fates of Ishmael and Ahab. The author might even choose to develop this thesis through some explanatory remarks that provide a road map to the paper. For example, the author may follow that thesis with the following sentences: Like Narcissus, Ahab pursues his own reflection so insistently that it leads to his death. Ishmael, on the other hand, is willing to see beyond the self and recognize the soul's dependence on others. This recognition saves him.

Outlines

While developing a strong, thoughtful thesis early in your writing process should help focus your paper, outlining provides an essential tool for logically shaping that paper. A good outline helps you see—and develop—the relationships among the points in your argument and assures you that your paper flows logically and coherently. Outlining not only helps place your points in a logical order but also helps you subordinate supporting points, weed out any irrelevant points, and decide if there are any necessary points that are missing from your argument. Most of us are familiar with formal outlines that use numerical and letter designations for each point. However, there are different types of outlines; you may find that an informal outline is a more useful tool for you. What is important, though, is that you spend the time to develop some sort of outline—formal or informal.

Remember that an outline is a tool to help you shape and write a strong paper. If you do not spend sufficient time planning your supporting points and shaping the arrangement of those points, you will most likely construct a vague, unfocused outline that provides little, if any, help with the writing of the paper. Consider the following example.

Thesis: Ishmael's version of the Narcissus myth is the "key" to understanding the different fates of Ishmael and Ahab. Like Narcissus, Ahab pursues his own reflection so insistently that it leads to his death. Ishmael, on the other hand, is willing to see beyond the self and recognize the soul's dependence on others. This recognition saves him.

    I. Introduction and thesis

   II. Ahab
        A. Ahab's reflections
        B. Ahab and Pip

  III. Moby Dick
        A. Moby Dick and Ahab

   IV. Starbuck
        A. Starbuck's assessment of Ahab
        B. Starbuck's sense of family

    V. Ishmael
        A. Ishmael's dependence on others
        B. Ishmael sees beyond the self
        C. Ishmael and Queequeg's coffin

```
VI. Queequeg
      A. Relationship with Ishmael
      B. Queequeg and his coffin


VII. Conclusion
```

This outline has a number of flaws. First of all, the major topics labeled with the Roman numerals are not arranged in a logical order. If the paper's aim is to show how the Narcissus myth explains the difference between the fates of Ishmael and Ahab, it makes sense that both of these characters might function as major headings in an outline for this paper. It is not clear, however, why the writer includes characters like Moby Dick, Starbuck, Pip, and Queequeg as major sections of this outline. It seems clear that all these characters might play a role in the paper, but they are misplaced in this outline. The fact that the author plans to discuss Queequeg's coffin before the discussion of Queequeg clearly demonstrates a problem with this organization. Similarly, under section III the author includes a subsection labeled A but fails to include any other subsections. An outline should not include an A with out a B, a 1 without a 2, etc. Still further, none of these sections provide much information about the content of the argument, and it seems likely that the writer has not given sufficient thought to the content of the paper. A better start to this outline might be:

```
Thesis: Ishmael's version of the Narcissus myth is
the "key" to understanding the different fates of
Ishmael and Ahab. Like Narcissus, Ahab pursues his own
reflection so insistently that it leads to his death.
Ishmael, on the other hand, is willing to see beyond
the self and recognize the soul's dependence on others.
This recognition saves him.


      I. Introduction and thesis


      II. Ahab
          A. Ahab and the self
              1.Ahab's    identity   represented   by
                 imagery  of  depth—echoes  of  the
                 Narcissis myth
```

2. Ahab understands that the pursuit of self is death
3. Ahab sees self reflected back everywhere
4. Moby Dick as a double or reflection of Ahab—quest as a quest for self

B. Ahab and others
1. In his quest he spurns human interdependence; chapter 108, "Ahab and the Carpenter"
2. Occasionally sees past own reflection
3. Relationships with Pip and Starbuck as rejected chances for redemption or salvation

III. Ishmael
A. Ishmael and the self—depression pushes him to sea; quest as a death wish (chapter 1, "Loomings")
B. Ishmael and others
1. Queequeg allows Ishmael to realize need for human interdependence
2. Ishmael's developing philosophy of community and mutuality

IV. The respective fates of Ahab and Ishmael
A. Ahab pulled into the depths and drowned, lashed to Moby Dick
B. Ishmael redeemed, reborn from the depths on Queequeg's coffin

V. Conclusion

This new outline would prove much more helpful when it came time to write the paper.

An outline like this could be shaped into an even more useful tool if the writer fleshed out the argument by providing specific examples from the text to support each point. Once you have listed your main point and your supporting ideas, develop this raw material by listing related supporting ideas and material under each of those main headings. From there, arrange the material in subsections and order the material logically.

For example, you might begin with one of the theses cited above: Although Bartleby is an "inscrutable" character, he can be productively interpreted as a symbol of poverty and of the biblical reminder that "ye have the poor always with you" (King James Bible Matthew 26:11). In order to start to shape a paper around this thesis, you should try to sort out the reasons why you think that Bartleby can be productively read as a symbol of the poor. These reasons could become the major supporting points in your essay and might function as headings in your outline. Under each of those headings you could then list ideas that support that particular point. In the outline below, the writer begins to support his thesis by suggesting that because Bartleby is literally poor, this may allow him to function as a symbol of the poor. From there, the author notes aspects of the story that might support an assertion that Bartleby is a symbolic character. Melville's echoes of biblical passages help the writer to see a meaning for the story in the interaction between the narrator and Bartleby as symbol. These topics form the three major headings of the outline. Note, too, that the outline below also includes references to particular parts of the text that help to support the argument. An informal outline, then, might look like this:

Thesis: Although Bartleby is an "inscrutable" character, he can be productively interpreted as a symbol of poverty and of the biblical reminder that "ye have the poor always with you" (Matthew 26:11).

Introduction

Bartleby as literally poor
- Bartleby as worker
- Bartleby as homeless
- Bartleby's savings fit in a bandanna
- Bartleby's poor diet
    ○ Poor diet probably creates the pallor that is mentioned frequently, and

this pallor probably is a reflection of poor health

Bartleby as a symbol of poverty and the poor
- Never goes out; has no existence or life outside the office
- "he was always there" seems an obvious echo of Matthew 26:11 (and Melville uses a lot of biblical echoes)

Story is about the treatment of the poor and our responsibilities; can see this in the relationship between narrator and Bartleby
- Matthew 26:11 is an echo of Deuteronomy 15:11, which gives instructions about how to treat the poor
- Once Bartleby stops working, the narrator struggles with relationship and brings up ethical questions ("What shall I do? I now said to myself, buttoning up my coat to the last button. What shall I do? what ought I do? what does conscience say I should do with this man, or rather ghost?" (2422)
- Calling Bartleby a "ghost" reflects the relationship between the two. Bartleby "haunts" the narrator just as poverty haunts the wealthy (through ethical questions)
- Like poverty, Bartleby proves a difficult and persistent problem
  - Narrator's easy fixes do not work
  - Narrator describes Bartleby abstractly as representing "misery" and "organic ill" that cannot be resolved. Therefore, he tries to "be rid of it."
    - Narrator moves but cannot escape responsibility ("you are responsible for the many you left there.")

■ Narrator still denies responsibility—
echoes Peter's denial of Christ

Conclusion

"Bartleby" reminds us of our responsibility
to the poor and reminds us that the problem
of poverty will always exist. Perhaps the
narrator realizes this. He finally visits
Bartleby in prison—perhaps another biblical
echo (King James Matthew 25:36, "I was in
prison, and ye came unto me.")

You would set about writing a formal outline with a similar process,
though in the final stages you would label the headings differently. A
formal outline for a paper that argues the thesis about business in "Bartleby" and "The Paradise of Bachelors and the Tartarus of Maids" cited
above might look like this:

Thesis: In "Bartleby, the Scrivener," and "The Paradise
of Bachelors and the Tartarus of Maids" human values
are destroyed by the values of business. This is most
clearly seen in the effects upon the workers, Bartleby
and the maids who work in the paper mill.

I. Introduction and Thesis

II. "Bartleby, The Scrivener"
   A. Setting: Wall Street, which is driven by
      business
      1. The story's subtitle, "A story of
         Wall Street"
      2. Offices at No. —— Wall Street share
         qualities with the "Paradise of
         Bachelors"
         a. all male
         b. narrator is lawyer like those at
            Temple Bar; is self-indulgent,
            especially at beginning

    B. Effects

       1. On narrator

          a. Narrator does not know how to treat Bartleby after he ceases to work, and he wavers between human values ("sons of Adam") and business values ("scandalizing my professional reputation")

          b. Finally decides to be rid of Bartleby

       2. On Bartleby

          a. Isolates—imagery of walls

          b. Renders him invisible—screens and language of ghostliness

          c. Dehumanizes—no history; no full name; no existence outside of office

          d. sickens—imagery of pallor

          e. kills—cadaverous; Bartleby as stillbirth

III. "The Paradise of Bachelors and the Tartarus of Maids"

    A. Setting of second part: the paper mill

       1. Similarly sterile

          a. Maids and bachelors

          b. Imagery of barrenness contrasts with sexual imagery

       2. Machines as God-like

          a. Girls "ruled" by machines

          b. The "great machine" as "mystical," prophetic, "a miracle"

    B. Effects

       1. On Cupid—hardens Cupid ("cruel-heartedness of this usage-hardened boy")

       2. On "the maids"—similar to those on Bartleby

a. Dehumanizes—serve machinery; animal imagery ("like so many mares . . ."); sexual imagery and rape; parallels between girls and paper
   b. Sickens—imagery of whiteness and pallor ("consumptive pallor")
   c. Kills—"So, through consumptive pallors of this bland, raggy life, go these white girls to death"; building as sepulchre
   d. renders them sterile—emphasis on status as maids; tour of mill ends with imagery of birth (of paper), another kind of stillbirth

IV. Conclusion
   A. In both stories, reams of paper are produced at the expense of human beings
   B. Both stories also chart the effects of business on those who could be in a position to change the situation (and who bear responsibility)
   C. Discuss stories as Melville's commentary on the effects of commerce and the need for change

As with the previous example, the thesis provided the seeds of a structure, and the writer was careful to arrange the supporting points in a logical manner, showing the relationships between the ideas in the paper.

Body Paragraphs

Once your outline is complete, you can begin drafting your paper. Paragraphs, units of related sentences, are the building blocks of a good paper, and as you draft you should keep in mind both the function and the qualities of good paragraphs. Paragraphs help you chart and control the shape and content of your essay, and they help the reader see your organization and your logic. You should begin a new paragraph whenever you move from one major point to another. In longer, more complex essays, you might use a group of related paragraphs to support major points. Remember that in addition to being adequately developed, a good paragraph is both unified and coherent.

Unified Paragraphs

Each paragraph must be centered on one idea or point, and a unified paragraph carefully focuses on and develops this central idea without including extraneous ideas or tangents. For beginning writers, the best way to ensure that you are constructing unified paragraphs is to include a topic sentence in each paragraph. This topic sentence should convey the main point of the paragraph, and every sentence in the paragraph should relate to that topic sentence. Any sentence that strays from the central topic does not belong in the paragraph and needs to be revised or deleted. Consider the following paragraph about Bartleby's poverty. Notice how the paragraph veers away from the main point when it strays into discussion of Bartleby's refusal to work and his habit of staring at walls:

> To begin with, Bartleby is, quite literally, poor. He is a law copyist, a worker. During the course of the story, the narrator discovers that Bartleby is also homeless. Stopping by his offices on a Sunday morning, the narrator finds that Bartleby has locked the door from the inside. The narrator says that he "surmised that for an indefinite period Bartleby must have ate, dressed, and slept in my office, and that too without a plate, mirror, or bed." He continues: "What miserable friendlessness and loneliness are here revealed! His poverty is great; but his solitude, how horrible!" (2412). The lawyer also discovers another sign of Bartleby's poverty—his "savings bank" is "an old bandanna handkerchief" (2414). The scrivener's poor diet also seems to indicate his poverty. "He lives, then, on ginger-nuts," the narrator observes, "never eats a dinner, properly speaking; he must be a vegetarian then; but no; he never eats even vegetables, he eats nothing but ginger-nuts" (2410). Not only does Bartleby

```
refuse to eat, but as the story progresses, he refuses
(or "prefers") not to work. Often he just stares at
walls in a "dead-wall revery" (2416). Ginger Nut seems
to summarize Bartleby well when he says, "I think, sir,
he's a little luny" (2410).
```

While the paragraph begins solidly, and the first sentence provides its central theme, the author soon goes on a tangent. If the purpose of the paragraph is to demonstrate Bartleby's literal poverty, the scrivener's refusal to work and his "dead-wall revery" are tangential here. These points may find a place later in the paper, but they should be deleted from this paragraph.

Coherent Paragraphs

In addition to shaping unified paragraphs, you must also craft coherent paragraphs, paragraphs that develop their points logically with sentences that flow smoothly into one another. Coherence depends on the order of your sentences, but it is not strictly the order of the sentences that is important to paragraph coherence. You also need to craft your prose to help the reader see the relationship among the sentences. In addition to shaping unified paragraphs, you must also craft coherent paragraphs, paragraphs that develop their points logically with sentences that flow smoothly into one another.

Consider the following version of the paragraph about Bartleby's poverty. Notice how the writer uses the same ideas as the paragraph above, but this time she only provides material that is relevant to the question of Bartleby's poverty. However, this paragraph, though it is unified, fails to help the reader see the relationships among the points. Consequently, it lacks coherence and clarity:

```
Bartleby is, quite literally, poor. He is a law copyist,
a worker. During the course of the story the narrator
discovers that Bartleby is homeless. The narrator says
that he "surmised that for an indefinite period Bartleby
must have ate, dressed, and slept in my office, and
that too without a plate, mirror, or bed." He continues:
"What miserable friendlessness and loneliness are
here revealed! His poverty is great; but his solitude,
how horrible!" (2412). The lawyer discovers Bartleby's
```

"savings bank" is "an old bandanna handkerchief" (2414). The scrivener has a poor diet. "He lives, then, on ginger-nuts, never eats a dinner, properly speaking; he must be a vegetarian then; but no; he never eats even vegetables, he eats nothing but ginger-nuts" (2410). When the young scrivener first arrives at the office door, the lawyer describes him as "pallidly neat" (2407), and he later calls the copyist "thin and pale." The narrator frequently describes Bartleby as "cadaverous."

This paragraph demonstrates that unity alone does not guarantee paragraph effectiveness. The argument is hard to follow because the author fails both to show connections between the sentences and to indicate how they work to support the overall point.

A number of techniques are available to aid paragraph coherence. Careful use of transitional words and phrases is essential. You can use transitional flags to introduce an example or an illustration (*for example, for instance*), to amplify a point or add another phase of the same idea (*additionally, furthermore, next, similarly, finally, then*), to indicate a conclusion or result (*therefore, as a result, thus, in other words*), to signal a contrast or a qualification (*on the other hand, nevertheless, despite this, on the contrary, still, however, conversely*), to signal a comparison (*likewise, in comparison, similarly*), and to indicate a movement in time (*afterward, earlier, eventually, finally, later, subsequently, until*).

In addition to transitional flags, careful use of pronouns aids coherence and flow. If you were writing about *The Wizard of Oz*, you would not want to keep repeating the phrase *the witch* or the name *Dorothy*. Careful substitution of the pronoun *she* in these instances can aid coherence. A word of warning, though: When you substitute pronouns for proper names, always be sure that your pronoun reference is clear. In a paragraph that discusses both Dorothy and the witch, substituting *she* could lead to confusion. Make sure that it is clear to whom the pronoun refers. Generally, the pronoun refers to the last proper noun you have used.

While repeating the same name over and over again can lead to awkward, boring prose, it is possible to use repetition to help your paragraph's coherence. Careful repetition of important words or phrases can lend coherence to your paragraph by reminding readers of your key points. Admittedly, it takes some practice to use this technique effectively. You may find that reading your prose aloud can help you develop an ear for effective use of repetition.

To see how helpful transitional aids are, compare the paragraph below to the preceding paragraph about Bartleby's poverty. Notice how the author works with the same ideas and quotations but shapes them into a much more coherent paragraph whose point is clearer and easier to follow:

> To begin with, Bartleby is, quite literally, poor. He is a law copyist, a worker. During the course of the story the narrator discovers that Bartleby is also homeless. Stopping by his offices on a Sunday morning, the narrator finds that Bartleby has locked the door from the inside. The narrator says that he "surmised that for an indefinite period Bartleby must have ate, dressed, and slept in my office, and that too without a plate, mirror, or bed." He continues: "What miserable friendlessness and loneliness are here revealed! His poverty is great; but his solitude, how horrible!" (2412). The lawyer also discovers another sign of Bartleby's poverty—his "savings bank" is "an old bandanna handkerchief" (2414). The scrivener's poor diet also seems to indicate his poverty. "He lives, then, on ginger-nuts," the narrator observes, "never eats a dinner, properly speaking; he must be a vegetarian then; but no; he never eats even vegetables, he eats nothing but ginger-nuts" (2410). Perhaps as a result of this poor diet, Bartleby's health suffers. He is frequently described as "pale" and "pallid." When the young scrivener first arrives at the office door, the lawyer describes him as "pallidly neat" (2407), and he later calls the copyist "thin and pale." Similarly, the narrator's frequent descriptions of Bartleby as "cadaverous"—for example his "cadaverously gentlemanly nonchalance" (2413) and "his mildly cadaverous reply" (2415)—reinforce this belief that Bartleby is ill, and they foreshadow his eventual death by starvation.

Similarly, the following paragraph from a paper on the effects of business in "Bartleby" and "The Paradise of Bachelors and the Tartarus of

Maids" demonstrates both unity and coherence. In it, the author draws connections between the two stories as he points to the many ways that the girls in the paper mill are dehumanized.

> The paper mill on Woedolor Mountain affects the "maids" who work there in much the same way that Wall Street affects Bartleby. Like Bartleby, the maids are dehumanized, and the narrator provides a great deal of imagery that suggests this dehumanization. At one point, he describes the girls as slaves who "served" the machinery "mutely and cringingly as the slave serves the Sultan" (2448). Just a page later, he says that they stood "like so many mares haltered to the rack" (2449). Additionally, the imagery of the scythes "vertically thrust up" before the girls seems to figure their situation as a metaphorical rape (2449). Finally, the extended parallels that the narrator draws between the girls and the paper that they produce also suggests just how thoroughly they have been dehumanized. Like the paper, they are silent and blank, and he repeatedly emphasizes their blankness. In fact, the girls are all so emptied of individuality that they all seem interchangeable.

Introductions

Introductions present particular challenges for writers. Generally, your introduction should do two things: capture your reader's attention and explain the main point of your essay. In other words, while your introduction should contain your thesis, it needs to do a bit more work than that. You are likely to find that starting that first paragraph is one of the most difficult parts of the paper. It is hard to face that blank page or screen, and as a result, many beginning writers, in desperation to start somewhere, start with overly broad, general statements. While it is often a good strategy to start with more general subject matter and narrow your focus, do not begin with broad sweeping statements such as, Business is everywhere, or Throughout the course of history business has flourished. Such sentences are nothing but empty filler. They begin to fill the blank page, but they do nothing to advance your argument. Instead, you should try to gain your readers' interest. Some writers like to begin with a pertinent quotation or with a relevant question. Or, you might begin with an introduction of the topic you will discuss. If you are writing about Melville's treatment of the ethics of business, for example, you might begin by talking about business and industry in 19th-century America. Another common trap to avoid is depending on your title to introduce the author and the text you are writing about. Always include the work's author and title in your opening paragraph.

Compare the effectiveness of the following introductions:

1. Throughout the course of history, business has flourished. Many people wonder about the values of business, though. Herman Melville was one of those people. He wondered about what business does to people. These two stories show that he wondered about business.

2. As business and industry thrived in 19th-century America, many activists began to question the values that drove these businesses. Their attitudes were reflected in some of the literature of the time. Herman Melville's varied experiences in youth gave him firsthand experience with both clerical and physical labor, since he spent time working as a clerk in an office and as a hand on whaling ships. Many of his writings draw from his experiences and comment on the effects of business and industry on the individual. Two stories in particular, "Bartleby, the Scrivener" and "The Paradise of Bachelors and the Tartarus of Maids," comment on business's detrimental effects on humanity. In both stories, human values are destroyed by the values of business. This is most clearly seen in the effects upon the workers, Bartleby, and the maids who work in the paper mill.

The first introduction begins with a boring, overly broad sentence, comments vaguely on Melville's attitudes, and then moves abruptly to the thesis. Notice, too, how a reader deprived of the paper's title does not know the title of the stories that the paper will analyze. The second introduction works with the same material and thesis, but provides more detail, and is, consequently, much more interesting. While it begins broadly, it does focus on business in 19th-century America. It explains Melville's connections to business and industry, and moves on to its thesis, which includes the titles of the works to be discussed.

The paragraph below provides another example of an opening strategy. It begins by introducing the author and the text it will analyze, and then it moves on to briefly introduce relevant details of the story in order to set up its thesis:

> The narrator of Herman Melville's "Bartleby, the Scrivener," calls Bartleby "unaccountable" and "inscrutable." Like the narrator, many readers also find it nearly impossible to explain Bartleby and his function in the story. In part, this difficulty results from the way Melville has drawn his title character. The scrivener seems to function as a symbolic character in a rather realistic story, and like any symbol, Bartleby represents many things at once. Although he is strange and "inscrutable," Bartleby can be productively read as a symbol of poverty and of the biblical reminder that "ye have the poor always with you" (Matthew 26:11). While this interpretation does not exhaust Bartleby's meaning, it can help readers to see a meaning in the story and to understand the narrator's complicated relationship with the scrivener.

Conclusions

Conclusions present another series of challenges for writers. No doubt you have heard the old adage about writing papers: "Tell us what you are going to say, say it, and then tell us what you've said." While this formula does not necessarily result in bad papers, it does not often result in good ones, either. It will almost certainly result in boring papers (especially boring conclusions). If you have done a good job establishing your points in the body of the paper, the reader already knows and understands your argument. There is no need to merely reiterate. Do not just summarize your main points in your conclusion. Such a boring and mechanical conclusion does nothing to advance your argument or interest your reader. Consider the following conclusion to the paper about business in "Bartleby" and "The Paradise of Bachelors and the Tartarus of Maids":

> In conclusion, Melville shows that business can be bad. Both Bartleby and the "maids" are dehumanized by their work. Finally, Bartleby dies, and Melville makes it clear that the maids will die as a result of their consumption, too. In both stories, humans are destroyed by work.

Besides starting with a mechanical and obvious transitional device, this conclusion does little more than summarize some of the main points of the outline (it does not even touch on all of them). It is incomplete and uninteresting.

Instead, your conclusion should add something to your paper. A good tactic is to build upon the points you have been arguing. Asking "why?" often helps to draw further conclusions. For example, in the paper discussed above, you might speculate or explain why Melville chooses to point out the detrimental effects of business. What does he hope to accomplish through his portraits of Bartleby and the girls in the paper mill? Another method of successfully concluding a paper is to speculate on other directions in which to take your topic, and tie it into larger issues. It might help to envision your paper as just one section of a larger paper. Having established your points in this paper, how would you build upon this argument? Where would you go next? The following conclusion to the paper comparing "Bartleby" and "The Paradise of Bachelors and the Tartarus of Maids" begins by reiterating some of the main points of the paper, but does so in order to speculate about Melville's purpose:

> While the work that Bartleby does is quite different from that of the maids in the paper mill, both stories show the dehumanizing effects of business. In both stories, reams of paper are produced at the expense of human beings. Bartleby dies of starvation, and the maids are chained to a life of servitude that will end in death. Each text, though, goes beyond an examination of the workers, providing a glimpse of the effects of business on those who might have the power to make a difference. The narrator of Bartleby vacillates between the values

of business and human values. While business values seem
to get the better of him when he moves and abandons
Bartleby at his offices, perhaps the fact that he visits
him in prison shows that he has had a change of heart.
Similarly, the final passage of the text may provide
evidence of a change of heart. After all, he feels the
need to tell Bartleby's story. Similarly, the narrator in
"The Paradise of Bachelors and the Tartarus of Maids,"
feels compelled to share the maids' story. Clearly, he
is moved and appalled by the situation of these girls.
It also seems as though he sees his own role in their
exploitation. Perhaps Melville, in his commentary on the
dehumanizing effects of business, might find some hope
in these men. If they do recognize the roles that they
play in the dehumanization of the working class, perhaps
they will begin to sow the seeds of change.

Similarly, in the following conclusion to the paper on Bartleby as a
symbol of poverty, the author draws from the earlier discussion about
the story's imagery in order to speculate about Bartleby's long-term
effects upon the narrator:

The narrator finally finds that he cannot be rid of
his human obligations to Bartleby, and he seems to
realize the magnitude of those obligations when he
speaks of being held to the "terrible account" (2423).
He visits Bartleby in prison. Perhaps here Melville
echoes Matthew 25:36, "I was in prison, and ye came unto
me" (King James Bible). On the last of these visits, the
narrator finds Bartley starved to death, and when the
prison grub-man asks "does he live without dining?" the
narrator responds, "Lives without dining." The narrator
is correct in his assessment here. Bartleby "lives"
even after his death. From the beginning, Bartleby
seemed more like a ghost than a flesh-and-blood man,
and even in death he continues to haunt the narrator's
conscience. This haunting explains the narrator's
decision to tell Bartleby's story. His narrative is a

kind of confession from an "eminently safe man" (2403) who prefers peace, prudence, and method, prefers to have nothing "invade [his] peace" (2403). His confession reminds readers that, like Bartleby, who is *always there*," poverty will continue to haunt and challenge humanity. Perhaps that explains the narrator's final exclamation: "Ah Bartleby! Ah Humanity!" (2427).

Citations and Formatting

Using Primary Sources

As the examples included in this chapter indicate, strong papers on literary texts incorporate quotations from the text in order to support their points. It is not enough for you to assert your interpretation without providing support or evidence from the text. Without well-chosen quotations to support your argument you are, in effect, saying to the reader, "Take my word for it." It is important to use quotations thoughtfully and selectively. Remember that the paper presents *your* argument, so choose quotations that support *your* assertions. Do not let the author's voice overwhelm your own. With that caution in mind, there are some guidelines you should follow to ensure that you use quotations clearly and effectively.

Integrate Quotations:

Quotations should always be integrated into your own prose. Do not just drop them into your paper without introduction or comment. Otherwise, it is unlikely that your reader will see their function. You can integrate textual support easily and clearly with identifying tags, short phrases that identify the speaker. For example:

> According to the narrator, Cupid is "a usage-hardened boy."

While this tag appears before the quotation, you can also use tags after or in the middle of the quoted text, as the following examples demonstrate:

> "I would prefer not to," Bartleby replies.

> "To such a degree may malign machinations and deceptions impose," Don Benito says to Delano. "So far may even the

best man err, in judging the conduct of one with the recess of whose condition he is not acquainted."

You can also use a colon to formally introduce a quotation:

Ginger Nut's assessment of Bartleby is quite clear: "I think, sir, he's a little *luny*."

When you quote brief sections of poems (three lines or fewer), use slash marks to indicate the line breaks in the poem:

As the poem ends, Melville speaks once again of the swallows: "While over them the swallows skim/And all is hushed at Shiloh."

Longer quotations (more than four lines of prose or three lines of poetry) should be set off from the rest of your paper in a block quotation. Double-space before you begin the passage, indent it 10 spaces from your left-hand margin, and double-space the passage itself. Because the indentation signals the inclusion of a quotation, do not use quotation marks around the cited passage. Use a colon to introduce the passage:

At first, the narrator is hesitant to dismiss Bartleby:

He is useful to me. I can get along with him. If I turn him away, the chances are he will fall in with some less indulgent employer, and then he will be rudely treated, and perhaps driven forth miserably to starve. Yes. Here I can cheaply purchase a delicious self-approval. To befriend Bartleby; to humor him in his strange willfulness will cost me little or nothing, while I lay up in my soul what will eventually prove a sweet morsel for my conscience.

Soon this generosity passes.

Melville's poem begins by providing an image of the
battlefield:

    Skimming lightly, wheeling still,
    The swallows fly low
    Over the field in clouded days,
    The forest-field of Shiloh—

This first image seems peaceful.

It is also important to interpret quotations after you introduce
them and explain how they help advance your point. You cannot
assume that your reader will interpret the quotations the same way
that you do.

Quote Accurately

Always quote accurately. Anything within quotations marks must be the
author's exact words. There are, however, some rules to follow if you need
to modify the quotation to fit into your prose.

1. Use brackets to indicate any material that might have been
   added to the author's exact wording. For example, if you need to
   add any words to the quotation or alter it grammatically to allow
   it to fit into your prose, indicate your changes in brackets:

       The narrator struggles with ethical questions,
       and he wonders what his "conscience [says he]
       should do."

2. Conversely, if you choose to omit any words from the quotation,
   use ellipses (three spaced periods) to indicate missing words or
   phrases:

       In the first paragraph of *Moby-Dick*, Ishmael
       describes the mood that prompted him to go
       to sea: "Whenever I find myself growing grim
       about the mouth; whenever it is a damp, drizzly
       November in my soul . . . then I account it

```
high time to get to sea as soon as I can. This
is my substitute for pistol and ball."
```

3. If you delete a sentence or more, use the ellipses after a period:

```
The setting at the beginning of Benito Cereno
foreshadows many of the work's themes: "The morning
was one peculiar to that coast. Everything was
mute and calm; everything gray . . . . The sky
seemed a gray surtout . . . . Shadows present
foreshadowing deeper shadows to come."
```

4. If you omit a line or more of poetry, or more than one paragraph of prose, use a single line of spaced periods to indicate the omission:

```
Foemen at morn, but friends at eve—
. . . . . . . . . . . . . . . . .
(What like a bullet can undeceive!)
But now they lie low,
While over them the swallows skim
And all is hushed at Shiloh.
```

Punctuate Properly

Punctuation of quotations often causes more trouble than it should. Once again, you just need to keep these simple rules in mind.

1. Periods and commas should be placed inside quotation marks, even if they are not part of the original quotation:

```
Ahab sees himself reflected in the coin: "The
firm tower, that is Ahab; the volcano, that is
Ahab."
```

The only exception to this rule is when the quotation is followed by a parenthetical reference. In this case, the period or comma goes after the citation (more on these later in this chapter):

```
Ahab sees himself reflected in the coin: "The
firm tower, that is Ahab; the volcano, that is
Ahab" (332).
```

2. Other marks of punctuation—colons, semicolons, question marks, and exclamation points—go outside the quotation marks unless they are part of the original quotation:

```
Why does Delano believe that the incident was
"but a sort of love-quarrel, after all"?
   After the incident, Delano says to himself,
"Ah, this slavery breeds ugly passions in man.—
Poor fellow!"
```

Documenting Primary Sources

Unless you are instructed otherwise, you should provide sufficient information for your reader to locate material you quote. Generally, literature papers follow the rules set forth by the Modern Language Association (MLA). These can be found in the *MLA Handbook for Writers of Research Papers* (sixth edition). You should be able to find this book in the reference section of your library. Additionally, its rules for citing both primary and secondary sources are widely available from reputable online sources. One of these is the Online Writing Lab (OWL) at Purdue University. OWL's guide to MLA style is available at http://owl.english.purdue.edu/owl/resource/557/01/. The Modern Language Association also offers answers to frequently asked questions about MLA style on this helpful Web page: http://www.mla.org/style_faq. Generally, when you are citing from literary works in papers, you should keep a few guidelines in mind.

Parenthetical Citations

MLA asks for parenthetical references in your text after quotations. When you are working with prose (short stories, novels, or essays) include page numbers in the parentheses:

```
Ahab sees himself reflected in the coin: "The firm
tower, that is Ahab; the volcano, that is Ahab" (332).
```

When you are quoting poetry, include line numbers:

Melville's poem begins peacefully: "Skimming lightly, wheeling still, / The swallows fly low / Over the field in clouded days" (1–3).

Works Cited Page

These parenthetical citations are linked to a separate works cited page at the end of the paper. The works cited page lists works alphabetically by the authors' last name. An entry for the above reference to Melville's *Moby-Dick* would read:

Melville, Herman. *Moby-Dick*. New York: Norton, 2002.

The *MLA Handbook* includes a full listing of sample entries, as do many of the online explanations of MLA style.

Documenting Secondary Sources

To ensure that your paper is built entirely upon your own ideas and analysis, instructors often ask that you write interpretative papers without any outside research. If, on the other hand, your paper requires research, you must document any secondary sources you use. You need to document direct quotations, summaries or paraphrases of others' ideas, and factual information that is not common knowledge. Follow the guidelines above for quoting primary sources when you use direct quotations from secondary sources. Keep in mind that MLA style also includes specific guidelines for citing electronic sources. OWL's Web site provides a good summary: http://owl.english.purdue. edu/owl/resource/557/09/.

Parenthetical Citations

As with the documentation of primary sources, described above, MLA guidelines require in-text parenthetical references to your secondary sources. Unlike the research papers you might write for a history class, literary research papers following MLA style do not use footnotes as a means of documenting sources. Instead, after a quotation, you should cite the author's last name and the page number:

"The famous Fayaway of *Typee* is a charming and sympathetic creature. Lovely to look at, uninhibited, tender, sensual, she understands better than any of the other *Typees* Tommo's needs and desires" (Douglas 297).

If you include the name of the author in your prose, then you would include only the page number in your citation. For example:

According to Ann Douglas, "Fayaway of Typee is a charming and sympathetic creature. Lovely to look at, uninhibited, tender, sensual, she understands better than any of the other Typees Tommo's needs and desires" (297).

If you are including more than one work by the same author, the parenthetical citation should include a shortened yet identifiable version of the title in order to indicate which of the author's works you cite. For example:

Gilmore argues that from "the American realities of 1851, Melville creates a fictional setting where everything has become marketable and can be converted into money" (*American Romanticism* 114).

Similarly, and just as important, if you summarize or paraphrase the particular ideas of your source, you must provide documentation:

Ahab uses mechanistic imagery in the final hunt for the whale. This imagery demonstrates his hunger for power (Marx 299).

Works Cited Page

Like the primary sources discussed above, the parenthetical references to secondary sources are keyed to a separate works cited page at the end of your paper. Here is an example of a works cited page that uses the examples cited above. Note that when two or more works by the same author are listed, you should use three hypens followed by a period in the subsequent entries. You can find a complete list of sample entries in the *MLA Handbook* or from a reputable online summary of MLA style.

WORKS CITED

Douglas, Ann. *The Feminization of American Culture.* New York: Knopf, 1978.

Gilmore, Michael T. *American Romanticism and the Marketplace.* Chicago: U of Chicago P, 1985.

——. "Hawthorne and the Making of the Middle Class." *Rethinking Class: Literary Studies and Social Formations.* Eds. Wai-chee Dimock and Michael T. Gilmore. New York: Columbia UP, 1994. 215–238.

Marx, Leo. *The Machine in the Garden: Technology and the Pastoral Ideal in America.* New York: Oxford UP, 1967.

Plagiarism

Failure to document carefully and thoroughly can leave you open to charges of stealing the ideas of others, which is known as plagiarism, and this is a very serious matter. Remember that it is important to include quotation marks when you use language from your source, even if you use just one or two words. For example, if you wrote, Fayaway provides unmoralized pleasure for Tommo, you would be guilty of plagiarism, since you used Douglas's distinct language without acknowledging her as the source. Instead, you should write: Fayaway provides "unmoralized pleasure" for Tommo (Douglas 297). In this case, you have properly credited Douglas.

Similarly, neither summarizing the ideas of an author nor changing or omitting just a few words means that you can omit a citation. Ann Douglas's book *The Feminization of American Culture* contains the following passage about the character of Fayaway in Melville's *Typee*:

> There are no women of any kind to speak of in *Redburn and White-Jacket*, and the only women in *Typee* and *Omoo* are Polynesians who pose few challenges to the protagonists. The famous Fayaway of *Typee* is a charming and sympathetic creature. Lovely to look at, uninhibited, tender, sensual, she understands better than any of the other Typees Tommo's needs and desires. She offers exactly what the American Victorian lady would deny her male counterpart: unmoralized pleasure.

Below are two examples of plagiarized passages:

There are few women in books like *Redburn*, and the island women in *Typee* and *Omoo* do not challenge Melville's male characters. These women, especially Fayaway, provide sympathy and pleasure. They are unlike the women of Victorian America because they offer unconstrained sexual pleasure without the guilt of Victorian society.

The island women in *Typee* and *Omoo* do not challenge Melville's male characters. Fayaway is charming and sympathetic, and she understands Tommo's needs and desires. Unlike American Victorian women, she offers unmoralized pleasure. (Douglas 297)

While the first passage doesn't use Douglas's exact language, it duplicates her idea and uses the structure of her argument without citing her work. This constitutes plagiarism. The second passage has shortened her passage, changed some wording, and included a citation, but some of the phrasing ("charming and sympathetic," "unmoralized pleasure") is Douglas's. The first passage could be fixed with a parenthetical citation. Because some of the wording remains the same, though, the second would require the use of quotation marks in addition to a parenthetical citation. The passage below represents an honestly and adequately documented use of the original passage:

As Ann Douglas indicates, the island women in *Typee* and *Omoo* do not challenge Melville's male characters. Fayaway is "a charming and sympathetic creature" who "understands . . . Tommo's needs and desires." Unlike American Victorian women, she offers what Douglas calls "unmoralized pleasure." (Douglas 297)

This passage acknowledges Douglas's idea and her argument, and it uses quotation marks to indicate her precise language.

While it is not necessary to document well-known facts, often referred to as "common knowledge," any ideas or language that you take from someone else must be properly documented. Common knowledge generally includes the birth and death dates of authors or other well-documented facts of their lives. An often-cited guideline is: If you can find the information in three sources, it's common knowledge. Despite this guideline, it is, admittedly, often difficult to know if the facts you uncover are common knowledge or not. When in doubt, document your source.

Sample Essay

Sara White
Ms. Sterling
English 160
May 26, 2008

"HE WAS ALWAYS THERE":
BARTLEBY AS A SYMBOL OF THE POOR

The narrator of Herman Melville's "Bartleby, the Scrivener" calls Bartleby "unaccountable" and "inscrutable." Like the narrator, many readers also find it nearly impossible to explain Bartleby and his function in the story. In part, this difficulty results from the way Melville has drawn his title character. The scrivener seems to function as a symbolic character in a rather realistic story, and, like any symbol, Bartleby represents many things at once. Although he is strange and "inscrutable," Bartleby can be productively read as a symbol of poverty and of the biblical reminder that "ye have the poor always with you" (King James Bible Matthew 26:11). While this interpretation does not exhaust Bartleby's meaning, it can help readers to see a meaning in the story and to understand the narrator's complicated relationship with the scrivener.

To begin with, Bartleby is, quite literally, poor. He is a law copyist, a worker. During the course of the story, the narrator discovers that Bartleby is also homeless. Stopping by his offices on a Sunday morning, the narrator finds that Bartleby has locked the door from the inside. The narrator says that he "surmised that for an indefinite period Bartleby must have ate, dressed, and slept in my office, and that too without a plate, mirror, or bed." He continues: "What miserable friendlessness and loneliness are here revealed! His poverty is great; but his solitude, how horrible!" (2412). The lawyer also discovers another sign of Bartleby's poverty—his "savings bank" is "an old bandanna handkerchief" (2414). The scrivener's poor diet also seems to indicate his poverty. "He lives, then, on ginger-nuts," the narrator observes, "never eats a dinner, properly speaking; he must be a vegetarian then; but no; he never eats even vegetables, he eats nothing but ginger-nuts" (2410). Perhaps as a result of this poor diet, Bartleby's health suffers. He is frequently described as "pale" and "pallid." When the young scrivener first arrives at the office door, the lawyer describes him as "pallidly neat" (2407), and he later calls the copyist "thin and pale." Similarly, the narrator's frequent descriptions of Bartleby as "cadaverous"—for example his "cadaverously gentlemanly nonchalance" (2413) and "his mildly cadaverous reply" (2415)—reinforce this belief that Bartleby is ill, and they foreshadow his eventual death by starvation.

These physical, tangible reminders of Bartleby's poverty help to develop his status as a symbol of poverty, and understanding him as a symbol of poverty can help readers to see a coherent meaning for "Bartleby, the Scrivener." Bartleby begins to seem less realistic and more symbolic when readers realize that he never leaves the office at all. The narrator frequently remarks on the places that Bartleby does not visit—"he never visited any refectory" (2414); he "never went out for a walk" (2414). At one point, he remarks, "I observed that he never went to dinner; indeed . . . he never went any where. As yet I had never of my personal knowledge known him to be outside of my office" (2410). In an almost surreal way, Bartleby seems to have no existence outside of his work. As the title implies, his character has been reduced to a single dimension. He is a worker—Bartleby, the scrivener. And the narrator tells us that, as a worker in the offices of No. —— Wall Street, Bartleby is always there:

"One prime thing was this,—he was always there;—first in the morning, continually through the day, and the last at night" (2412). This phrase, which Melville italicizes, evokes the famous biblical passage from Matthew 26:11, "For ye have the poor always with you" (King James Bible). This passage from Matthew echoes an Old Testament verse from Deuteronomy that gives explicit teaching about the treatment of the poor: "For the poor shall never cease out of the land: therefore I command thee, saying, Thou shalt open thine hand wide unto thy brother, to thy poor, and to thy needy, in thy land" (King James Bible Deuteronomy 15:11). "Bartleby, the Scrivener," is filled with biblical references, and it repeatedly asks questions about the responsibilities that individuals owe to one another, so it seems reasonable to think that these passages can help readers to understand the messages behind the text.

Even though Bartleby at first seems a perfect worker who has no life or existence beyond the office, he soon ceases to work. When this happens, the narrator begins a long struggle to understand his new relationship with Bartleby. At one point, he says, "What shall I do? I now said to myself, buttoning up my coat to the last button. What shall I do? what ought I do? what does conscience say I *should* do with this man, or rather ghost?" (2422). When he calls Bartleby a "ghost," the lawyer seems to reference Bartleby's pallor, that very real reminder of his poverty and his poor health. The lawyer develops this imagery, frequently speaking of Bartleby as a kind of ghost. Just two paragraphs earlier, for example, he calls the scrivener an "apparition" and an "intolerable incubus." This language of ghostliness also characterizes the lawyer's new "relationship" with Bartleby. Poor, homeless Bartleby haunts the narrator just as the specter of poverty haunted the well-off who worked on Wall Street. And like the omnipresent poor, Bartleby raises serious ethical questions for the lawyer.

Earlier in the story, when Bartleby was still willing to do some work, the narrator muses:

> He is useful to me. I can get along with him. If I turn him away, the chances are he will fall in with some less indulgent employer, and then he will be rudely treated, and perhaps driven forth miserably to starve. Yes. Here I can cheaply purchase a delicious self-approval. To befriend Bartleby; to humor him in his strange willfulness, will cost me little or nothing, while I lay up in my soul what will eventually prove a sweet morsel for my conscience. (2410)

As the story progresses, Bartleby becomes more difficult; humoring him becomes much more costly, and the narrator can no longer view his relationship with the scrivener as "a sweet morsel for [his] conscience" that is "cheaply purchase[d]." The ethical questions of what he "ought" to do, what his "conscience [says he] should do" really begin to tax the narrator. He offers Bartleby 20 dollars as a kind of severance package; he offers to help him find his family; he offers to help Bartleby find suitable employment; and he even offers to take Bartleby home. But like the problem of poverty, Bartleby refuses to be easily solved.

Clearly, and justifiably, frustrated with Bartleby, the narrator now tries to ignore the problem that Bartleby poses. He says:

> My first emotions had been those of pure melancholy and sincerest pity; but just in proportion as the forlornness of Bartleby grew and grew to my imagination, did that same melancholy merge into fear, that pity into repulsion. So true it is, and so terrible too, that up to a certain point the thought or sight of misery enlists our best affections; but, in certain special cases, beyond

that point it does not. They err who would assert
that invariably this is owing to the inherent
selfishness of the human heart. It rather proceeds
from a certain hopelessness of remedying excessive
and organic ill. To a sensitive being, pity is not
seldom pain. And when at last it is perceived that
such pity cannot lead to effectual succor, common
sense bids the soul to be rid of it. (2414)

Realizing that the problem of Bartleby, like the
problem of poverty, is difficult and persistent, the
narrator tries various ways to "be rid of it." He tries
to ignore Bartleby, and he finally tries to run away
from Bartleby by vacating his offices. Neither of these
tactics work. After the lawyer has moved his business
to another office, the new occupant of No. —— Wall
Street approaches the narrator. The interchange between
the two lawyers is important:

> "Then sir," said the stranger, who proved a lawyer,
> "you are responsible for the man you left there.
> He refuses to do any thing; he says he prefers not
> to; and he refuses to quit the premises."
>   "I am very sorry, sir," said I, with assumed
> tranquility, but an inward tremor, "but really,
> the man you allude to is nothing to me—he is no
> relation or apprentice of mine, that you should
> hold me responsible for him." (2423)

The visitor reminds the narrator that he does bear a
responsibility to Bartleby. Yet, despite his earlier
recognition that "both I and Bartleby were sons of
Adam" (2414), the narrator repeatedly denies this
responsibility, obviously echoing Peter's denial of
Christ in Mark 14:68.
    The narrator finally finds that he cannot be rid
of his human obligations to Bartleby, and he seems
to realize the magnitude of those obligations when he

speaks of being held to the "terrible account" (2423). He visits Bartleby in prison. Perhaps here Melville echoes Matthew 25:36, "I was in prison, and ye came unto me" (King James Bible). On the last of these visits, the narrator finds Bartley starved to death, and when the prison grub-man asks, "does he live without dining?" the narrator responds, "Lives without dining." The narrator is correct in his assessment here. Bartleby "lives" even after his death. From the beginning, Bartleby seemed more like a ghost than a flesh-and-blood man, and even in death he continues to haunt the narrator's conscience. This haunting explains the narrator's decision to tell Bartleby's story. His narrative is a kind of confession from an "eminently safe man" (2403) who prefers peace, prudence, and method, prefers to have nothing "invade [his] peace" (2403). His confession reminds readers that like Bartleby who is "*always there*," poverty will continue to haunt and challenge humanity. Perhaps that explains the narrator's final exclamation: "Ah Bartleby! Ah Humanity!" (2427).

WORKS CITED

The Bible, King James Version. 20 November 2006. Electronic Text Center. University of Virginia Library. 1 August 2007. <http://etext.virginia.edu/kjv.browse.html>.

Melville, Herman. "Bartleby, the Scrivener." *The Heath Anthology of American Literature.* Vol. 1. 3rd ed. Ed. Paul Lauter. Boston and New York: Houghton Mifflin: 1998. 2410–2427.

HOW TO WRITE ABOUT HERMAN MELVILLE

AN OVERVIEW

THE SHAPE of Melville's career, both before and after his death, seems to be marked by a struggle with reputation. More correctly, his career has been marked by a struggle with reputations, for Melville's writing elicited a surprisingly wide range of responses from the reading public. For contemporary students—who may know only of Melville's status as a "great" American writer and the author of *Moby-Dick*—the history of his literary reception might prove surprising. His first work, *Typee: A Peep at Polynesian Life,* was published when Melville was just 27 and was based on his own experiences living among the Typee people on the Marquesan island of Nukuheva. *Typee* initiated Melville's life-long struggle with reception and reputation. Melville proved a master of adventure and suspense. The narrator, Tommo, jumps ship and avoids capture as he travels across the island, eventually finding himself in the territory of the Typees, who have a reputation as brutal and savage cannibals. As Tommo lives peaceably among these people, Melville dangles the ever-present threat of cannibalism and violence. The book sold well, and many reviews praised it as an adventure narrative that provided a realistic glimpse into the ways of a people long regarded as "savages." The *London Times* noted that *Typee* was "endowed with freshness and originality to an extent that cannot fail to exhilarate the most enervated and *blasé* of circulating-library loungers." At the same time, the book spawned another thread of response. Because Melville challenged Western missionary efforts and colonialism, some reviewers found the book offensive. As a response to the vehement criticism of the religious press,

Melville's American publishers pressured Melville to "revise" the second edition of *Typee*. Despite these negative responses, *Typee*, along with its "sequel," *Omoo*, accorded Melville a complex literary reputation, one far different from his current status as an esteemed, canonical author. On one hand, he was an instant literary success, a minor celebrity. Still further, the book's discussion of the sexual freedoms of the Typee people turned Melville into something like the 19th-century equivalent of a rock star, a man of fame, talent, and sexual frankness.

This strong start to Melville's career would haunt him for most of his life. As he matured, his interests changed, and he wished to write books that were different from *Typee* and *Omoo*. While Melville longed to travel in new literary directions, his reading public wanted and expected more adventure narratives. He complained to Nathaniel Hawthorne in an 1851 letter, "What 'reputation' H. M. has is horrible. Think of it! To go down to posterity is bad enough, any way; but to go down as a 'man who lived among the cannibals'!" Throughout the rest of his career Melville would struggle against his initial success and the expectations of the reading public. After his marriage, as a man with a growing family, Melville would feel the pressure of public acclaim even more, for he became acutely aware that he could be assured of an income only if he pleased the reading public. That 1851 letter to Hawthorne provides a great deal of insight into both Melville's financial conundrum and his attitude toward the reading public. He touches on the matter of finances as he describes his revision of *Moby-Dick*: "In a week or so, I go to New York, to bury myself in a third-story room, and work and slave on my 'Whale' while it is diving through the press. *That* is the only way I can finish it now,—I am so pulled hither and thither by circumstances. . . . Dollars damn me; and the malicious Devil is forever grinning in upon me, holding the door ajar. . . . What I feel most moved to write, that is banned,—it will not pay. Yet, altogether, write the *other* way I cannot. So the product is a final hash, and all my books are botches." Earlier in the letter he comments on the wants of the reading public and his ability to make a living: "Try to get a living by the Truth—and go to the Soup Societies. . . . Truth is ridiculous to men." When *Moby-Dick* went to publication, it clearly demonstrated the new directions in which Melville hoped to travel, but his readership, anxious for more of the stuff from which *Typee* was made, was disappointed. On the whole, the book was poorly received and poorly understood. While Melville's friend Evert A. Duyckinck could praise *Moby-Dick* as "a most remarkable sea-dish—an intellectual chowder of romance, philosophy, natural history, fine writing, good feeling, bad sayings," most responses were more in keeping with the reviewer for the London *Athenaeum,* who declared the work "an ill-compounded mixture of romance and matter-of-fact," and complained that "the idea of a connected and collected story has obviously visited and abandoned its writer again and again in the course of composition."

Melville's 1850 essay "Hawthorne and His Mosses" affords a more thorough glimpse into the author's ideas about popularity and truth-telling, and he seems to argue that they are antithetical. He claims that Hawthorne and Shakespeare are "masters of the great Art of Telling the truth," but the "common eye," the "superficial skimmer of pages," does not appreciate their genius. Hawthorne is "too deserving of popularity to be popular." Of Shakespeare he maintains, "few men have time, or patience, or palate, for the spiritual truth as it is in that great genius." Nevertheless, despite his reverence for Shakespeare, Melville refuses to worship him as the pinnacle of literary achievement. As he argues for the establishment of a uniquely American literature, he says, "if Shakespeare has not been equaled, he is sure to be surpassed, and surpassed by an American born now or yet to be born." Perhaps Melville was slyly insinuating something about his own potential; perhaps he aspired to surpass Shakespeare and become the "literary Shiloh of America."

Surely to many modern students of American literature Melville has been firmly ensconced in that position. After spending most of his adult life trying to outrun the expectations created by the success of *Typee,* battling the indifference and hostility of the reading public, and confronting the harsh economic realities of authorship, Melville's literary reputation turned around more than 30 years after his death. During the 1920s, scholars and literary critics rediscovered and reassessed his work, spawning the "Melville Renaissance." Currently, his reputation precedes him, and many students know him only as the author of *Moby-Dick,* a novel that seems large, dense, difficult, and "boring."

If you come to Melville armed only with an awareness of this reputation, you may be surprised by what you discover in your own encounters with the author and his texts. Melville's early life experiences were not easy. While he was of affluent parentage, his father found himself bankrupt when Melville was 11, and less than two years later Allan Melvill was dead. In the wake of the family tragedy, Herman Melville worked at a number of jobs in an effort to support his family and himself. In the span of seven years, Melville had worked as a bank clerk, as a clerk for his older brother's fur store, as a teacher, and as a farmhand. In 1839, he went to sea, and before he returned to Boston in 1844 he served on a merchant ship, on whalers, and on a naval ship. While the work was hard and the environment often brutal, Melville's voyages took him to places many people will never see. He traveled to Britain, Hawaii, South America, the Marquesas, Tahiti, and the Galápagos Islands. The people and the places that Melville experienced during these years populate his fiction, and though Melville might cringe at the comparison, reading his work is akin to watching the Discovery Channel. Written in the wake of Charles Darwin's visit to the Galápagos aboard the HMS *Beagle,* "The Encantadas" provides a different glimpse of the desolate landscape of the Galápagos Islands, their famous "antediluvian-looking," "really wondrous" tortoises appearing like a refrain throughout the work. If *Moby-Dick* is heavily laden with dense philosophical passages, it also exposes the whaling industry as one of history's dirty jobs, for Melville depicts the rendering of whales as brutal, gory, bloody, and dangerous. In chapter 96, "The Try-Works," he tells of the practice of using "tried out . . . crisp, shrivelled blubber . . ." as fuel for the fire used in the rendering process. "These fritters feed the flames," he says. "Like a plethoric burning martyr . . . once ignited, the whale supplies his own fuel and burns by his own body." And he adds, "Would that he consumed his own smoke! for his smoke is horrible to inhale. . . . It has an unspeakable, wild, Hindoo odor about it, such as may lurk in the vicinity of funeral pyres." And in *Typee* he paints the edenic landscape of the Marquesas and provides a "peep" into the world of the Typee people. And, as his first readers realized in 1846, he laces the book with adventure and suspense.

Modern students are also often surprised by Melville's humor. *Typee* begins with anecdotes about cross-cultural encounters, including a story of a tribal queen who, during a military ceremony aboard a Western ship, raised her skirts to show her tattoos to a tattooed sailor. Similarly, consider the encounter that appears toward the end of "Bartleby, the Scrivener." The narrator has been called back to his former offices because the new tenant cannot get rid of Bartleby. When he enters, the narrator encounters his perplexing former employee:

> Going up stairs to my old haunt, there was Bartleby silently sitting upon the banister at the landing.

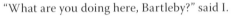

"What are you doing here, Bartleby?" said I.

"Sitting upon the banister," he mildly replied.

Along with the adventure and the humor, the serious side of Melville remains. Even in his "popular" works, such as *Typee*, he engages serious and weighty questions. Never one to blindly accept the common beliefs and practices of his culture, he challenges Western missionary work in the South Pacific in this first book, and he criticizes Western colonialism, a practice he argues that was destroying the people and the paradises of the South Seas. Throughout his career, he continued to challenge other beliefs and practices sacrosanct in his culture: traditional Christian beliefs, the superiority of "civilization," the benefits of industrialism and business, and the viability of Reconstruction after the Civil War. As a reader, you may be surprised how strikingly modern Melville seems. Many of the issues and concerns he addresses still have modern relevance. In works such as *Benito Cereno* and *Typee,* he asks readers to consider questions of race and to reevaluate racial stereotypes. Certainly our world still feels the effects of the colonialism that Melville critiques in *Typee*. *Moby-Dick*, "Bartleby, the Scrivener," and "The Paradise of Bachelors and the Tartarus of Maids" can all be read as critiques of the principles of business and industry, and the same principles seem to lay behind modern business practices. Finally, as the United States fights on foreign soil today, it is hard not to see the relevance of some of the questions *Billy Budd* asks about the sometimes violent collision between war and human rights.

If you are a reader coming to Melville for the first time, forget his modern reputation as a "great" American writer and the author of *Moby-Dick*. Instead, read his work as the effort of a man who lost his father when he was 12 and who was forced into the world where he met people from all walks of life and visited places that few of us will ever have the opportunity to see. Remember that, above all, he strived to tell the truth in a world that was often loath to hear the truths he told. Keep in mind the words of the 20th-century poet Marianne Moore, whose poem "Poetry" seems to give advice to the unwilling reader:

I, too, dislike it: there are things that are important beyond all this fiddle.

Reading it, however, with a perfect contempt for it, one discovers in it after all, a place for the genuine.

Melville's work is full of the "genuine," and if you read with an eye for the genuine, you will find plenty of material from which to build strong, insightful, and interesting papers.

TOPICS AND STRATEGIES

The paragraphs below should help you generate ideas for papers on Melville's works. The topic suggestions below provide broad ideas for essays about themes, characters, literary forms, language, and imagery. In addition, they should guide your thinking about the cultural context of both Melville and his works, suggesting historical and philosophical topics for consideration. Remember that these topics are quite broad; they give you a general framework to guide you as you read, reread, and analyze the text or texts that you will write about. You will need to narrow the focus of your paper, constructing an analytical thesis and bearing in mind the proposed length of your paper.

Themes

Readers often begin analysis of a work of literature by asking what the work is about; these questions lead to the theme of the work. In order to write about themes, you need not only determine what the work is about, but also what it says about that particular theme. If you have observed that industrialism seems to be a central theme in "The Paradise of Bachelors and the Tartarus of Maids," you will need to determine what Melville says about industrialism in this work. You may find that examining other elements of the text—such as character and imagery—will help to develop an understanding of Melville's themes.

Sample Topics:

1. **America and democracy:** Examine Melville's interest in America and American democracy in his works. What does he say about America, its values, and its position in the world order?

   In "Hawthorne and His Mosses" Melville speaks of the necessity for an American literature, and nearly every one of his major works could be read as a commentary on America, its characteristics and its values. Clearly, the country, its past and its future, constitute the major focus of *Battle-Pieces,* but even works that initially seem to have little to do with America and democracy could be read as commentaries on Melville's homeland. *Billy Budd*, for instance, is set aboard a British man-of-war during the 18th century, but it deals with questions of war, revolt, and human rights and was written in the wake of the American Civil War. *Benito Cereno*, though it takes place in the waters off South America aboard a Spanish ship, centers on American attitudes and values through its portrait of the American captain, Delano.

2. **Paradise and the fall:** Analyze the theme of Eden and the fall throughout Melville's writing. Why is this theme so prominent in his work?

You might find connections between Melville's imagery of paradise and his handling of America as a subject. Does the nation function as a paradise in any of his work? What qualities mark the Edens of Melville's fiction? Where and how does he portray the fall from paradise? You may find it suggestive to explore the relationship between Eden and the theme of innocence. How are the two connected? Similarly, Melville seems almost as interested in portraying metaphorical hells in his fiction. "The Paradise of Bachelors and the Tartarus of Maids" clearly works on the contrast between paradise and hell, and "The Encantadas" portrays an infernal, "fallen" world.

3. **God and religion:** What does Melville's portrayal of God and of religion suggest about his worldview and his belief system?

Melville's first published work, *Typee*, critiqued Western missionaries and their work in the South Seas. *Moby-Dick* is similarly unkind to traditional Christianity. While Melville was raised in the Dutch Reformed Church and knew the tenets of Calvinism, his worldview, finally, seems at odds with the religion of his youth. Hawthorne once said of him, "He can neither believe, nor be comfortable in his unbelief; and he is too honest and courageous not to try to do one or the other." How does Melville's work provide evidence of his deep ambivalence about God, religion, and religious practices?

4. **Nature and humanity's relationship with nature:** Examine Melville's works for evidence of his attitudes toward nature. How does he characterize the relationship between nature and humanity?

This question relates to an exploration of Melville's attitude toward God, for both topics ask you to examine Melville's worldview. Readers have argued that the white whale embodies both nature and God, and you could easily focus an entire paper on Melville's conception of nature in *Moby-Dick*. You might find that it is helpful to ground such an exploration in the theories of transcendentalism, which Melville knew and was probably responding to. Similarly, a good deal of "The Encantadas" focuses on nature and the natural world, and, toward the end of that work, Melville explores the connection between the "fallen" natural world of the Galápagos and the humans who visit or inhabit the island.

Character

Characters can provide a way to analyze texts because readers often react to them as they would to real people. As you develop a focus for a paper on Melville's treatment of character, you might begin by considering your own reaction to the characters. Did you sympathize with a particular character? Why or why not? From there, you should develop your analysis, by examining the characters' language and behavior. Evaluate their relationships with other characters as well as the imagery associated with them. If you are planning a paper that analyzes characters in a few works, you should look for patterns. Are there characteristics that mark the bachelors of Melville's fiction? What are they? Why does Melville seem drawn to the figure of the bachelor, and how does he use his bachelors in his texts? As you draw conclusions about patterns in character development, you can begin to shape a thoughtful thesis for an essay.

Sample Topics:

1. **Melville's bachelors:** Melville's major works are populated largely by men, and he seemed particularly interested in the figure of the bachelor. Examine some of Melville's bachelors, and draw some conclusions about his use of these figures. What do

these men represent for Melville? Does he use them to reflect on some of his themes? Does he use them to comment on issues of gender and sexuality, or does their function seem tied to other social issues?

Readers have long noted Melville's interest in the figure of the bachelor. What do you notice about Melville's bachelors? Do they all seem to possess the same characteristics and play the same roles in the social milieus that he creates? "The Paradise of Bachelors and the Tartarus of Maids" provides an obvious starting place for such an investigation, and the conclusions that you draw from an analysis of this work should help you develop a more extended evaluation of Melville's use of the bachelor figure. Other bachelor figures include the narrator from "Bartleby, the Scrivener," as well as some of Melville's sailors and ship captains. You might also note that some of the ships from Melville's works are labeled as bachelors: *The Bachelor's Delight* in *Benito Cereno*, for example, and the *Bachelor* of *Moby-Dick*. How might a consideration of these "bachelors" and their crew help to develop your analysis of Melville's bachelors?

2. **Foundlings and orphans:** Melville populates his fiction with orphans and foundlings. Why does Melville use characters without clear parentage or heritage so frequently? What significance or conclusions can you draw about Melville's frequent use of these figures? Why does he return to them again and again? Does his treatment of the foundling reveal anything about his interests or the themes of his fiction?

While Melville was not an orphan, he was just 12 when his once wealthy father, Allan Melvill, died bankrupt in 1832. Melville and his older brother, Gansevoort, left school to help provide for their family. The fatherless Melville was forced into the adult world when he was just a child, and this experience clearly had a profound influence on the writer. It seems likely that the recurring figure of the orphan or the foundling is tied to the experience of Melville's youth. Orphans and fatherless characters figure prominently in his work; Ahab, Pip, and Billy

Budd provide prominent examples. In addition, you might find it helpful to explore the many characters who, though they are not definitely marked as orphans or foundlings, seem to be without a past or a clear position in society—Bartleby and Ishmael, for instance. How are these characters related to the orphans of Melville's work? You might also think of other characters, such as Babo and Queequeg, who seem to have no clear place in Western society. What do these characters share with the orphans and the outcasts of Melville's work? Are issues of race related to the issues that Melville raises through his treatment of orphans and foundlings in his fiction?

3. **Western and non-Western characters:** Explore Melville's portrayal of non-Westerners in his fiction. How and why does he portray these characters for his American audience?

Melville's experiences at sea and abroad provided him with the opportunity to meet people of different races and cultures. Perhaps more than any other American writer of his time, he provided portraits of these people in his fiction. *Typee, Moby-Dick,* and *Benito Cereno* provide the most obvious starting places for this topic. Clearly, you should consider issues of race and of racial prejudice. Does Melville seem to be free of the racial prejudices of his time, or does he seem to participate in them? Consider, too, how the point of view of the fiction affects the portrayal of characters such as Babo, Queequeg, or any of the Typees. *Typee* and *Moby-Dick* both include first-person narrators, and *Benito Cereno* works through a complicated use of perspective or point of view.

History and Context

Melville's work is rooted in 19th-century America, and it reflects an interest in the politics, events, and philosophies of his time. Background reading on antebellum America, on Melville's biography, and on the social issues and events of his day will provide context for his treatment of history and culture. Similarly, Melville was a copious and analytical reader, and if you know something about the books and authors he read, you will have more insight into his work. Whether you are exploring the influence of Melville's reading or the effects of the political, economic, and social issues of 19th-century America, remember that your historical and contextual research should inform your analysis of Melville's texts. Your paper should focus on the literature, exploring the influence of history and context on the work.

Sample Topics:

1. **Melville's reading:** Explore the effect of Melville's reading on his writing.

   Melville read copiously. He grew up in the Dutch Reformed Church, and he knew his Bible well. All of his writings reflect his knowledge of the Bible, and many refer explicitly to individual biblical passages or biblical characters. *Moby-Dick*, "Bartleby, the Scrivener," and *Billy Budd* should prove particularly suggestive. Similarly, Melville was well read in classic British authors such as Shakespeare, Milton, and Spenser. He also read widely from travel and adventure narratives and knew what others had said about the places that he visited and wrote about. All of this reading left a clear mark on his own work. His knowledge of Shakespeare permeates many of his works, especially *Moby-Dick* and *Billy Budd.* Milton's *Paradise Lost* echoes loudly throughout *Battle-Pieces* as Melville contemplates the Civil War and its effects. Spenser's *Fairie Queene* provides most of the epigrams for the individual sketches for "The Encantadas." If you are interested in Melville's use of travel and adventure narratives, you may find it useful to explore his methods and strategies in adapting some of these narratives. *Moby-Dick*, *Typee*, "The Encantadas," and *Benito Cereno* should all provide plenty of material for such explorations.

2. **Melville's own history at sea:** Explore the connection between Melville's writing and his own travels and his experiences at sea.

   Melville served aboard whale ships, merchant ships, and a naval ship. He lived among the native inhabitants of Nukuheva in the Marquesas and he visited Hawaii, Tahiti, and the Galápagos. During his travels, he met people of many different races from many different cultures. Clearly his experiences at sea affected his writing. While *Typee* seems to be most directly drawn from his own life, works such as *Moby-Dick* and "The Encantadas" are also rooted in Melville's life. A paper on this topic might examine Melville's strategies for recasting his own experiences and his methods of reshaping them into fiction.

3. **The Civil War:** While most of Melville's major works were published prior to the American Civil War, the conflict clearly affected his later work. Explore the effect of the Civil War on Melville's writing.

Melville turned to poetry during his later years. Some scholars speculate that this change was the result of the poor reception of his fiction. Whatever his reasoning for trying his hand at poetry, Melville's first published collection (though not the first collection that he wrote or tried to publish) was *Battle-Pieces*, which centered on the war and its effects. Clearly, you cannot explore the effect of the war on Melville without closely studying this volume. *Billy Budd*, which Melville was still revising when he died, also seems inspired by the tensions and issues of the war. Though it is set aboard a British man-of-war during the 18th century, it addresses questions of revolt and revolution, war, and the fall from innocence, all of which Melville tackled in *Battle-Pieces.*

Philosophy and Ideas

Another way to examine Melville's writing is through its engagement with social ideas or philosophies. Melville's work sometimes makes direct reference to the ideas of past philosophers, such as Rousseau and Locke. At other times, he engages the philosophies of his time. Much of his work seems to address the thinking and the worldview of transcendentalists such as Emerson. Perhaps Melville's most thoroughgoing philosophical interest concerns epistemological questions. Many of his texts explore the connection between perception and understanding, and he continually emphasizes the relationship between observation and knowledge. As Pip says after watching his shipmates contemplate the gold doubloon on the *Pequod*'s mast: "I look, you look, he look; we look, ye look, they look."

Sample Topics:

1. **Perception and understanding:** What kind of commentary does Melville make about the relationship between perception and understanding? What does he say about what humans know and how humans know?

   Clearly, the nature of human understanding and its link to individual perception is a central concern in *Moby-Dick,* but this philosophical concern also runs throughout Melville's work. Perception and understanding are also central to *Benito Cereno,* "Bartleby, the Scrivener," and "The Paradise of Bachelors and the Tartarus of Maids." You could easily examine other Melville texts in an investigation of this philosophical theme.

2. **Transcendentalism:** Explore Melville's response to or his treatment of the philosophy of transcendentalism expressed by such thinkers as Ralph Waldo Emerson.

   In a May 1851 letter to Nathaniel Hawthorne, Melville wrote: "In reading some of Goethe's sayings . . . I came across this, 'Live in the all.' That is to say, your separate identity is but a wretched one,—good; but get out of yourself, spread and expand yourself, and bring to yourself the tinglings of life that are felt in the flowers and the woods, that are felt in the planets Saturn and Venus, and the Fixed Stars. What nonsense!" In his postscript to the letter, though, Melville returns to that concept: "N.B. This 'all' feeling, though, there is some truth in. You must often have felt it, lying on the grass on a warm summer's day. Your legs seem to send out shoots into the earth. Your hair feels like leaves upon your head. This is the *all* feeling. But what plays the mischief with the truth is that men will insist upon the universal application of a temporary feeling or opinion."
   Melville's description of this "all feeling" seems to share a good deal with Emerson's transcendental ideas, especially those

expressed in his work *Nature*. Literary scholars have pointed particularly to a few elements in *Nature* that seem to have a direct bearing on *Moby-Dick*, including Emerson's focus on sight and perception. Nor are Melville's explorations of and reactions to transcendentalism limited to *Moby-Dick*. You might find that as Melville comments on God and the natural world he is also reacting to transcendental notions of God, nature, and the universe. *Battle-Pieces*, "The Encantadas," and "The Paradise of Bachelors and the Tartarus of Maids" might prove particularly useful for a paper on Melville and transcendentalism.

3. **The noble savage:** His travels and his interactions with native people in the South Seas caused Melville to reconsider ideas about civilization and savagery. In *Typee*, he addresses Rousseau's notion of the "noble savage" who is innocent, good, and free from the corrupting influence of civilization. Explore Melville's treatment of the noble savage in his fiction.

In order to address this question, you should familiarize yourself with the philosophy of the noble savage. The concept of the uncivilized innocent is often associated with the writings of Jean-Jacques Rousseau and romantic philosophy, though it has it roots in the Enlightenment. Clearly, *Typee* provides a starting point for such an exploration. Certainly, *Moby-Dick* is also relevant, especially given its treatment of Queequeg and its contemplation of notions of civilization and savagery. Melville's treatment of these ideas in these earlier texts may have implications for later texts such as *Benito Cereno* and *Billy Budd*.

4. **Colonization and political structure:** Explore Melville's commentary on colonization and human political structures.

Melville's treatment of colonization and colonialism is related to his ideas about savagery and civilization, but his examination of human political structures develops this investigation even further. Having arrived in Nukuheva when the French were colonizing the Marquesas, Melville critiqued colonialism in *Typee*. Interestingly, the seventh and ninth sketch of

"The Encantadas" explore the idea of colonization in more abstract terms, and this work also considers the efficacy and the legitimacy of various human political structures. Given Melville's interest in American democracy, "Hawthorne and His Mosses," *Benito Cereno*, and *Battle-Pieces* might also prove fruitful for a paper that explores Melville's commentary on political structure.

Form and Genre

Examining the structure or the form of a text can also provide insight into its meanings, and you can build insightful papers from such an analysis. Melville's habit of incorporating his own experiences into his fiction consistently presents a challenge for readers because it tends to test traditional definitions of the novel and the short story. Similarly, Melville's first-person narrators further complicate his use of these genres. Thinking analytically about the form and the structure of Melville's works can provide important insights into Melville's themes and purposes.

Sample Topics:

1. **Melville's challenges to traditional generic forms:** Explore the ways in which Melville's works challenge traditional conceptions of genres such as the novel and the short story.

   In a paper on form and genre, you might want to think about the building blocks of Melville's works and to consider how he shapes and structures the works from those materials. *Typee,* for example, draws from Melville's biography and incorporates elements of fiction, memoir, biography, and travel writing. Consequently, the work is hard to classify. *Moby-Dick,* now commonly thought of as a powerful novel, shifts narrative point of view, partakes of the elements of drama, and includes lengthy philosophical passages. All of these elements seem to violate accepted novelistic conventions. "The Encantadas," one of Melville's magazine pieces, clearly incorporates some of the elements of fiction, and yet its structure and style seem to separate it from more traditional magazine fiction. Consider why Melville played with, stretched, and challenged these forms. What purposes do his nontraditional structures serve?

2. **Narrative voice:** Examine the narrative voice in some of Melville's works and explore how voice and point of view affect the meaning of the texts.

While you should always consider the narrative point of view when you read a text, such analysis is especially important to an understanding of Melville's works. It is important not to confuse the narrator with the author. If you conflate Melville and the narrator of "Bartleby," you will misunderstand the points and purposes of the story. Consider the first-person narrators as characters in Melville's fiction and analyze how and why they think, act, and speak as they do. Similarly, in works that are told in the third person, you should think about what that third person knows and what he shares. Is the third-person narrator omniscient? Does he limit what the reader sees and knows of the characters? Why would Melville decide to tell a story from the particular narrative point of view that he chooses?

Language, Symbols, and Imagery

Writers craft and build their art through careful use of language, and careful attention to Melville's language will provide you with insight into his ideas. Students who are alert to the nuances of language and imagery have a much more vivid understanding and appreciation of a work, and their papers often provide penetrating analysis of the effects of an author's use of language and imagery. If you have read widely from Melville's work, you will begin to see familiar patterns of imagery. He often used color imagery, and the contrast of light and dark, in particular, recurs frequently in his work. Similarly, he often employed animal imagery in his fiction. As you analyze the imagery of his texts, consider the common or traditional connotations of such language. Does Melville rely on these traditional or common meanings, or does he develop or change them? What are the effects of the changes that he makes? Develop your analysis of imagery and symbolism by drawing connections to the themes or meaning of a work. How does an understanding of Melville's figurative language enhance a reader's understanding of his meanings or purposes?

Sample Topics:

1. **Color imagery:** Examine Melville's use of color imagery. Pay particular attention to his use of light and dark. How and why does he employ this imagery?

   In "Hawthorne and His Mosses," Melville praises the darkness of Hawthorne's fiction, and he writes of the "blackness, ten times black" that shrouds the "hither side of Hawthorne's soul." The imagery of blackness and darkness was important for Melville, and he uses that same imagery often in his own work. You might start, then, by examining the philosophy of fiction that Melville expresses in "Hawthorne and His Mosses." *Moby-Dick*, published soon after this essay, also uses much of the same imagery. While the book obviously centers on white and whiteness, Melville makes clear the connections between the imagery of whiteness and its dark opposite. "The Paradise of Bachelors and the Tartarus of Maids," "The Encantadas," *Benito Cereno*, "Bartleby, the Scrivener," and *Typee* all use the imagery of light and dark, and any of these texts could form the basis of an essay on Melville's use of color imagery.

2. **Animal imagery:** Analyze Melville's use of animal imagery. How and why does he use animal imagery?

   While your first thought about animal imagery in Melville might be his infamous white whale, there are a great many ways to explore Melville's use of animal imagery. Obviously, Moby Dick functions as a symbol in the novel that bears its name, and a thorough analysis of the whale and its function in the novel could support numerous papers. Shark imagery, too, becomes important in *Moby-Dick*, and Melville returns to this imagery late in his career in *Battle-Pieces*. You could analyze the recurring images of tortoises in "The Encantadas," and animal imagery plays important roles in *Benito Cereno* and *Billy Budd*. The author's use of animal imagery often reflects his attitudes toward humanity or toward individual characters; at other times it communicates broad philosophical concerns.

3. **Tattoos and bodily markings:** Examine Melville's use of tattoos and bodily markings. How would you characterize his use of this imagery?

Tattoos and tattooing play an important role in *Typee*, and Tommo comments extensively on the Typees' tattoos. A scene at the end of the book portrays Tommo's reaction when an artist wants to tattoo Tommo's face. In *Moby-Dick*, Melville continues to explore tattooing and bodily marking through his treatment of Queequeg as well as through the marks on the bodies of Ahab, Ishmael, and Moby Dick. You could continue to trace Melville's attention to bodily marking into his later fiction if you explore "The Paradise of Bachelors and the Tartarus of Maids" and "The Encantadas." Conversely, in "Bartleby," the scrivener's pallor, the absence of bodily marking, seems relevant to Melville's points about Bartleby and his place in society.

Compare and Contrast Essays

Comparing and contrasting elements in or across works provide a common and often effective strategy for developing an essay. Examining the author's language or techniques in one text often suggests important questions about another work. Why, for example, does Melville adapt the narratives of others in *Moby-Dick, Benito Cereno,* and "The Encantadas"? What insight into the meanings of the texts does a comparative analysis of his sources provide? Considering the whys behind such comparisons and contrasts, though, is extremely important. If you do not craft a thesis that proposes an answer to such questions, your paper is likely to become little more than a list of interesting—or not so interesting—similarities and differences. Teachers dread these papers because they have no apparent purpose or organizing principle. Whether you choose to compare and contrast elements within a work, elements across Melville's work, or whether you are comparing Melville's works to those of another author, be sure that you structure your paper around an analytical thesis that makes a point or an argument about the similarities and differences that you have observed.

Sample Topics:

1. **Examining elements across Melville's work:** Compare and contrast Melville's use or treatment of a particular element—theme, character type, philosophy, or pattern of imagery—in two or more of his works.

   You might begin work on this topic by selecting an element that you find particularly interesting or engaging and then examining that element across Melville's work. Perhaps you found his treatment of madness intriguing in your reading of *Moby-Dick*. You could begin to develop a focus for your paper by asking questions about his use of madness in other works. You may have noticed that the ship's surgeon in *Billy Budd* questions Captain Vere's sanity when he decides to convene the drum-head court, and at the beginning of chapter 21, the narrator questions how one distinguishes sanity from insanity. Could similar questions be posed about Ahab and his pursuit of Moby Dick? Do Vere and Ahab share any qualities?

2. **Analyzing elements within a work:** Much of Melville's work allows for comparative analysis of elements within the work. Choose one such element and develop an argument about Melville's use of that element.

   Just as you might analyze Melville's treatment of madness across his work, you could easily explore his treatment of that same theme within a work. In *Moby-Dick*, Pip, Elijah, Gabriel, and Ahab are described as mad. Certainly, though, Ahab's madness seems to be qualitatively different from that of the others. You might, then, explore how madness functions within the text. Why is madness so prevalent in the novel, and why might Melville have populated his novel with these characters?

3. **Relating Melville's work to that of another author:** Compare or contrast the work of another author with Melville's writing.

   In order to construct a productive analysis, you should think of the purpose behind your choice of authors. Why do you want to compare these two particular authors? What do you hope to show through your analysis? Keep in mind the projected length of your essay and focus your topic accordingly. You could write a great deal about the nature of symbolism in *Moby-Dick* and *The Scarlet Letter*, for instance, but the subject is far too broad to handle in a short paper. You might have more success comparing the treatment of gender issues in "The Paradise of Bachelors and the Tartarus of Maids" with that in Hawthorne's "The Birth-Mark." Or you might want to compare Melville's treatment of innocence in *Billy Budd* with Hawthorne's treatment of the same theme in *The Marble Faun* or "My Kinsman, Major Molineux." If you are interested in Melville's view of nature, you might find that the work of Emerson provides an interesting comparison. Rebecca Harding Davis's *Life in the Iron Mills* could provide an interesting text to compare to Melville's work. Similarly, Whitman's commentaries on democracy and on the Civil War also provide good material for comparison with Melville's treatment of the same themes.

Bibliography and Online Resources

Arvin, Newton. *Herman Melville.* New York: William Sloane, 1950.

Bickley, R. Bruce. *The Method of Melville's Short Fiction.* Durham: Duke UP, 1975.

Bloom, Harold. *Herman Melville's* Billy Budd, *"Benito Cereno," "Bartleby, the Scrivener," and Other Tales.* New York: Chelsea House, 1987.

Broadhead, Richard. *Hawthorne, Melville, and the Novel.* Chicago: U of Chicago P, 1973.

Brown, Gillian. *Domestic Individualism: Imagining Self in Nineteenth-Century America.* Berkeley: U of California P, 1990.

Bryant, John. *Melville and Repose.* New York: Oxford UP, 1993.

Cameron, Sharon. *The Corporeal Self: Allegories of the Body in Melville and Hawthorne.* Baltimore: Johns Hopkins UP, 1981.

Campbell, Donna. "Herman Melville." *American Authors.* 22 November 2006. Washington State University. 17 May 2007. <http://www.wsu.edu/~campbelld/amlit/melville.htm>.

Cassuto, Leonard. *The Inhuman Race: The Racial Grotesque in American Literature and Culture.* New York: Columbia UP, 2006.

Coffler, Gail. *Melville's Allusions to Religion: A Comprehensive Index and Glossary.* New York: Praeger Publishers, 2004.

Delbanco, Andrew. *Melville: His World and His Work.* New York: Knopf: 2005.

Dimock, Wai-chee. *Empire for Liberty: Melville and the Poetics of Individualism.* Princeton, NJ: Princeton UP, 1989.

Dryden, Edgar. *Monumental Melville: The Formation of a Literary Career.* Stanford, CA: Stanford UP, 2004.

———. *Melville's Thematics of Form: The Great Art of Telling the Truth.* Baltimore: Johns Hopkins UP, 1968.

Fisher, Marvin. *Going Under: Melville's Short Fiction and the American 1850s.* Baton Rouge: Louisiana State UP, 1977.

Fogle, Richard Harter. *Melville's Shorter Tales.* Norman: U of Oklahoma P, 1960.

———. *The Wake of the Gods: Melville's Mythology.* Stanford, CA: Stanford UP, 1963.

Gilmore, Michael T. *American Romanticism and the Marketplace.* Chicago. U of Chicago P, 1985.

Gunn, Giles. *A Historical Guide to Herman Melville.* Oxford: Oxford UP, 2005.

Hayes, Kevin J. *Melville's Folk Roots.* Kent, Ohio: Kent State UP, 1999.

Hayford, Harrison, and Hershel Parker. *Melville's Prisoners.* Evanston, IL: Northwestern UP, 2003.

Howard, Leon. *Herman Melville: A Biography.* Berkeley: U of California P, 1951.

Irwin, John. *American Hieroglyphics: The Symbol of the Egyptian Hieroglyphics in the American Renaissance.* New Haven, CT: Yale UP, 1980.

Karcher, Carolyn. *Shadow over the Promised Land: Slavery, Race, and Violence in Melville's America.* Baton Rouge: Louisiana State UP, 1980.

Kelley, Wyn. *A Companion to Herman Melville.* Oxford: Blackwell, 2006.

Levin, Harry. *The Power of Blackness: Hawthorne, Poe, Melville.* New York: Knopf, 1964.

Levine, Robert S. *The Cambridge Companion to Herman Melville.* Cambridge: Cambridge UP, 1998.

———. *Conspiracy and Romance: Studies in Brockden Brown, Cooper, Hawthorne, and Melville.* New York: Cambridge UP, 1989.

Lewis, R. W. B. *The American Adam: Innocence, Tragedy and Tradition in the Nineteenth Century.* Chicago: U of Chicago P, 1955.

The Life and Works of Herman Melville. Available online. URL: http://www.melville.org/melville.htm#Whois. Downloaded May 17, 2007.

Martin, Robert K. *Hero, Captain, and Stranger: Male Friendship, Social Critiques and Literary Form in the Novels of Herman Melville.* Chapel Hill: U of North Carolina P, 1986.

Marx, Leo. *The Machine in the Garden: Technology and the Pastoral Ideal in America.* New York: Oxford UP, 1967.

Matthiessen, F. O. *American Renaissance: Art and Expression in the Age of Emerson and Whitman.* New York: Oxford UP, 1941.

Milder, Robert. *Exiled Royalties: Melville and the Life We Imagine.* New York: Oxford UP, 2006.

Miller, James E. *A Reader's Guide to Herman Melville.* New York: Octagon, 1973.

Newman, Lea Bertani Vozar. *A Reader's Guide to the Short Stories of Herman Melville.* Boston: Hall, 1986.

Otter, Samuel. *Melville's Anatomies: Bodies, Discourse, and Ideology in Antebellum America.* Berkeley: U of California P, 1998.

Parker, Hershel. *Herman Melville.* 2 vols. Baltimore: Johns Hopkins UP, 1996, 2002.

Post-Lauria, Sheila. *Correspondent Colorings: Melville in the Marketplace.* Amherst: U of Massachusetts P, 1996.

Renker, Elizabeth. *Strike Through the Mask: Herman Melville and the Scene of Writing.* Baltimore: Johns Hopkins UP, 1996.

Reuben, Paul. PAL: Chapter 3: "Herman Melville. Perspectives in American Literature—A Research and Reference Guide—An Ongoing Project." Available online. URL: http://web.csustan.edu/english/reuben/pal/chap3/melville.html. Downloaded on October 25, 2007.

Rogin, Michael Paul. *Subversive Genealogy: The Politics and Art of Herman Melville.* New York: Knopf, 1983.

Rowe, John Carlos. *Literary Culture and U.S. Imperialism.* New York: Oxford UP, 2000.

———. *Through the Custom-House: Nineteenth-Century American Fiction and Modern Theory.* Baltimore: Johns Hopkins UP, 1982.

Sandborn, Geoffrey. *The Sign of the Cannibal: Melville and the Making of a Postcolonial Reader.* Durham, NC: Duke UP, 1998.

Sealts, Merton M., Jr. *Melville's Reading.* Columbia: U of South Carolina P, 1988.

Steelye, John. *Melville: The Ironic Diagram.* Evanston, IL: Northwestern UP, 1970.

Stern, Milton R. *Critical Essays on Herman Melville's Typee.* Boston: G. K. Hall, 1982.

Sundquist, Eric. *To Wake Nations: Race in the Making of American Literature.* Cambridge, MA: Belknap P of Harvard UP, 1993.

Thompson, Lawrance. *Melville's Quarrel with God.* Princeton, NJ: Princeton UP, 1952.

TYPEE

READING TO WRITE

MELVILLE'S FIRST book, *Typee*, simultaneously anticipates and belies the rest of Melville's literary career. Unlike *Moby-Dick*, *Typee* and its sequel, *Omoo*, sold relatively well and afforded the young author notoriety and some degree of financial success. Melville's early life at sea provided necessary experience and material for *Typee*. And yet, later in his life, Melville seemed to view the book as a sort of literary stepchild, apparently wishing to break free of the strong connection in the public mind between the author and his first, and best-selling, book. Despite Melville's later ambivalence, and despite the vast differences in the two books, readers can glimpse topics in *Typee* that Melville would develop in *Moby-Dick*. And in more recent years, with the increased interest in the portrayal of colonialism and Western imperialism in literature, readers have found a new appreciation for *Typee* and some of its major themes.

Based on Melville's experience living among the inhabitants of the Typee Valley on the Marquesan island of Nukuheva, *Typee* challenged American notions about the West's relationships with primitive cultures. Most apparently, the book challenges the urge to "civilize" these cultures. In chapter 2 of *Typee*, when the whaling ship *Dolly* first encounters the inhabitants of Nukuheva, readers can see the origins of this commentary as the narrator Tommo begins to introduce some of the islanders and their culture. As the *Dolly* sails into the bay of Nukuheva, Tommo observes the "numerous canoes" that push off to greet the ship. He soon observes that "among the number of natives . . . not a single female was to be seen." Tommo quickly informs readers that he later learned of the custom of "taboo," which prohibited women from riding in canoes.

Thus, he already begins to educate his audience about the ways of this little-known culture. He then begins to sketch a portrait of the numerous young women who swim toward the *Dolly*: "I almost fancied they could be nothing else than so many mermaids:—and like mermaids they behaved too." And as these "swimming nymphs" board the ship in welcome, Tommo continues:

> The 'Dolly' was fairly captured; and never I will say was a vessel carried before by such a dashing and irresistible party of boarders! The ship taken, we could not do otherwise than yield ourselves prisoners, and for the whole period that she remained in the bay, the 'Dolly,' as well as her crew, were completely in the hands of the mermaids.
>
> In the evening after we had come to an anchor the deck was illuminated with lanterns, and this picturesque band of sylphs, tricked out with flowers, and dressed in robes of variegated tappa, got up a ball in great style. These females are passionately fond of dancing, and in the wild graces and spirit of their style excel everything that I have ever seen. The varied dances of the Marquesan girls are beautiful in the extreme, but there is an abandoned voluptuousness in their character which I dare not attempt to describe.
>
> Our ship was now wholly given up to every species of riot and debauchery. Not the feeblest barrier was interposed between the unholy passions of the crew and their unlimited gratification. The grossest licentiousness and the most shameful inebriety prevailed, with occasional and but short-lived interruptions, through the whole period of her stay. Alas, for the poor savages when exposed to the influence of these polluting examples! Unsophisticated and confiding, they are easily led into every vice, and humanity weeps over the ruin thus remorselessly inflicted upon them by their European civilizers. Thrice happy are they who, inhabiting some yet undiscovered island in the midst of the ocean, have never been brought into contaminating contact with the white man.

Perhaps the first thing that readers notice about this passage is Tommo's playful tone. Clearly the "shoal" of young girls presents no real threat to the ship, and yet Tommo uses the language of invasion to describe the girls' ascent onto the *Dolly*. Once the women have boarded, Tommo says that the *Dolly* was "fairly captured," "taken," and that the sailors had to "yield [themselves] prisoners." Both ship and crew, the first paragraph concludes, "were completely in the hands of the mermaids." The tone is playful, and the sailors are clearly willing "prisoners" of these beautiful young women. Indeed, Tommo's description reads like the beginnings of a sailor's sexual fantasy. Readers familiar with the course of the book's action, though, might connect this pleasurable entrapment with Tommo's later situation. Once he has escaped the *Dolly* and ventured into the Typee Valley, Tommo finds himself in a veritable Eden, a pleasure paradise. Soon, despite the beauty of the valley, the kind treatment he receives, and the attentions of Fayaway and Kory-Kory, Tommo begins to speak of himself as a captive, a prisoner. How does this early passage, where the ship is "fairly captured" by the "mermaids," anticipate Tommo's situation later in the text?

These connections should encourage you to examine this early description of the young women in more detail. You might consider Tommo's description of them as "mermaids" and "sylphs" more thoroughly. Once again, these descriptions seem marked by their connections to male fantasy, and yet they do more to characterize the women and their culture. Is it significant that both mermaids and sylphs (like the nymphs to whom Tommo earlier compared the women) are mythological? How might this fact contribute to the element of male fantasy? Consider, too, what other implications their mythological status might hold for the passage. Does their unreality say anything about the paradise that Nukuheva appears to be? Does it say anything about Western conceptions and understandings of the Marquesas and their inhabitants? Still further, consider the connections between the sylphs and nature. (*Sylph* is derived from the Latin *sylvesris,* meaning "of the forest.") What does the connection between these women and the water and the forest imply about them and the other inhabitants of the island? Similarly, you might think about how the descriptions of the women and their dancing help to develop these implications. How are the descriptions of the women as "beautiful in the extreme," "passionately fond of dancing," and the "wild grace and spirit of their style" related to the portrait of the islanders that Tommo develops in this passage?

Still further, careful readers will notice just how quickly the power dynamic implied in Tommo's playful language of capture and occupation is overturned. While the women are figured as the captors and the men the "prisoners," the sailors, not the "savages" prove to be the aggressors, for the "riot and debauchery" aboard the *Dolly* are clearly driven by the "unholy passions" of the sailors. When Tommo speaks of these "unholy passions of the crew and their unlimited gratification" he portrays a scene of rape. These implications are only strengthened at the passage's end, where he extends the implications of abuse, extrapolating from the crew's treatment of the nymphs to Western treatment of the islanders: "Alas, for the poor savages when exposed to the influence of these polluting examples! Unsophisticated and confiding, they are easily led into every vice, and humanity weeps over the ruin thus remorselessly inflicted upon them by their European civilizers." Alert readers will notice how Melville overturns conventional 19th-century understanding savagery and civilization. The savage becomes the "poor savage," the victim, who, as "[un]sophisticated and confiding" and "easily led," seems innocent and childlike. By contrast, the "European civilizers" are the victimizers, "polluting" and "remorselessly inflict[ing]" ruin upon the paradise of the "poor savage." No wonder, then, that Melville ends the passage with a profoundly anticolonial statement: "Thrice happy are they who, inhabiting some yet undiscovered island . . . have never been brought into contaminating contact with the white man."

Melville's philosophy here clearly runs counter to 19th-century America's understanding of its position in the world. Along with the French and the British, the United States was claiming "undiscovered" territories as its own. In the process of colonizing these territories, Americans imported their values and their religion. These missionary efforts are a central target in *Typee.* Similarly, it is hard to read Melville's description of the "poor savages . . . exposed to the influence of [the] polluting examples" of the "European civilizers" without thinking of American history and the example of the American Indians. This, too, is a comparison that Melville would draw later in *Typee.* While he seems so eager to challenge traditional Western notions of civilization and savagery, Melville also shows an awareness of his audience and its values. While Tommo draws comparisons between rape and colonization and imperialism quite explicitly, he "dare[s] not attempt to describe" the "abandoned voluptuousness" of the Marquesan girls' dancing. Such overt self-censoring proved a successful way to speak of the sexual freedom of the Marquesan cultures without overtly offending Melville's reading public. And yet, his overt attacks on missionary efforts in the Marquesas came under a great deal of public criticism, forcing Melville to "revise" *Typee* for its second American edition. Modern readers who are alert to

Melville's treatment of audience and important themes such as the "ruin remorselessly inflicted . . . by European civilizers" should find plenty of material in *Typee* for strong, analytical papers.

TOPICS AND STRATEGIES

This section of the chapter provides you with broad topic ideas that should help you develop an essay on *Typee*. Remember that these topics are just springboards for your own exploration; you will need to focus your analysis and develop your own specific thesis.

Themes

As the Reading to Write portion of this chapter indicates, European attempts to "civilize" the "savages" of the South Sea Islands provide one of the dominant themes of *Typee*. This theme is broad, though, and you might choose to focus papers in a number of different ways. You might focus specifically on Melville's treatment of missionary efforts in the South Seas; you might focus on the imagery of exploitation and rape that Tommo uses in the passage cited above; or you might focus on the parallels between the history of the American Indian and Western activities in the South Sea Islands. You could also find quite a few other themes to analyze in a paper on *Typee*. The Reading to Write section also commented on the many connections between *Moby-Dick* and *Typee*, and the two books do share many themes. You could choose to explore the treatment of tattooing in *Typee*, since it plays a major role in Tommo's descriptions of the Typee people and their culture. Clearly, other aspects of their culture, including cannibalism and taboo, could serve as fruitful topics for a theme-based paper. Be sure that your paper makes a specific assertion about the treatment of theme in the text and is not just a series of observations connected to a theme.

Sample Topics:

1. **Civilization:** Perhaps the major theme of *Typee* is the clash of two cultures, the "civilized" West and the "primitive state of society" (chapter 17). Despite his application of such 19th-century terms as *cannibal* and *savage* to the Typees, Melville's attitude seems to run counter to the prevailing antebellum American attitudes about the South Sea Islands and the

process of "civilization." In chapter 26, as he discusses Mehevi, the Typee king, Tommo says, "May Heaven for many a year preserve him . . . if a hostile attitude will secure his lovely domain from the remorseless inflictions of South Sea civilization." What, in Melville's eyes, is wrong with American and European efforts to "civilize" the "savage" cultures of the South Sea Islands? How does he present his argument through Tommo's experiences living among the Typee?

In order to develop a response to this question, you should carefully examine the portraits of the individual islanders as well as his portraits of some of the Westerners. Beyond these individual portraits, consider Tommo's many explicit comparisons between the "primitive state of society" and "Civilization" (chapter 17). There are many passages in the book that provide explicit social analysis. What does Western civilization bring to islands like Nukuheva? What effects does it have upon the "savages" who live on these islands? In a number of places, he presents commentary on this issue through his descriptions of events on Tahiti and the Sandwich (Hawaiian) Islands. In what ways does he figure these islands as reflections of Nukuheva's future? Think about why Melville evaluates the process of civilization as he does. In his views, what drives and desires propel the Western urge to civilize? Obviously, you cannot thoroughly assess Melville's analysis of the confrontation between "primitive" society and "civilization" without analyzing his treatment of missionaries and missionary work in the South Seas. How are missionary efforts linked to the advance of civilization? What, according to Melville, drives and motivates the Christian missionary efforts in the South Seas? You might also note how explicitly Melville draws attention to the meanings of such words as *savage* and *civilized*. In chapter 17, Tommo says, "The term 'savage' is, I conceive, often misapplied." You might consider whether more modern terms like *imperialism* or *colonization* could aptly describe the civilizing process that Melville depicts in *Typee*.

2. **Eden and the fall:** Throughout *Typee*, Tommo paints the Typee
   Valley as a kind of Eden. Examine the Typee Valley's status as
   a "paradisiacal abode" (chapter 26). What are its benefits, and
   what are its drawbacks? Can *Typee* be read as an argument in
   favor of the idea of the fortunate fall?

   You should probably begin thinking about this issue by tracing
   the many ways that Melville develops the associations between
   the Typee Valley and Eden. What qualities allow this island
   world to appear so Edenic? How does Melville develop these
   associations? Consider, too, what the inhabitants of the Typee
   Valley share with Adam and Eve. In what ways do they seem
   prelapsarian? You should also see if you can draw connections
   between this Edenic world and Tommo's decision to flee it. Why
   does Tommo decide to escape? Is the looming threat of cannibalism his only motivation? Does this paradise have any other
   drawbacks? How is the language of enchantment related to the
   theme of paradise? How do the Typee Valley's associations with
   enchantment and spells reflect on its Edenic qualities? How do
   they help to explain Melville's treatment of the valley?

3. **Cannibalism:** In chapter 4, Tommo says of the Typees: "their
   very name is a frightful one; for the word 'Typee' in the Marquesan dialect signifies a lover of human flesh." Throughout the
   text, though, Tommo's belief in, as well as his attitude toward,
   the Typees' status as cannibals remains in constant flux. How
   does Melville use the threat of cannibalism in *Typee*?

   To address this question, you need to consider both Tommo's
   attitudes and Melville's apparent attitudes and purposes. Such
   a consideration is complicated by the complex relationship
   between Tommo and his creator. You must try to sort out just
   how closely Tommo reflects Melville's experiences and his
   ideologies. What do the two share? When do they separate?
   Clearly, like Tommo, Melville knew of the Typee's reputation
   for fierceness and cannibalism, and clearly his attitudes about
   the islanders changed after his residence there. Similarly, after

spending some time among the Typees, Tommo's fears of being cannibalized are calmed by the treatment he receives. And yet, by the book's end, he believes that he sees sufficient evidence of the Typees' cannibalistic ways, and he once again begins to fear for his own safety. Consider if Melville projects his own attitudes on Tommo here, or if the two are separate. Tommo witnesses some disturbing scenes near the book's close, but are the shrunken heads and the human "bones still fresh with moisture, and with particles of flesh clinging to them" clear evidence of human cannibalism? What are readers to think of Tommo and his reaction? Why does Melville refuse to definitively settle the question of the Typees' cannibalism? As you sort through these issues and questions, you should also think about Melville's purpose and his strategies as an author.

4. **Tattooing/bodily marking:** Tommo directs a good deal of attention both to the Typee custom of tattooing and to their tattoos themselves. Near the book's end, Karky the tattoo artist tries to tattoo Tommo. Why does Tommo respond with horror to the prospect of being tattooed? What does his reaction say about the book's treatment of the art of tattooing?

   Any analysis of the theme of tattooing in *Typee* must closely consider the scene in chapter 30 when Karky tries to tattoo Tommo's face. You should closely examine Tommo's description of Karky and his work. In what ways is Karky portrayed as an artist? What other patterns of language seem to work against this portrayal of the artist and his work? Examine Tommo's horror at Karky's proposal. Why does he react as he does? Why does he offer his arm for tattooing as a kind of compromise? What does the language of this scene, particularly when Karky "continued his attack upon [Tommo's] face," suggest? You should also draw connections between this scene and Tommo's other discussions of tattooing throughout the text. His descriptions of the tattoos of Kory-Kory, Marnoo, and Fayaway are particularly relevant.

5. **Taboo:** Throughout *Typee*, Tommo remains mystified by the Typee system of taboo, which he discusses at some length in

chapter 30. He calls taboo "inexplicable" and "capricious," but also "all-controlling." Examine the treatment of taboo. While it seems that neither Tommo nor Melville thoroughly understand the meaning and the implementation of the system of taboo, how does Melville's text manage to comment on taboo and its function?

Obviously, a paper that tackles this subject should begin with this lengthy discussion of taboo in chapter 30. Although this passage occurs near the end of *Typee*, Tommo has encountered the perplexing rules of taboo throughout his stay in the Typee Valley. Examine these encounters in some detail. Consider how the word and the concept of taboo are used in the valley. Consider who imposes the restrictions of taboo and who is restricted by it. What can you conclude about the Typees, their religion, and their system of government though an analysis of taboo in *Typee*?

6. **Storytelling and the creation of narrative:** In his preface to *Typee*, Melville makes a plea for both the veracity of his text as well as its ability to entertain: "Yet, notwithstanding the familiarity of sailors with all sorts of curious adventure, the incidents recorded in the following pages have often served, when 'spun as a yarn,' not only to relieve the weariness of many a night-watch at sea, but to excite the warmest sympathies of the author's shipmates." Consider how *Typee* continues this theme of the power and the effects of storytelling.

Even a cursory familiarity with the history of *Typee* shows how important the tension between story and truth, fact, or history is. Numerous early readers doubted the veracity of Melville's book because it seemed too well crafted to have been written by a "common sailor." In other words, it seemed more like "story" than "truth." Even in the process of composing and then of revising, Melville knew that questions of veracity would prove important to his success. With that history in mind, you might find it interesting to explore his commentary in *Typee* on the power and the veracity of storytelling and on the slippage between "story" and "truth." To shape this sort of inquiry, you should pay close attention to Tommo's many references to stories and storytelling. Examine the sailor's yarns that he hears and shares. Examine his references to fairy tales in *Typee*. Concurrently, examine what he has to say about the published narratives about the South Sea Islands. How factual does he find these narratives to be? What kind of power resides in the stories? What kind of power resides in the published narratives? Similarly, you might analyze how Melville "shapes" his own history in his book. How does he rely on the strategies and the forms of fiction as he conveys his own experiences? This kind of inquiry will overlap with some of the topics in the Form and Genre section of this chapter.

7. **Gender:** Tommo spends a great deal of time discussing gender norms in the Typee Valley. How might this focus allow you to read *Typee* as a commentary on gender roles and culture's effect on them?

A paper that addresses *Typee*'s treatment of gender could focus on numerous elements in the text. Clearly, Tommo spends a good deal of time speaking about the free, uninhibited sexuality of the Typees. He seems especially to focus on the natural and unconstrained sexuality of the young women. At the same time, though, Tommo speaks admiringly of many of the young men. This is especially so in his descriptions of Marnoo. How might you read his treatment of Typee sexuality as a commentary on Western attitudes toward sexuality and gender roles? Still further, you should examine Tommo's description of the institution of marriage on Typee. How might this commentary help to develop this line of inquiry? Additionally, Tommo frequently comments upon the role of women in this society. Examine his comments about the restrictions placed upon women by the system of taboo as well as his commentary on women and work on the island. Consider, too, his brief description of Tinor, Kory-Kory's mother. Any of these examinations could help you to develop a thoughtful paper on the topic of gender in *Typee*.

Character

Peopled as it is with interesting and exotic characters, *Typee* presents many opportunities for papers on character. Papers on Melville's portrayal of Tommo, for example, could be shaped in a number of ways. You may be interested in Tommo's voice as the narrator and his relationship to Western society, or you may be intrigued by his desire to leave the tropical paradise of the Typee Valley. Similarly, characters such as Fayaway and Toby could also prove effective topics for a paper on character. In a strong and effective paper, you should be sure to examine the character from many possible angles. In *Typee*, it is important to remember that, as the narrator, Tommo always serves as a mediating consciousness. In his dealings with the Typee characters, his interpretations are often marred by his own prejudices and his inability to communicate effectively in the Typee language. Be sure to keep these facts in mind as you plan a paper about character in *Typee*.

Sample Topics:

1. **Tommo:** *Typee* is clearly rooted in Melville's own experience in the South Seas, and sometimes the distinction between Tommo and his author is difficult to sort out. Despite this blurring between author and narrator, how might you read *Typee* as a psychological allegory that charts Tommo's development?

   Clearly, this question asks you to think about the fictional aspects of this text more than its nonfictional qualities. And one way to envision a response to this question is to think about the elements that *Typee* shares with fairy tales (a genre that Melville references in chapter 27). When Tommo first glimpses the Typee Valley in chapter 7, he says, "Over all the landscape there reigned the most hushed repose, which I almost feared to break lest, like the enchanted gardens in the fairy tale, a single syllable might dissolve the spell." Consider how Tommo's journey to and his return from the Typee Valley emulate the structure of many fairy tales. ("Little Red Riding Hood" and "Hansel and Gretel" come to mind immediately.) What does the landscape share with these tales? How might this landscape and the journey be read symbolically? Similarly, consider Tommo's relationships with other characters, especially his relationships with Toby, Kory-Kory, Marnoo, and Mehevi. Think about the significance of Tommo's name as well as the significance of his leg wound. Both could serve symbolic functions. You would also do well to examine the language used to describe the Typee Valley throughout the book. How is this language significant? Finally, you should think about how such a reading helps to explain Tommo's decision to flee Nukuheva and return to "civilization." How have his experiences in the Typee Valley changed Tommo?

2. **Toby:** As Tommo is drawn from Melville himself, Toby is based on Melville's shipmate Richard Tobias Greene, who jumped ship with Melville and journeyed with him into the Typee Valley. Thus, there is factual material that underlies Toby's portrait and his leave-taking from the valley. And yet, as is the case with the character of Tommo, Toby is also a fictionalized character. What is the significance of Toby and his role in *Typee*?

It is difficult to assess Toby's role without considering him in relation to Tommo. You should first consider the allure of Toby. What draws Tommo to him? Why does he seem an appropriate "partner of [Tommo's] adventure" (chapter 5)? How is Toby's background and his history significant? What is Toby's role as the two men journey over the mountains and into the Typee Valley? What is the effect of Toby's disappearance from the valley?

3. **Fayaway:** Examine the role of Fayaway in *Typee*. Does she function as more than just an exotic love interest for Tommo?

In many ways, this question relates to the question about gender as a theme in *Typee*. Fayaway in many ways seems to exemplify the qualities of all the Typee women, and so a study of her character could also develop into a study of *Typee*'s treatment of gender, gender roles, and sexuality. On the other hand, you could consider Fayaway's role in Melville's fictional narrative. Although Tommo claims, "This picture is no fancy sketch; it is drawn from the most vivid recollections of the person delineated," scholars have noted that some of Melville's depictions of Fayaway are probably not based in fact. This is especially so of Tommo's descriptions of his boat rides with Fayaway in which she stands in the front of the boat, using her wrap of tappa as a sail. There is, modern scholars argue, no lake in the Typee Valley. Why, then, would Melville have invented scenes like this? What function do they serve?

History and Context

Melville's own experiences and his culture provide the most interesting context for *Typee*, since the book is drawn from his time living among the Typee people. Consequently, examining the connections between Melville's biography and his book could prove an engaging subject. Similarly, since the book so explicitly references and denounces some predominant Western ideologies of Melville's time, you might find that both his political commentary and his audience's reaction to *Typee* provide the basis for numerous papers about the book's history and the context. Good biographies of Melville should provide you with a good place to begin research on these topics. Similarly, some of the textual studies of *Typee* and its complicated editorial history can provide important insights that should help develop papers on the book's history and context.

Sample Topics:

1. **Melville's own time in Typee:** Melville's young life was full of nautical adventure. He signed on to the whaler *Acushnet* in January 1841, then jumped ship on the South Sea island of Nukuheva in June 1842 after 18 months aboard the whaling ship. After living among the Typee people on Nukuheva for four weeks, Melville shipped aboard another whaler, the *Lucy Ann,* and, along with other sailors, participated in a mutiny in Tahiti. Melville crafted *Typee* from his experiences among the Typee. In what ways does the text seem biographical, and in what ways does it seem to be something very different?

   Obviously, this question shares a good deal of territory with the discussion of genre that follows, and yet this question asks you to consider Melville's real-life experiences in relation to his text. Part of the difficulty of grappling with this question is that, apart from *Typee* itself, there is little in the way of biographical

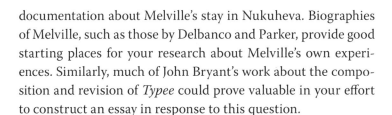

documentation about Melville's stay in Nukuheva. Biographies of Melville, such as those by Delbanco and Parker, provide good starting places for your research about Melville's own experiences. Similarly, much of John Bryant's work about the composition and revision of *Typee* could prove valuable in your effort to construct an essay in response to this question.

2. **Prior narratives of the South Seas:** Throughout *Typee*, Melville makes use of, and uses overt references to, numerous published accounts of the South Sea Islands. To what use does Melville put these texts? Why does he make such overt reference to them?

   As scholars John Bryant, Geoffrey Sanborn, Samuel Otter, and Robert Milder have pointed out, Melville drew from numerous published accounts, including Charles S. Stewart's *Visit to the South Seas* and David Porter's *Journal of a Cruise Made to the Pacific Ocean.* In his introduction to the Penguin edition of *Typee,* Bryant notes that Melville also drew from missionary accounts of the South Sea Islands. You might find it fruitful to look at Stewart and Porter's works and compare their assessment of the islands and the islanders to Melville's. Similarly, you should read Melville's text closely to see how it comments rather explicitly upon these other texts. What do his references tell us about these texts and their relation to and effects upon Western attitudes? How do these references help readers to understand Melville's purpose in *Typee*?

3. **The textual history of *Typee*:** *Typee* has a complex and vexing textual history. The original British and American editions have some substantial differences, and reactions among the American reading public resulted in a "revised" American edition. Melville's revisions for this last edition were made largely in response to pressure from Christian readers and reviewers who were offended by his treatment of missionaries. In his correspondence with Evert A. Duyckinck, Melville shows his discomfort with the process of "revision," calling the new edition a "Revised (Expurgated?—Odious word!) Edition of Typee." Is it fair to call the revised American edition of *Typee* an expurgated text?

Critic John Bryant has published a good deal of textual scholarship on *Typee*, and the Penguin edition of the book contains an introduction, explanatory commentary, and appendixes by Bryant that provide thorough insight into the textual emendations of what Bryant calls this "fluid text." In order to consider this topic thoroughly, you should analyze the statements that Melville is making about Protestant missionary efforts in the Polynesian Islands and consider how the textual changes affect his commentary. Similarly, you might wish to study his next book, *Omoo*, which continues the theme of missionaries and conversion.

4. **Melville's 19th-century audience and its effect:** Despite its challenges to traditional American ideologies about gender, sexuality, and religion, there are other ways in which *Typee* seems clearly to be aimed at a 19th-century reading public. Where do you see the imprint of the values of an antebellum American audience?

While a response to this question could address the textual emendations discussed in the previous question, there are other ways to develop this topic. Perhaps the most fruitful approach might be to examine the book's treatment of gender and family. A belief in the values of domesticity reigned in middle-class American culture in the 19th century. This cult of domesticity centered moral value in the home and the family. Consider how Melville was able to write about sexuality in a relatively overt way (for the 19th century) in *Typee*. Examine, for example, his portrait of Fayaway and his relationship with her. What elements in his portrait of the Typees allowed him to "get away with" such relatively overt treatment of female sexuality?

Philosophy and Ideas

Clearly, Melville addresses the idea of the "noble savage," untouched by civilization, in *Typee*, and this subject informs a major philosophical motif in the book. Additionally, *Typee*, like nearly all of Melville's work, asks questions about the ways that humans come to know and to understand. Since Tommo spends time immersed in a culture that he knows only by reputation, and since he gains only the most rudimentary understanding of the language, this topic is especially clear in *Typee*.

Sample Topics:

1. **The idea of the noble savage:** Consider *Typee* as an argument about the romantic notion of the "noble savage" who is innocent, good, and free from the corrupting influence of civilization. Is *Typee* an argument in favor of the concept of the noble savage?

   In order to address this question, you should familiarize yourself with the concept of the noble savage. The notion of the uncivilized innocent is often associated with the writings of Jean-Jacques Rousseau and romantic philosophy, though it has it roots in the Enlightenment. In what ways do the Typees seem to be the embodiments of this concept? Similarly, you might want to examine the writing of Captain James Cook, who sailed to the South Seas in the 18th century and whose writing seems to espouse the idea of the noble savage. Tommo comments on Cook in *Typee*. Consider, too, how the language of paradise and Eden is interwoven with this concept in *Typee*. The concept of the noble savage seems to be at odds with the Christian belief in original sin. How, then, do these competing ideologies shed light on the "paradise" of the Typee Valley? Clearly, you must also take into account Tommo's rhetoric about civilization and "civilized barbarity" (chapter 17) and the related issue of missionary work. Finally, how does Tommo's ultimate decision to flee Typee and return to civilization reflect on this theme?

2. **Perception and understanding:** In speaking of the religious ceremonies of the Typees, Tommo says, "I saw everything, but could comprehend nothing" (chapter 24). While the complexities of Typee religion and taboo remain unclear to Tommo, it is clear that he comes to comprehend many things differently as a result of his stay in the Typee Valley. Consider *Typee* as a commentary on human perception and comprehension.

   Because Tommo has such limited understanding of the Typee language, his understanding of Typee culture, values, and behavior is all the more dependent on his eyesight. Nowhere is this more apparent than in his struggles to reach some definite conclusion about the Typees' reputation as cannibals. Consider how much of his evidence of their cannibalism is based on visual clues—the human bones in the ceremonial vessel and the glimpse he thinks he gets of the white man's head. How definitive is such evidence? Examine, too, his commentary on the scarcity of "first hand" accounts of cannibalism. In addition, you should examine the text for instances when Tommo speaks about the process of seeing and interpreting. When he discusses Kory-Kory's tattoos in chapter 11, for example, he says that "they were a little curious to my unaccustomed sight." This statement might imply that Tommo's sight becomes acclimated to the sites of the Typee Valley. What effect does this change in vision have upon Tommo?

Form and Genre

Based as it is in Melville's own history, *Typee* presents numerous challenges to ideas about form and genre. Perhaps the most obvious, and the most important, is the question of *Typee*'s relationship to traditional literary genres. Classifying this book is difficult since it is a complicated blend of biography and fiction. How closely is Tommo connected to Melville? How much of the narrator is a literary creation? How "true" is Tommo's experience to Melville's? Even if you could definitively answer questions like these, other, more philosophical, questions remain. What, finally, is the relationship between autobiography and fiction? Autobiography uses the techniques of fiction in order to shape the facts of a life into a story. Where does *Typee* fall in the continuum between autobiography, memoir, and novel? These are the sort of questions that should inform any paper on *Typee* and genre.

Sample Topics:

1. **Fact or fiction—*Typee* and genre:** While modern scholars often praise *Moby-Dick* for stretching the boundaries of the novel, *Typee*'s relationship to traditional literary genres is even more complicated. *Typee* is difficult to classify because it blends autobiography, fiction, anthropology, travel literature, and personal essay. While few modern readers would hesitate to call *Moby-Dick* a novel, most are unwilling to classify *Typee* as a novel (unlike literary scholars from the early part of the 20th century). While the biographical nature of *Typee* is undeniable,

Melville clearly uses many of the strategies and techniques of fiction. He shapes and invents a plot; he sketches and develops characters. Construct a paper that argues for *Typee*'s classification as a particular genre of writing. Is it novel, autobiography, travel literature, or something altogether different?

This question obviously requires that you familiarize yourself with the characteristics of different genres of writing. You might look at a good handbook of literary terms in order to find thorough definitions of such genres as the novel or autobiography. You should also bear in mind that this question cannot be answered definitively. Your job is to make the most coherent argument that you can, while demonstrating your knowledge of the various genres and of *Typee*. You should also think about some of the realities of autobiography. Writers of autobiographies tell their stories from a particular perspective, shaping the facts of their lives to make specific points or to construct a particular view of themselves. Generally, such authors are intently aware of their prospective audience. Think about your life story as you would tell it to your friends. Consider how you might write your life differently if you were writing for your parents. Do you think that Melville is trying to paint a particular kind of portrait of himself in *Typee* through his creation of Tommo? Was he responding to his understanding of the expectations of his audience? You might also find it interesting to explore the genre of travel writing. Critic Janet Giltrow makes a strong argument that Melville was working within the conventions of 19th-century travel writing.

2. ***Typee* as captivity narrative:** Tommo's initial glimpse of the Typee Valley seems to promise a stay in paradise, and the hospitality of the Typees at first seems to support his initial impression. Before long, though, Tommo realizes that the Typees are unwilling to let him leave, and he begins to speak of his "captivity" on the island. When Marnoo tells him in chapter 18 that the Typees will not allow him to depart, Tommo says, "still it increased my anxiety to escape from a captivity, which, however endurable, nay, delightful it might be in some respects,

involved in its issues a fate marked by the most frightful contingencies." This language presents still another possible classification for *Typee*—the captivity narrative. Examine *Typee* as such a narrative.

The captivity narrative is a distinctly American genre that has its roots in accounts of Puritan settlers captured by Native Americans. Mary Rowlandson's *Narrative of the Captivity and Restoration of Mrs. Mary Rowlandson . . .* is perhaps the most famous example of the genre. Generally, though not always, these narratives told the story of women, and generally they worked to uphold the "civilized," Christian values of their society. While captivity narratives are based in fact, they were generally shaped to make an ideological point. You might want to consider what elements *Typee* shares with these traditional captivity narratives. Besides the fact that Tommo speaks of his condition as "captivity," what else does he share with the protagonists of earlier captivity narratives? Consider also how the theme of civilization and civilized values is treated in *Typee*. Similarly, you should think about the story line of the book. While not all captives choose to be "restored" to their community, the traditional captivity narrative emphasized the captive's restoration. How would you compare that story line to that of *Typee*? Do you think that he is "restored" by the end of the book? You might also want to analyze the ways that their "savage" captors imperil the female subjects of traditional captivity narratives. Is Tommo imperiled in similar ways?

Language, Symbols, and Imagery

Because Melville takes his own adventures and shapes them into fiction in *Typee*, he employs many elements of fiction, including imagery and symbols. Think about the ship that takes Tommo from home to the paradise of the Marquesas. How might the *Dolly* function symbolically? Similarly, you could examine the imagery of sleep and dreams in *Typee*. No matter what kind of imagery you chose to explore, you would do well to consider the relationship between imagery and themes in the book. How does Melville use the imagery to help develop or to reflect on some of the text's themes?

Sample Topics:

1. **The *Dolly* and its function:** In the early chapters of the book, readers see a bit of Tommo's life aboard the *Dolly*. Examine the role of the *Dolly* in *Typee*. How does it function, and what might it represent?

Melville's portrait of the *Dolly* is drawn from his experiences aboard the *Acushnet*, and clearly the early chapters of the narrative set up and explain Tommo's decision to "run away." Life on the *Dolly* is in no way enticing or pleasant. In order to craft an essay in response to this question, though, you should think of the ship symbolically. Consider what the *Dolly* represents. In order to do this, you should think about why life aboard the *Dolly* is so unbearable that Tommo "chose rather to risk [his] fortunes among the savages of the island than to endure another voyage" (chapter 4). What else might share the *Dolly*'s negative qualities? You might develop this line of argumentation if you consider the contrast implicit in Tommo's choice. How is life aboard the ship and life with the "savages of the island" different? How does this difference relate to the book's larger theme of civilization and its treatment of the relationship between "civilized" people and "savages"?

2. **Imagery of sleep and dreams:** In chapter 2, as the *Dolly* approaches the Marquesas, Tommo speaks of the "languor" and the "spell" that seem to affect the ship. This spell of languor introduces a theme that will run through the text, since Tommo frequently notes a similar atmosphere in the Typee Valley. Examine the language of sleep, dreams, and enchantment in *Typee*. How does this language function?

You might begin by noting the connection between this sleepiness and the notion of a "spell." How are the two alike, and how are they different? What connotations or associations does the idea of a spell suggest? Further, you might think about the literary reference that Melville seems to be making here, as the atmosphere aboard the ship seems to echo the passage in the *Odyssey* where Odysseus visits the land of the Lotus-Eaters. Other authors have used this episode in their works, including Alfred, Lord Tennyson, whose poem "The Lotos Eaters" was written just 13 years before *Typee*. Examining these works might help you to develop a paper on Melville's use of this imagery in *Typee*. You might also want to consider how this imagery reflects upon or develops some of the book's themes. How, for example, might it be related to the theme of civilization? How does it reflect upon the Edenic qualities of the Typee Valley? How might Melville's use of this imagery help you to contextualize Tommo's ultimate decision to escape the Typee Valley?

Compare and Contrast Essays

Because *Typee* draws on Melville's early experiences at sea as does so much of his fiction, it presents many opportunities to construct compare and contrast papers. This chapter has already indicated numerous connections between *Typee* and *Moby-Dick*. *Billy Budd*, too, provides ample room for comparison. Similarly, *Typee* addresses a number of other subjects that Melville treated across a wide range of his fiction. Always keep in mind that your project in a compare and contrast paper is to draw some conclusions. Your thesis should present an assertion about the similarities and differences that your paper works to support. Do not just present a list of similarities and differences.

Sample Topics:

1. **The confrontation between civilization and innocence:** Examine Melville's treatment of the confrontation between civilization and innocence in *Typee* and another of his works. What comment does he make in his treatment of this theme?

   This topic requires that you consider the definition of "innocence." Are the "savage" Typees "innocent," according to Melville? Can a people be both cannibalistic and innocent? What in *Typee* seems to mark the Typees as innocent? *Billy Budd* is probably the most likely text for comparison since Melville clearly marks Billy as an innocent who runs afoul of the rules of "civilized" society. If you examine these two texts, it might be especially interesting to explore whether Melville's commentary on this theme changed over the course of his career; *Typee* was his first published book, and *Billy Budd* was published after his death. While the connections might not be quite so apparent at first, you could also develop an essay on this topic through a comparison with "Bartleby, the Scrivener," *Benito Cereno*, or "The Paradise of Bachelors and the Tartarus of Maids."

Another way to approach this question is to compare this theme in *Typee* and in another 19th-century work. *The Marble Faun* by Nathaniel Hawthorne (who was a close friend of Melville) presents the young Italian Donatello as a faun living in the human world of 19th-century Rome. In many ways, Donatello is uncivilized, as are the Typees. And like the Typees, Donatello seems both innocent and violent.

2. **The values of the Typees and *Moby-Dick*:** Melville revisited many of the themes of *Typee* in *Moby-Dick*, and many scholars describe his treatment of these themes in the latter work as a more mature treatment. Choose one of the shared themes and analyze Melville's use of it in the two books.

   Some of the topics you might choose include the theme of civilization versus savageness and the treatment of tattoos and bodily markings. Clearly, this question asks you to examine Queequeg and his relationship with Ishmael in *Moby-Dick*. Queequeg, himself a South Sea islander, suggests a more complex treatment of the notions of "savageness" that Melville began to explore in *Typee*. Who is Queequeg? What kinds of values does he embody? In what ways is he like the Typees? In what ways is he "savage," and in what ways is he "civilized"? How does he affect Ishmael?

3. **Melville's use of the theme of enchantment:** Compare Melville's use of the theme of enchantment in *Typee* and another of his works. How and why does he use this theme? Does he use it toward the same purpose in both works?

   It might prove particularly interesting to compare the theme of enchantment in *Typee* and "The Encantadas," which bears the subtitle "the Enchanted Isles." Indeed, both texts profile "enchanted" isles, but the nature of the enchantment seems very different in each. Why? You might also want to explore the ways that Melville treats the notion of enchantment in portions of *Moby-Dick*. Should you choose to examine *Moby-Dick* in relation to this theme, you would do well to limit the scope of your essay. You might, for instance, choose just one chapter that seems to deal with the idea of enchantment or trace the theme as it applies to one character. *Benito Cereno*, too, might prove an interesting text for comparison here. When Delano boards the *San Dominick*, the narrator says that boarding a strange ship produces "something of the effect of enchantment." How might you consider Delano's experience aboard the *San Dominick* one of enchantment?

4. **Critiques of Christianity and 19th-century texts:** *Typee* clearly criticizes Protestant missionary efforts in the South Seas, and in so doing it offers a critique of the missionaries' Christian values. Compare *Typee*'s critique of Christianity with that of another 19th-century text.

You might develop a paper in response to this topic by examining *Typee* in relation to "Bartleby, the Scrivener." Clearly, Melville sees both the evangelizing efforts of the missionaries in *Typee* and the charity of "Bartleby's" narrator as suspect. You could easily move beyond Melville's work in response to this topic. Many abolitionist texts, for example, call into question the "Christianity" of slaveholding Christians. Stowe's *Uncle Tom's Cabin* and Frederick Douglass's *Narrative of the Life of Frederick Douglass, an American Slave* present two possibilities for comparison.

5. **Melville's bachelors:** In his portrait of the Hoolah Hoolah ground and the Ti, Melville presents a world "secured . . . from the imaginary pollution of a woman's presence." Compare this sacred space with the other bachelor realms that populate his fiction.

While "The Paradise of Bachelors and the Tartarus of Maids" presents an obvious choice for comparison, other texts might provide material relevant to this question. Consider how many male enclaves appear in Melville's texts. Nearly all the ships in his fiction are populated only by men. Similarly, only men labor in the office at No. —— Wall Street in "Bartleby." As you examine these spaces, notice how frequently Melville actually refers to bachelors and bachelors' quarters. What does he associate with these realms populated exclusively by men?

Bibliography and Online Resources for *Typee*

Bryant, John, ed. *A Companion to Melville Studies.* New York: Greenwood, 1986.

———. Introduction. *Typee: A Peep at Polynesian Life.* By Herman Melville. New York: Penguin, 1996.

———. *The Fluid Text.* Ann Arbor: U of Michigan P, 2002.

———. *Melville and Repose.* New York: Oxford UP, 1993.

Bryant, John, and Robert Milder, eds. *Melville's Evermoving Dawn.* Kent, OH: Kent State UP, 1997.

Coffler, Gail. *Melville's Allusions to Religion: A Comprehensive Index and Glossary.* New York: Praeger Publishers, 2004.

Delbanco, Andrew. *Melville: His World and His Work.* New York: Knopf, 2005.

Dimock, Wai-chee. *Empire for Liberty: Melville and the Poetics of Individualism.* Princeton, NJ: Princeton UP, 1989.

Douglas, Ann. *The Feminization of American Culture.* New York: Knopf, 1978.

Dryden, Edgar. *Monumental Melville: The Formation of a Literary Career.* Stanford, CA: Stanford UP, 2004.

Ellis, Juniper. "Engendering Melville." *Journal of Narrative Theory* 29 (1999): 62–84.

Giltrow, Janet. "Speaking Out: Travel and Structure in Herman Melville's Early Narratives." *American Literature* 52 (1980): 18–32.

Gunn, Giles. *A Historical Guide to Herman Melville.* Oxford: Oxford UP, 2005.

Hayford, Harrison, and Hershel Parker. *Melville's Prisoners.* Evanston, IL: Northwestern UP, 2003.

Herbert, T. Walter. *Marquesan Encounters: Melville and the Meaning of Civilization.* Cambridge, MA: Harvard UP, 1980.

Karcher, Carolyn. *Shadow over the Promised Land: Slavery, Race, and Violence in Melville's America.* Baton Rouge: Louisiana State UP, 1980.

Lawrence, D. H. *Studies in Classic American Literature.* New York: Viking, 1964.

Maroviz, Sanford E. *Melville Among the Nations: Proceedings of an International Conference,* Volos, Greece, July 2–6, 1997. Kent, OH: Kent UP, 2001.

Martin, Robert K. *Hero, Captain, and Stranger: Male Friendship, Social Critiques and Literary Form in the Novels of Herman Melville.* Chapel Hill: U of North Carolina P, 1986.

Milder, Robert. *Exiled Royalties: Melville and the Life We Imagine.* New York: Oxford UP, 2006.

Miller, James E. *A Reader's Guide to Herman Melville.* New York: Octagon, 1973.

Otter, Samuel. *Melville's Anatomies: Bodies, Discourse, and Ideology in Antebellum America.* Berkeley: U of California P, 1998.

Parker, Hershel. *Herman Melville.* 2 vols. Baltimore: Johns Hopkins UP, 1996, 2002.

Porter, David. *Journal of a Cruise Made to the Pacific Ocean.* Philadelphia, 1815. Reprint, New York: Wiley & Halsted, 1822. Available online. URL: http://www.galapagos.to/TEXTS/PORTER-1.HTM. Downloaded on November 4, 2007.

Renker, Elizabeth. *Strike Through the Mask: Herman Melville and the Scene of Writing.* Baltimore: Johns Hopkins UP, 1996.

Rogin, Michael Paul. *Subversive Genealogy: The Politics and Art of Herman Melville.* New York: Knopf, 1983.

Rowe, John Carlos. *Literary Culture and U.S. Imperialism.* New York: Oxford UP, 2000.

Samson, John. *White Lies Melville's Narratives of Facts.* Ithaca, NY: Cornell UP, 1989.

Sandborn, Geoffrey. *The Sign of the Cannibal: Melville and the Making of a Postcolonial Reader.* Durham, NC: Duke UP, 1998.

Schueller, Malini Johar. "Indians, Polynesians, and Empire Making: The Case of Herman Melville." In *Genealogy and Literature.* Ed. Lee Quinby. Minneapolis: U of Minnesota P, 1955. 48–67.

Sealts, Merton M., Jr. *Melville's Reading.* Columbia: U of South Carolina P, 1988.

Steelye, John. *Melville: The Ironic Diagram.* Evanston, IL: Northwestern UP, 1970.

Stern, Milton R. *Critical Essays on Herman Melville's* Typee. Boston: G. K. Hall, 1982.

Stewart, Charles S. *A Visit to the South Seas, in the US Ship* Vincennes, *During the Years 1829 and 1830.* New York: John P. Haven, 1831; rpt. New York: Prager, 1970.

Wardrop, Daneen. "The Signifier and the Tattoo: Inscribing the Uninscribed and the Forces of Colonization in Melville's *Typee*." *ESQ* 47 (2002): 135–61.

"HAWTHORNE
AND HIS MOSSES"

READING TO WRITE

THERE IS little doubt that Melville's relationship with Nathaniel Hawthorne affected the course of Melville's life and the direction of his
writing. Not long after his initial meeting with Hawthorne in 1850, Melville published the essay "Hawthorne and His Mosses" in Evert Duyckinck's New York *Literary World.* The essay is part literary review and part
commentary on America and its literary scene. Melville fictionalized
parts of the essay; he claims that he had not met the author of *Mosses
from an Old Manse,* and he creates an alternative identity for himself,
claiming that he is a Virginian visiting in Vermont. His admiration for
Hawthorne, though, is clearly genuine, and in his review of the elder
writer's collection of tales, Melville articulates his own ideas about literary genius and the "Art of Telling the Truth." Consider how much the
following, often quoted, passage about the "blackness" of Hawthorne's
fiction tells about Melville's own worldview and about his beliefs in the
methods of fiction:

> For spite of all the Indian-summer sunlight on the hither side of Haw-
> thorne's soul, the other side—like the dark half of the physical sphere—is
> shrouded in a blackness ten times black. But this darkness but gives more
> effect to the ever-moving dawn, that forever advances through it, and cir-
> cumnavigates his world. Whether Hawthorne has simply availed himself
> of this mystical blackness as a means to the wondrous effects he makes it
> to produce in his lights and shades; or whether there really lurks in him,
> perhaps unknown to himself, a touch of Puritanic gloom,—this I can-

not altogether tell. Certain it is, however, that this great power of blackness in him derives its force from its appeals to that Calvinistic sense
of Innate Depravity and Original Sin, from whose visitations, in some
shape or other, no deeply thinking mind is always and wholly free. For,
in certain moods, no man can weigh this world, without throwing in
something, somehow like Original Sin, to strike the uneven balance. At
all events, perhaps no writer has ever wielded this terrific thought with
greater terror than this same harmless Hawthorne. Still more: this black
conceit pervades him, through and through. You may be witched by his
sunlight,—transported by the bright gildings in the skies he builds over
you;—but there is the blackness of darkness beyond; and even his bright
gildings but fringe, and play upon the edges of thunder-clouds.

In this passage, Melville introduces the notion of blackness that is so
important for any understanding of this essay. Hawthorne's soul, he says,
"is shrouded in a blackness, ten times black." The first job of any reader
of this passage is to try and make sense of this imagery, to try to understand with some precision what Melville represents through this image
of blackness. You might first notice that he introduces the idea of Hawthorne's blackness through its opposite, "the Indian-summer sunlight on
the hither side of Hawthorne's soul." What is the relationship between
the light and the dark in Hawthorne? Why does Melville use the image
of a planet or a moon, "the physical sphere," to describe Hawthorne's
soul? What does that image suggest about the relationship between the
light and the dark in Hawthorne and his writing? Is it significant that
the "Indian-summer sunlight" is on the "hither" side of Hawthorne's
soul, while his darker side lies on the further side of his soul? At first it
seems that in mentioning these two opposing sides of the author Melville
might be emphasizing the sunlight and the brightness in Hawthorne, for
he claims that the darkness "gives more effect to the ever-moving dawn
that . . . circumnavigates his world." Without the darkness, he seems to
say, the brightness would not be so brilliant and clear. It should not take
long, though, for a careful reader to see that it is not the brightness and
the sunlight that interests Melville. Toward the end of the passage, when
he again contrasts the bright and the dark in Hawthorne, he says that the
reader "might be witched by his sunlight,—transported by the bright gildings in the skies he builds over you;—but there is a blackness of darkness
beyond; and even his bright gildings but fringe, and play upon the edges

of thunder-clouds." The darkness, the "thunder-clouds" are primary and central, and the sunlight is but "gilding," a deceptively pleasing surface application. Similarly, he argues that the reader is "witched" or deluded by the sunlight, but the blackness "pervades him, through and through."

Having thus established the centrality of the blackness of Hawthorne, you will need to do more analysis in order to try to understand what Melville means when he uses this term. Melville labels this blackness "mystical." Why does he choose that term? According to the *American Heritage Dictionary,* two possible meanings for the word *mystical* are "of or having a spiritual reality or import not apparent to the intelligence or senses," and "of, relating to, or stemming from direct communion with ultimate reality or God." Is Melville suggesting, then, that Hawthorne's darkness communicates some spiritual truth? If so, how is that spiritual truth connected to the idea of "Puritanic gloom" and "that Calvinistic sense of Innate Depravity and Original Sin, from whose visitations . . . no deeply thinking mind is always and wholly free"? Does the blackness in Hawthorne stem from the recognition of humanity's fallen nature? While Melville seems to indicate that this is so, in the next sentence he modifies his reference to the doctrine of "innate Depravity and Original Sin," saying that "in certain moods, no man can weigh this world, without throwing in something, somehow like Original Sin." In his movement from the idea of original sin to "something, somehow like Original Sin," Melville seems to move away from the idea of original sin. If Hawthorne's blackness does not represent the darkness within humanity, but only "something, somehow like" it, what precisely does it represent? Where do Hawthorne and Melville locate the darkness in the world? Does Melville imply that this darkness is somehow larger and more ominous than original sin? Is that why he indicates that the thoughts of such "deeply thinking men" are "terrific"? What are the connotations of *terrific* here? How are they linked to Melville's assertion that Hawthorne "wield[s] this terrific thought with . . . terror"? To understand something of Melville's conception of the blackness of Hawthorne should help you to understand Melville's arguments in "Hawthorne and His Mosses." Similarly, if you understand something of Melville's worldview, his belief that "no deeply thinking mind is always and wholly free" from the "terrific" realization of the blackness in the world, you will understand something of the philosophy that motivated a great deal of *Moby-Dick,* which he was to publish within the year.

TOPICS AND STRATEGIES

This section of the chapter provides you with broad topic ideas that should help you develop an essay on "Hawthorne and His Mosses." Remember that these topics are just springboards for your own exploration; you will need to focus your analysis and develop your own specific thesis.

Themes

While Hawthorne and his collection of stories, *Mosses from an Old Manse,* are the announced topics of this piece, Melville treats a number of themes in this wide-ranging essay. For example, Shakespeare and his works play a major role in the essay. Similarly, in his argument about Hawthorne's genius, Melville soon advocates for a national American literature. This theme, in turn, connects to his consideration of the difficulty of telling the truth in literature when he states, "You must have plenty of sea-room to tell the Truth in; especially, when it seems to have an aspect of newness, as America did in 1492." If you choose to explore one of these themes in your paper, you should carefully trace Melville's treatment of that theme throughout the essay, and you would do well to consider how one theme affects another as Melville develops his argument. You will probably find it difficult to explore Melville's call for a national literature, for example, without at least considering what he says about truth telling in literature.

Sample Topics:

1. **A national literature:** Toward the end of his essay, Melville begins to argue for a national literature. He urges, "let us away with this . . . flunkeyism toward England." Why does Melville believe that a national literature is desirable, even necessary?

   To write a response to this question you will need to consider Melville's attitudes toward America, democracy, and authorship. Start with an examination of Melville's instructions for writing like an American. "[N]o American writer," he says, "should write like an Englishman, or a Frenchman; let him write like a man, for then he will be sure to write like an American." In Melville's ideology, what does it mean to "write like a man"? Why would the ability to "write like a man" rather than like an "Englishman, or a Frenchman" guarantee that one would write like an American? You will also need to explore Melville's attitudes toward and beliefs about America. How does "Mosses" characterize America socially, politically, and culturally? Examine, too, what Melville has to say about authorship. What is the relationship between nation and author? What role does the author play in the world? Finally, Melville makes much of democracy and "republican progressiveness" in this essay, and yet he explicitly argues that American writers need not "studiously cleave to nationality in their writings." Does he seem to argue for a relationship between American authorship and American democracy?

2. **"The great Art of Telling the Truth"**: In an 1851 letter to Hawthorne, Melville again touches on one of the major themes in this essay, truth: "Try to get a living by the Truth—and go to the Soup Societies. Heavens! Let any clergyman try to preach the Truth from its very stronghold, the pulpit, and they would ride him out of his church on his own pulpit banister. . . . Truth is ridiculous to men." And yet, in "Hawthorne and His Mosses," Melville indicates that both Shakespeare and Hawthorne were "masters of the great Art of Telling the Truth." What qualities allow these authors, and others like them, to be such successful truth tellers?

A thorough answer to this question must first examine the nature of truth. How does Melville characterize truth and reality? Look closely at the language and imagery Melville uses to describe truth and reality. What adjectives does he connect to truth? What metaphors does he use to describe it? What does his language indicate about the nature of truth and about humanity's relationship with truth? Why is the ability to tell the truth an "Art"? What strategies do these authors need to use in order to tell the truth? Besides Shakespeare and Hawthorne, who else does Melville argue is capable of communicating the truth? You might also find it helpful to explore Melville's descriptions of Shakespeare, Hawthorne, their works, and their reception by readers. How does a close examination of these passages help to develop your response?

Why, for instance, is the "mere critic" unable to fully appreciate Hawthorne's writing? Finally, you might consider whether this theme of truth telling is related to the theme of blackness that pervades both this essay and, particularly, its portrayal of Hawthorne.

3. **Authorship and the reading public:** In an 1851 letter to Hawthorne, Melville says, "I am told, my fellow-man, that there is an aristocracy of the brain. Some have boldly advocated and asserted it." In "Hawthorne and His Mosses," Melville makes it clear that both Shakespeare and Hawthorne were geniuses who belonged to just such an "aristocracy of the brain." How does Melville describe and/or envision the relationship between the genius author and his reading public? How is this relationship related to the ideas about democracy expressed in this essay?

Melville sets authors like Shakespeare and Hawthorne apart from other authors, and he clearly argues that the vast majority of their readers fail to understand the depth of their thoughts. Examine his comments about the popular reception of both Hawthorne and Shakespeare. What does the popular audience value in these authors? What does Melville value? Do Melville's comments about the popular audience's reception and understanding of these authors reflect upon his belief in "republican progressiveness"?

4. **Hawthorne's fiction:** In the final section of the essay, Melville writes briefly of Hawthorne's "Young Goodman Brown," saying, "it is, in itself, such a strong positive illustration of that blackness in Hawthorne, which I had assumed from the mere occasional shadows of it, as revealed in several of the other sketches." Read "Young Goodman Brown" carefully. Does it, in fact, embody the principle of blackness that Melville describes in this essay? Why or why not?

You must examine Melville's description of Hawthorne's blackness in some detail in order to address this question. What exactly does he mean when he says that "a blackness, ten times black" pervades Hawthorne's works? How does he describe this blackness? What other qualities in Hawthorne's fiction seem to be linked to this darkness? Additionally, you will need to read and analyze "Young Goodman Brown" in depth. What particular elements in Hawthorne's story seem particularly "black" to you? You should think about Hawthorne's use of imagery, setting, and his development of character. What, finally, is the story's point or purpose? Does this meaning support Melville's assertion that Hawthorne's fiction is marked by blackness?

History and Context

Melville places his argument in a particular historical context when he states that he had often heard of *Mosses from an Old Manse* and "even had it recommended to me by a tasteful friend, as a rare, quiet book, perhaps too deserving of popularity to be popular." This comment critiques the reading tastes and habits of his time, and much in the essay continues this critique. If you do some historical research on the reading habits and the best sellers of 19th-century America, you will see how thoroughly this essay is informed by its historical context. Similarly, if you examine biographies of Melville or look at some of his letters—particularly those to Hawthorne—you will find that Melville was troubled by the reading public's response to some of his own works. Understanding something of the literature of Melville's time as well as the reception that his own work received might help you to develop an interesting essay on the connections between "Hawthorne and His Mosses" and its historical context. Remember, though, that in such a paper your goal should be to illuminate the text, not merely to tell your reader about the historical context.

Sample Topics:

1. **Hawthorne and Melville:** In the final part of the essay, Melville writes, "But already I feel that this Hawthorne has dropped germanous seeds into my soul. He expands and deepens down, the more I contemplate him; and further, and further, shoots his strong New-England roots into the hot soil of my Southern soul." In the essay, Melville fictionalizes his relationship with Hawthorne. Melville was not a southerner, as he claims, and he had, in fact, met Hawthorne before he wrote this review. Clearly, though, Hawthorne and his writing did have a profound influ-

ence on Melville's writing, and he was soon to dedicate *Moby-Dick* to Hawthorne. Do some research about the relationship between Melville and Nathaniel Hawthorne. How is Melville's assessment of Hawthorne and his writing indicative of the relationship between the two authors? Where do you see the influence of Hawthorne's work upon Melville's writing?

There is a great deal of scholarship that discusses the relationship between these two authors, and quite clearly Hawthorne's work and his ideas affected Melville's writing. Similarly, it seems likely that the elder writer's works were also affected by Melville's writing. While you will need to explore biographical connections, a thorough answer to this rather broad question should be firmly rooted in the literature. You might begin by an exploration of the imagery that Melville uses in this essay. Is it related to the imagery that Hawthorne uses in *Mosses* or in other fiction by Hawthorne that Melville might have read by 1850? Similarly, do you see evidence that the thematic content of Hawthorne's fiction affected Melville's writing? Where and how do you see this influence?

2. **The reading public in Melville's day:** In the early paragraphs of this essay, Melville writes that *Mosses from an Old Manse* is "perhaps too deserving of popularity to be popular." Here and elsewhere in the essay, Melville critiques the reading tastes of his time. Compare Melville and Hawthorne's work with the popular best sellers of the 19th century. Do you agree with Melville when he argues that there is a qualitative gap between the popular literature of the day and the works by Hawthorne and Melville? How would you account for the differences between the two types of works?

This question asks you to consider quite a bit of literature and to ask some qualitative questions about that literature. As you consider whether one body of literature is "better" or "stronger" than another, you should also try to evaluate the standards of "good" literature that Melville is using here. Similarly, you might ask yourself whether the popular literature of the time reflects a particular set of standards or values. If so, how would you describe these standards? How do these sets of standards compare to your own assessment of "good" literature? Is "deserving" literature consistently undervalued? Is literature that is popular today "deserving"?

3. **Shakespeare in performance in Melville's day:** Melville came to appreciate Shakespeare through reading his works, not from seeing them performed onstage. "Hawthorne and His Mosses" gives readers some indication of Melville's assessment of stage productions of Shakespeare when he says, "For by philosophers Shakespeare is not adored as the great man of tragedy and comedy.—'Off with his head! So much for Buckingham!' this sort of rant, interlined by another hand, brings down the house,—those mistaken souls, who dream of Shakespeare as a mere man of Richard-the-Third humps, and Macbeth daggers." In this description, he targets the bowdlerized stage productions of Shakespeare's works in the 18th and 19th centuries. Research the stage productions of Shakespeare's plays from this time period. Do you agree with Melville that these productions diminished the power of the written works?

You will need to be familiar with Shakespeare's works in order to construct an adequate response to this question. You may find it helpful to focus on just one play. *Hamlet, King Lear, Macbeth,* or *Richard the Third* might work well. How were these plays altered or affected as they were staged in the 18th and 19th centuries? Why were they altered? How do the alterations affect the meanings and messages of the written texts?

Language, Symbols, and Imagery

Melville is best known as a writer of fiction, and astute readers will see the literary qualities that this essay shares with Melville's fiction. No reader can adequately understand his argument in "Hawthorne and His Mosses" without thoroughly considering Melville's use of imagery in the essay. Indeed, you could validly argue that imagery becomes the centerpiece of the essay when Melville describes Hawthorne and his writing through the metaphor of blackness. Any student who writes about this essay, no matter the paper's topic, should have some understanding of the way that Melville wields this particular metaphor. If you choose to write about the language or the imagery in this piece, you should begin by identifying a particular image or pattern of imagery that you find intriguing, and you should trace its use throughout the text. You should also ask some questions about the ways that Melville uses this imagery. Why, for example, does he use imagery to make his point? What does he gain by using this imagery rather than just making his point in unembellished prose? Be sure that a paper about imagery and language makes a particular argument or assertion about how or why Melville uses figurative language.

Sample Topics:

1. **Blackness:** Melville uses the metaphor of blackness to describe the power that lies behind Hawthorne's writing. On one side of Hawthorne's soul, he says, is "a blackness ten times black." What is this "blackness" that Melville describes, and why does it give Hawthorne such power?

   As the first part of this chapter suggests, you will need to work closely with the lengthy passage that introduces this idea of blackness, and you should also consider the relationship between blackness and light in this passage. You should also consider other places in the essay where Melville writes of blackness, and you will need to trace this image and similar imagery throughout the essay. For example, explore Melville's use of the imagery of darkness. How is this related to the notion of blackness? Who and what else share these qualities with Hawthorne? Consider, too, the relationship between blackness, genius, truth telling, and the imagery of depth. Are any of these qualities related? Finally, you should consider why Melville uses a metaphor to convey this aspect of Hawthorne and his writing.

2. **Imagery of depth:** Along with the image of blackness, Melville frequently uses the imagery of depth. After his description of Hawthorne's blackness, he argues that Hawthorne "is immeasurably deeper than the plummet of the mere critic." Why does Melville use the imagery of depth in this essay, and what does it represent?

American River College Library

You might begin your exploration of this subject by examining Melville's description of Hawthorne's depth more completely. To what does Melville link this depth? What does he argue is necessary to comprehend the depths of Hawthorne and his fiction? What does this passage imply about good literature? Does Melville use similar terms in other places in the essay? Similarly, examine the essay for other images of depth. How do these relate to Hawthorne and his literary achievement?

Compare and Contrast Essays

Melville uses imagery in "Hawthorne and His Mosses" that was common both in Hawthorne's fiction and in much of Melville's other work. Similarly, his comments about the role of the writer and about the need for a national literature reflect the concerns of other writers of his day. Thus, this essay provides many opportunities for compare and contrast essays. As you construct your essay, be sure that you avoid the most common pitfall of the compare and contrast essay: the laundry list. Remember that you should make an argument about the similarities and differences that you note between the works.

Sample Topics:

1. **Calls for an American literature:** Melville was not alone in his call for a national American literature. Compare his argument in favor of a national literature to that made by other authors of the American Renaissance.

   In response to this question you should consider the relationship that Melville describes between the nation and the author. What is the author's role in the project of nation building? What kinds of metaphors and images does he use to communicate this relationship? Why does he believe that American literature should be different from that of England? Why does he argue that America should "first praise mediocrity even, in her own children, before she praises . . . the best excellence in the children of any other land"? Compare Melville's beliefs to those expressed by Ralph Waldo Emerson in *Nature*. Why does Emerson believe that America must "have a poetry and philosophy of insight and not of tradition"? Are

Emerson's attitudes about America and its literature similar to Melville's? (Remember, too, that Melville included Emerson among his list of great American writers.) You might also examine Melville in relation to Walt Whitman's preface to the 1855 edition of *Leaves of Grass.*

2. **Other assessments of Hawthorne's work:** Melville finds genius, blackness, and depth in Hawthorne's writing, and he argues that "the world is mistaken in this Nathaniel Hawthorne." Examine other 19th-century evaluations of Hawthorne and his writing. Do you agree with Melville that the "world is mistaken" about Hawthorne? Do other reviewers find blackness, depth, and genius in him?

   Much of Hawthorne's work was reviewed in many of the same periodicals that reviewed Melville's work. Examine some of these reviews and compare what they have to say about Hawthorne to what Melville says in "Hawthorne and His Mosses." You might also find it interesting to see which of Hawthorne's shorter pieces critics mentioned. Do other assessments of *Mosses from an Old Manse,* for instance, comment on the same stories in the collection that Melville comments on? Another relevant work is Edgar Allan Poe's 1842 review of Hawthorne's *Twice Told Tales.*

3. **Authorship and the difficulty of truth telling:** In "Hawthorne and His Mosses," Melville calls Hawthorne and Shakespeare "masters of the great Art of Telling the Truth." Throughout the essay, he indicates that telling the truth can be difficult because the truth is often difficult. Often people cannot, or will not, hear the truth. Compare Melville's comments on the "Art of Telling the Truth" with other 19th-century authors' statements about truth and telling the truth.

   In order to focus a response to this question, you would do well to focus on the work of one other writer. While Hawthorne's work might be a good choice here, another interesting candidate might be Emily Dickinson's poems about poetry and about publication. Poem #1129 ("Tell all the Truth but tell it slant—"), 435 ("Much Madness is divinest sense—"), and #448 ("This was a Poet—It is That") are just three of many poems that might prove suggestive.

Bibliography and Online Resources for "Hawthorne and His Mosses"

Baym, Nina. "Melville's Quarrel with Fiction." *PMLA* 94 (1979): 909–923.

Delbanco, Andrew. *Melville: His World and His Work.* New York: Knopf, 2005.

Dryden, Edgar. *Melville's Thematics of Form: The Great Art of Telling the Truth.* Baltimore: Johns Hopkins UP, 1968.

Gilmore, Michael T. *American Romanticism and the Marketplace.* Chicago. U of Chicago P, 1985.

Howard, Leon. *Herman Melville: A Biography.* Berkeley: U of California P, 1951.

Kesterson, David B. "Hawthorne and Melville." Hawthorne in Salem. Available online. URL: http://www.hawthorneinsalem.com/ScholarsForum/HawthorneandMelville.html. Downloaded on September 20, 2007.

Markels, Julian. *Melville and the Politics of Identity.* Urbana: U of Illinois P, 1963.

"Melville and Hawthorne." Hawthorne in Salem. Available online. URL: http://www.hawthorneinsalem.com/Literature/Melville/Introduction.html. Downloaded on September 20, 2007.

"Melville and Nathaniel Hawthorne." The Life and Works of Herman Melville. Available online. URL: http://www.melville.org/hawthrne.htm. Downloaded on September 20, 2007.

Milder, Robert. *Exiled Royalties: Melville and the Life We Imagine.* New York: Oxford UP, 2006.

Parker, Hershel. *Herman Melville.* 2 vols. Baltimore: Johns Hopkins UP, 1996, 2002.

Stuart, John W. "The Hawthorne–Melville Relationship." Hawthorne in Salem. Available online. URL: http://www.hawthorneinsalem.com/ScholarsForum/MMD2461.html. Downloaded on September 20, 2007.

Vincent, Howard P. *The Trying-Out of* Moby-Dick. Boston: Houghton Mifflin, 1949.

MOBY-DICK

READING TO WRITE

IN CHAPTER 41 of *Moby-Dick*, Ishmael says, "No wonder, then . . . the outblown rumors of the White Whale did in the end incorporate with themselves all manner of morbid hints . . . which eventually invested Moby Dick with new terrors." This passage could well apply to the novel itself. Like the whale for which it is named, *Moby-Dick*'s reputation precedes it, and students often approach it fearfully. Perhaps this reputation is not entirely unjustified—both whale and book are large, complex, and intimidating. Yet, just as Ishmael tries to comprehend whales though examining their anatomical parts, you may begin to comprehend *Moby-Dick* by examining its parts. Even then, the whole of this vast book may seem unknowable. As Job 41:1 (to which Melville so frequently alludes) asks, "Canst thou draw leviathan with a hook? or his tongue with a cord which thou lettest down?" No essay on *Moby-Dick* can encompass the whole, and yet close analysis of the text's component parts can help you to craft an essay that can elucidate the books' themes and messages.

The first chapter, "Loomings," provides a strategic place to begin such an investigation, for it provides a good deal of insight into the novel's methods and meanings. In this chapter, the narrator, Ishmael, explains his decision to go to sea as a common sailor on a whaleboat. A careful reader will immediately take note of both the chapter's title and its famous first line, "Call me Ishmael." Both of these elements should frame your reading of the rest of the chapter. According to *The Oxford English Dictionary*, "to loom" means "To appear indistinctly; to come into view in an enlarged and indefinite form." Still further, "looming" carries connotations of threat or intimidation. Already, then, the chapter seems to announce foreshadowings or portents, and it seems to breed a vague sense of unease. Additionally, the Norton Critical Edition of *Moby-Dick* glosses the chapter's title in a footnote, explaining: "A nautical sense is land or ships beyond the horizon, dimly seen by reflection in peculiar weather conditions." While this meaning of the word also indicates a foreshadowing or foreknowledge, it also draws attention to the very nature of perception, for those loomings are seen only through reflection. As you continue to read the chapter, then, you might ask yourself how it foreshadows the events of the novel. Do you see particular images or themes for the novel as a whole? Still further, you might wonder whether the nautical sense of the word asks readers to think about the very process of perception. How is it that we can see something beyond the horizon? How reliable is such vision? "Loomings" carries yet another connotation that might be relevant for the reader of *Moby-Dick.* The word is also associated with the process of weaving something on a loom: "The action or process of 'mounting' the warp on the loom" (OED). The chapter title seems to evoke the metaphor of weaving for the act of storytelling, as Ishmael is about to weave together the story of Ahab's hunt for Moby Dick. You might assess the relevance of this metaphor and look for similar uses of it as you read Melville's novel.

Along with the chapter's title, its first sentence, "Call me Ishmael," should attract your attention. Consider what this simple sentence indicates about the text that will follow. Immediately Ishmael establishes himself as a first-person, participant narrator. Already you know that he is both character and storyteller, and thus you must analyze him as both a character and as a storyteller. Perhaps you might also ask about the phrasing of Ishmael's introduction. Since he says that readers should "call him" Ishmael, you might suspect that is not his given name. Why might he have chosen the name Ishmael and asked readers to call him that? What does the name tell us about Ishmael and his sense of self? Since the biblical Ishmael was an outcast (see Genesis 16:12), is the narrator also an outcast? If so, why is he an outcast? Readers also quickly learn something of Ishmael's style and tendencies as a storyteller. He begins his chapter telling of his reasons for going to sea. After explaining the draw of the sea, he links himself to the rest of humanity ("If they but knew it, almost all men in their degree, some time or other, cherish very nearly the same feelings toward the ocean with me"); he links the sea to the process of meditation ("Yes, as everyone knows, meditation and water are wedded for ever."); and he claims that the myth of Narcissus (which he alters) is "the key to it all." It does not take more than a few pages for readers to understand that Ishmael is a rambling and discursive storyteller and that the text he weaves is no straightforward seafaring adventure.

Having finally explained why he has gone to sea, Ishmael proposes to explain why he has gone to sea as a common sailor on a whaleboat. The final four paragraphs of "Loomings" introduce quite a few of the novel's themes and issues:

> But wherefore it was that after having repeatedly smelt the sea as a merchant sailor, I should now take it into my head to go on a whaling voyage; this the invisible police officer of the Fates, who has the constant surveillance of me, and secretly dogs me, and influences me in some unaccountable way—he can better answer than any one else. And, doubtless, my going on this whaling voyage formed part of the grand programme of Providence that was drawn up a long time ago. It came in as a sort of brief interlude and solo between more extensive performances. I take it that this part of the bill must have run something like this:
>
> "*Grand Contested Election for the Presidency of the United States.*
>
> "Whaling voyage by one Ishmael.
>
> **"BLOODY BATTLE IN AFFGHANISTAN."**
>
> Though I cannot tell why it was exactly that those stage managers, the Fates, put me down for this shabby part of a whaling voyage, when others were set down for magnificent parts in high tragedies, and short and easy parts in genteel comedies, and jolly parts in farces—though I cannot tell why this was exactly; yet, now that I recall all the circumstances, I think I can see a little into the springs and motives which being cunningly presented to me under various disguises, induced me to set about performing the part I did, besides cajoling me into the delusion that it was a choice resulting from my own unbiased freewill and discriminating judgment.
>
> Chief among these motives was the overwhelming idea of the great whale himself. Such a portentous and mysterious monster roused all my curiosity. Then the wild and distant seas where he rolled his island bulk; the undeliverable, nameless perils of the whale; these, with all the attending marvels of a thousand Patagonian sights and sounds, helped to sway me to my wish. With other men, perhaps, such things would not

have been inducements; but as for me, I am tormented with an everlasting itch for things remote. I love to sail forbidden seas, and land on barbarous coasts. Not ignoring what is good, I am quick to perceive a horror, and could still be social with it—would they let me—since it is but well to be on friendly terms with all inmates of the place one lodges in.

By reason of these things, then, the whaling voyage was welcome; the great flood-gates of the wonder-world swung open, and in the wild conceits that swayed me to my purpose, two and two there floated into my inmost soul, endless processions of the whale, and midmost of them all, one grand hooded phantom, like a snow hill in the air.

As the passage begins, readers learn about Ishmael's worldview. He claims that his reason for shipping aboard a whaling ship rather than a merchant ship could be better explained by "the invisible police officer of the Fates, who has the constant surveillance of me . . . and influences me in some unaccountable way." He further describes his decision as one formed by "the grand programme of Providence that was drawn up some time ago." In both these descriptions Ishmael indicates that his decisions were not his own; they were fated or predestined. An alert reader will notice, though, that these two descriptions seem to credit very different kinds of gods for the management of his life—the first references the Greek goddesses, the Fates, and the second reference to "Providence" seems to invoke a Christian concept of God. As if to underline that his decisions reflect not his own choices but a preordained fate, Ishmael says toward the end of the next paragraph, "now that I recall all the circumstances, I think I can see a little into the springs and motives which being cunningly presented to me under various disguises, induced me to set about performing the part I did, besides cajoling me into the delusion that it was a choice resulting from my own unbiased freewill and discriminating judgment." Free will, he says, is a fiction, a delusion. Clearly, by the end of the first chapter, Melville asks his audience to contemplate issues of free will versus fate. This philosophical theme runs throughout *Moby-Dick*. Similarly, given the apparently conflicting descriptions of "the Fates" and "Providence," you might wonder about the theology that underlies this belief. Does Ishmael express a type of Christian, Calvinistic belief about predestination, or is his worldview distinctly non-Christian? Still further, you might question whether his worldview reflects that of his author. Melville was raised in the Calvinistic Dutch Reformed Church. How might Ishmael's contemplation of free will and fate reflect Melville's own reaction to the religious traditions of his childhood?

Additionally, you may have noticed how Ishmael's meditation on free will and fate also tells you something very important about the narrative that is to follow. The first paragraph of the chapter clearly establishes that the ensuing narrative is a retrospective when Ishmael says, "Some years ago—never mind how long precisely . . ." But these paragraphs from the end of the chapter tell us that in recalling "all the circumstances" that led to his shipping aboard the *Pequod,* Ishmael believes that he "can see a little into the springs and motives" that motivated his choice. In other words, the Ishmael who narrates the events that are to follow believes that he understands the workings of the world better than the younger Ishmael whose story he narrates. You would be wise, then, to read *Moby-Dick* with an eye toward evaluating Ishmael and his growth. What does Ishmael learn during the course of his journey on the *Pequod*? How do you assess the learning that he undergoes? Examining these issues as you read should provide the basis for thoughtful papers about Ishmael and his narrative style.

Similarly, the language Ishmael uses to describe the workings of fate is also striking. Examine the use of stage language here. He speaks of the "grand programme of Providence," and he envisions and re-creates in the text the playbill that announces his "brief interlude and solo between more extensive performance." Still further, he speaks of the "stage managers, the Fates" who "put [him] down for this shabby part of a whaling voyage, when others were set down for magnificent parts in high tragedies, and short and easy parts in genteel comedies, and jolly parts in farces." Clearly, the language of the stage reflects Ishmael's apparent belief that the paths of human lives are somehow predestined and preordained. You might find his use of stage language suggestive of still other issues that might help to shape your reading of *Moby-Dick.* For instance, explore the significance of Ishmael's casting of his own life as a bit part in a drama. What precisely is his "part" in the story of Ahab's hunt for Moby Dick? By the novel's end, he seems to have identified his part and its purpose. Do you agree with his assessment? Further, how might his belief that our roles in life are predestined affect

Ishmael's telling of the story? Will it affect how he presents and assesses the other characters in his drama? How might it affect his technique? Approaching the text with questions like these prepares you to analyze elements of the book that have long been the subject of study. While *Moby-Dick* begins as a narrative of Ishmael's whaling adventure, before long the book moves into a much more dramatic mode, and many readers become aware that they seem to have lost Ishmael's voice. When the book moves into dramatic mode, it seems more like the written script of a drama rather than a novel. It includes stage directions and soliloquies. How might Ishmael's early use of dramatic language help you to make sense of these narrative shifts? Considering such questions might help you to formulate paper topics about form, genre, and narrative technique in *Moby-Dick*.

In the paragraph that follows Ishmael's description of his "shabby part," he introduces the "chief" motive—"the great whale himself." Here he might be describing Moby Dick, or he might be describing the whale as a species. Examine the language that he uses in his description. The whale is "chief" motive, "overwhelming idea," "portentous and mysterious monster." What do these descriptions imply about Ishmael's assessment of the whale? In what sense is the whale monstrous? Certainly, he is monstrous in size, and words like *overwhelming, portentous,* and *island bulk,* might help to reinforce the idea of the monstrous size of the whale. You might also notice, though, that Ishmael tells the reader that the whale "roused all my curiosity," and his language also seems to paint the whale as a riddle or a puzzle to be solved. He is "mysterious." Beyond this, "portentous" carries a great deal of suggestive meaning. Besides meaning "large" or "weighty," it also can mean "ominous" or "threatening," as well as "marvelous" or "extraordinary" (as well as "monstrous"). The whale, then, is both threatening and awe inspiring, and, consequently, it draws Ishmael. Still further, Ishmael says that the "overwhelming idea," the "nameless peril," of the whale entices him. What does he mean by that? It seems as though its very vastness and inscrutibility is what draws him. How might this be related to his desire for the "wild and distant" seas and his "ever-lasting itch for things remote"? In the first paragraph of "Loomings," Ishmael says he goes to sea "whenever it is a damp, drizzly November in my soul." The journey is a "substitute for pistol and ball." Might we see in the "itch for things remote," the lure of the whale, the "wild and distant seas," the desire to "perceive a horror, and . . . still be social with it" an echo of the kind of death wish that begins the chapter?

Ishmael magnifies and repeats the lure of the whale in the final paragraph of the chapter. "In the wild conceits that swayed [him] to[his] purpose" he lists the "endless processions of the whale" that "two and two . . . floated into my inmost soul." "[M]idmost of them all," he says, is "one grand hooded phantom, like a snow hill in the air." Here, at last, he seems to paint a portrait of Moby Dick, and here you might raise a number of questions. Why, for example, does he speak of Moby Dick as a "grand hooded phantom"? How does this description connect to his earlier descriptions of the whale? As a "phantom" and as a "snow hill in the air," Moby Dick seems both threatening and otherworldly. Similarly, the "hooded" nature of this "phantom" seems to suggest an elusive quality. This "hooded phantom" is veiled, somehow unknowable. Certainly, a close examination of this description of Moby Dick, coupled with an an analysis of Ishmael's descriptions of whales, lays the groundwork for your own evaluation of Moby Dick. Similarly, your interrogation of Ishmael's conception of the white whale should prepare you for the many epistemological issues raised in the novel as it takes stock of the varied characters' assessments of Moby Dick. Finally, a careful reader should also note that Ishmael says that the procession of whales "floated into my inmost soul." While Ishmael prepares for a journey outward into "things remote," the procession of whales moves inward. Perhaps then, the story that he is about to tell is the chronicle of both the physical journey of the whaling adventure and a journey inward into the soul of the outcast Ishmael.

Having read the opening pages of *Moby-Dick* attentively, you should be well prepared to approach the rest of the text. You should have questions about Ishmael and his narrative technique, human perceptions and evaluations of the whale, fate and free will, and form and genre. A thorough investigation into any of these topics should provide you with material that you can focus and shape into a successful paper topic.

TOPICS AND STRATEGIES

This section of the chapter provides you with broad topic ideas that should help you develop an essay on *Moby-Dick*. Remember that these topics are just springboards for our own exploration; you will need to focus your analysis and develop your own specific thesis.

Themes

As the previous section of this chapter points out, *Moby-Dick* explores many themes. To paraphrase Walt Whitman, this book is large, and it contains multitudes. Viable topics for thematic examination range from sociologically based investigations into race and human community to more philosophical inquiries about humanity's place in the natural world. To write a paper about thematic concerns in the novel, you should begin by identifying a theme that you found intriguing. From there, you should go back over the text carefully and attempt to draw some conclusions about Melville's treatment of that theme. If you are interested in the theme of the orphan in *Moby-Dick*, for example, you might begin by identifying the orphaned characters in the text. You might also explore what Ishmael and the rest of these characters have to say about orphanage. Consider why Melville has interwoven so many orphans into this text. You could also think about how this theme might function metaphorically. Do these orphans seem to represent something beyond themselves?

Sample Topics:

1. **Human community:** Ishmael begins "Loomings" with images of isolation and insularity. He presents himself as a depressed (if jocular) outcast, and he parallels his own situation to that of "all men" and with an image of the "insular" island of Manhattan. By the chapter's end, though, he presents images of community and fraternity. How might you read *Moby-Dick* as an argument for human community and fraternity, and for their political incarnation, democracy?

   One way to approach this topic is to consider the *Pequod* and the human interactions on board the ship. Many scholars have noted that Melville seems to present the whaleship as a micro-cosm of the world or as a microcosm of America. Look at the social structure on board the ship. How are the relationships officially structured? How do these relationships actually function on board the *Pequod*? What allows them to func-tion as they do? Chapters 26 and 27 (both titled "Knights and

Squires") should provide a good starting place for this investigation. Similarly, examine chapter 54, "The Town-Ho's Story." How does this interpolated tale reflect upon issues of human community and democracy? You should also find it helpful to explore the relationships among the individual members of the crew. Look at the relationships between Ishmael and Queequeg, Ahab and Pip, Ahab and Starbuck. You might also think about the dynamics between the *Pequod* and the other ships it meets. The chapters on the *Bachelor* and the *Rachel* are particularly relevant. Take into account the imagery and the language associated with this theme throughout the book. What phrases or images help to develop the commentary on human community, fraternity, and democracy? Images of isolation might also provide you with a framework for exploring ideas of human community. Analyze the theme of isolation in the work. How does it work in conjunction with the theme of fraternity and community?

2. **Birth and rebirth:** One of the final images of *Moby-Dick* is that of Ishmael buoyed up and saved by Queequeg's coffin. In chapter 127, "The Deck," Ahab contemplates the symbolism of the coffin turned life-buoy: "Here now's the very dreaded symbol of grim death, by a mere hap, made the expressive sign of the help and hope of most endangered life. A life-buoy of a coffin! Does it go further? Can it be that in some spiritual sense the coffin is, after all, but an immortality-preserver!" What does *Moby-Dick* say about birth and rebirth?

For a novel featuring many images of death, *Moby-Dick* is surprisingly full of images of birth, rebirth, and generation. To begin preparing a paper on this topic, review the novel for these images. How does Melville develop them? As Ahab's commentary on the life-buoy coffin suggests, these images are filled with metaphorical possibilities, and the theme of rebirth is especially fertile. Consider the carpenter's commentary on refitting the coffin in chapter 126, "The Life-Buoy." How does his dismay at this "cobbler's job" reflect upon these themes? Besides Ishmael (and the coffin), who or what else is birthed or reborn in *Moby-Dick*? What is the significance of these births/rebirths? What metaphorical significance do you see in them? You might consider their connections to the themes of religion, orphanage, and identity. Obviously, you will need to hone your focus significantly if you hope to write an effective paper on birth and rebirth in *Moby-Dick*.

3. **Economics and commodification:** Money, finance, buying, and selling permeate *Moby-Dick*. The novel makes it quite clear that whaling is an industry and that whales are products with great commercial value. How might you read *Moby-Dick* as a commentary on economics and the process of commodification?

You might take a paper on economics and commodification in *Moby-Dick* in a number of directions. Chapter 16, "The Ship," tells a lot about the industry of whaling, as do many of Ishmael's chapters on the killing and the rendering of whales. Read these carefully for Ishmael's (and, perhaps, for Melville's) commentary. Examine the language of economics. Look at the imagery used in the chapters on the rendering of the whales. You should also explore the significance of the doubloon that Ahab nails to the ships mast in chapter 36, "The Quarter-Deck." How does Melville use the doubloon to comment on economics and commodities?

On the other hand, you could examine the novel for related imagery of mechanization. How are these images related to the language of economics and commodity? How might this language allow you to develop a paper on this topic from an angle different from that suggested above? You could also think about how this theme intersects with the issue of symbolism discussed in the section of this chapter on Philosophy and Ideas. How might this connection be suggestive as you focus on a paper on Melville's treatment of economics and commodity in *Moby-Dick*?

4. **Orphans and orphanage:** *Orphan* is the final word of *Moby-Dick*, and the novel is populated by orphans or characters who feel themselves to be orphans—Ishmael, Pip, Ahab. Echoes of

this theme clearly occur throughout the book. Why does Melville return to this theme so often? What significance or conclusions can you draw from his use of this theme?

There are myriad ways of approaching this question. You could explore the status of any of the novel's more significant orphans, Ishmael, Pip, or Ahab. What effect does their status as orphans have on their characters and on the role they play throughout the course of the book? You could choose a broader focus, drawing conclusions about the abundance of orphans in the text. Or, you might wish to draw connections between this theme and others. For instance, what relation does this theme bear to the treatment of rebirth in the novel? Chapter 14, "The Gilder," should prove particularly suggestive. Similarly, you can relate the orphan theme to issues of democracy, politics, and nationalism or to identity in general. How might it provide commentary on or insight into any of these themes?

5. **Nature:** One way of interpreting Moby Dick as a symbol is to interpret the whale as an embodiment of nature. While this certainly is a legitimate way to view the title character, it can also limit the reader's understanding of both the whale's meaning and the text's treatment of nature as a theme. How might you read *Moby-Dick* as a commentary on nature and on humanity's relationship with nature?

This is a huge, complex question that will require substantial focusing if you are to write an effective essay. There are numerous ways of approaching this topic. As the question implies, you could examine Moby Dick as an embodiment of nature. This alone is a momentous task, for as a symbol the whale is multifaceted, and Ishmael provides readers with numerous opinions about Moby Dick, his meaning, and his nature. Obvious starting points for a paper that focuses on the whale as a symbol of nature are chapter 41, "Moby Dick," and chapter 42, "The Whiteness of the Whale." You would also need to explore chapter 36, "The Quarter-Deck," carefully. These are only starting places for this difficult topic.

You have quite a few other options for shaping a paper on this topic. Consider the novel's commentary about humans and their relationship with nature. This approach provides many possible avenues for study. You may choose to examine the whaling voyage and the relationship between the *Pequod*'s crew and their encounters with whales and sharks. How do these encounters figure the relationship between humans and nature? How complex is this relationship? How does Melville provide commentary on humanity's connection with nature through these encounters and the language that describes them? You could also write a paper that considers American history and the country's attitudes toward nature in the mid-19th century. Look at the mechanistic imagery that Melville uses. How is it significant? Examine the many times Melville discusses the sea through land imagery—fields and prairies. What is this significance of these descriptions?

Yet another approach might be to examine contrasting views of nature. Frequently expressing the unity between humanity and nature, the book presents views of nature derived from romantic philosophies. (Chapter 35, "The Mast-Head," provides a famous example.) And yet, the book also presents many examples of a starkly contrasting view of nature. (Ahab's apostrophe to the "dark Hindoo half of nature" in chapter 76, "The Dying Whale," and Queequeg's ejaculation that "de god what made shark must be one dam Ingin" in chapter 25, "The Whale as a Dish," provide just two well-known examples.) These are just a few possibilities for narrowing this very broad, but very important, topic.

6. **Religion:** Years after the publication of *Moby-Dick*, Nathaniel Hawthorne wrote of Melville: "He can neither believe, nor be comfortable in his unbelief; and he is too honest and courageous not to try to do one or the other." How does *Moby-Dick* provide evidence of Melville's deep ambivalence about God, religion, and religious practices?

Once again, this is a huge topic, and there are numerous ways of approaching it in order to forge a manageable paper topic. To explore Melville's treatment of God in *Moby-Dick,* you would do well to consider some of the concerns addressed in the previous discussion about nature as a theme. How might the contemplations of Moby Dick in chapter 42, "The Whiteness of the Whale," or in chapter 36, "The Quarter-Deck," provide evidence of Melville's crisis of belief? Similarly, you might explore the Calvinist God presented in Father Mapple's sermon in chapter 9. Many readers have connected this sermon to Melville's upbringing in the Dutch Reformed Church. Does this chapter comment on God, religion, or on Calvinism specifically? You could broaden such an investigation to explore Melville's treatment of other characters who espouse a particular religious tradition. You might examine Captain Peleg and Captain Bildad for example. Both are Quakers, though they seem to express their Quakerism quite differently. Early in the book, Ishmael speaks of his background in the "infallible Presbyterian Church" (chapter 10, "A Bosom Friend"), but ironically, he seems to stretch Presbyterian beliefs when he evokes the golden rule to justify his decision to join Queequeg in his religious ritual and "turn idolater." Still further, the text frequently invokes the word *cannibal* to refer to non-Christians. You could craft an effective paper that compares the text's many "cannibals" to its professed Christians. Ahab, too, could provide an interesting focus for a paper, especially if you examine his propensity for perverting religious rituals (as, for example, in his baptism of his harpoon in chapter 113, "The Forge"). Obviously, Starbuck provides a strong contrast to Ahab, and he is presented as a traditional Christian character. You might find it worthwhile to compare the two men, or you might focus a paper on Starbuck's Christianity and Melville's commentary on it.

7. **Race:** Readers have long noted the many races represented aboard the *Pequod.* How does Melville use the multiracial society aboard the whaling craft to comment on race in the 19th century?

The three harpooners—Queequeg, Tashtego, and Dagoo— all provide a substantial starting place for an exploration of race in *Moby-Dick*. Clearly, it seems significant that in the whaleboats each of the three "foreign" harpooners is paired with a white "leader" (Starbuck, Stubb, and Flask). Ahab and Fedallah form a similar pair. What significance do you see in these relationships? Many scholars see a commentary on slavery in Melville's treatment of Dagoo, Pip, and Fleece. Consider how chapter 89, "Fast Fish and Loose Fish," could help you to develop this approach. Do these racial "others" also provide a means to explore America's relationship with American Indians? How might such a reading work? Another approach to the issue of race in *Moby-Dick* would be to explore Queequeg's role. Analyze his relationship with Ishmael. Queequeg becomes a far less prominent figure once the hunt for Moby Dick begins. What do you make of this? Do Queequeg's tattoos have any bearing on this issue? Critic Geoffrey Sandborn argues quite convincingly that "in the mid-nineteenth century 'cannibal' was a relatively common racial epithet," rather than a comment on a character's eating habits. How does an exploration of the text's use of the terms *cannibal* and *savage* provide you with a way to explore *Moby-Dick*'s commentary on race?

8. **Madness:** Just as *Moby-Dick* presents readers with a plethora of orphaned characters, so madness seems to characterize its many characters. How and why does Melville use the theme of madness in *Moby-Dick*?

A paper that addresses this question could focus on Ahab and his exclusive fixation on the whale, but Ahab is not the only mad character. Examine the roles of Pip, Elijah, and Gabriel. How does their madness function within the text? Of these, Pip deserves special attention. What has caused Pip's madness? What are its effects? What effect does his madness have on those around him, and how is it significant? Still further, you may want to consider why madness is so prevalent and why Melville populated his novel with such characters.

A paper that explores Ishmael's journey into his "inmost self" might also consider his comment in chapter 11, "Nightgown," that "darkness" is necessary for a man to "feel his own identity aright." How does that darkness, both literal and metaphoric, help Ishmael on his journey inward? The early chapters of the book, often called the "land chapters," provide an essential beginning for an investigation of Ishmael's character. In some of these, readers learn of Ishmael even before he begins to contemplate his whaling voyage. Clearly, you must also analyze Ishmael's reaction to and relationship with Queequeg. Consider, too, his experience with Ahab and Moby Dick. How are these essential for his inward journey? Additionally, Ishmael often includes his own contemplations of selfhood and the relationship between the self and the other. These passages should prove provocative. Pay particular attention to chapter 35, "The Mast-Head"; chapter 72, "The Monkey Rope"; chapter 87, "The Grand Armada"; and chapter 94, "A Squeeze of the Hand." Finally, you should consider whether you believe Ishmael has grown in self-understanding by the novel's end. Is the Ishmael who narrates the book a different man from the younger version of himself described in "Loomings"?

2. **Ahab:** After discussing Ahab's madness in chapter 41, "Moby Dick," Ishmael says, "This is much, yet Ahab's larger, darker, deeper part remains unhinted." He develops this statement through a comparison with the underground ruins beneath Paris's Hotel de Cluny: "Winding far down from within the very heart of this spiked Hotel de Cluny where we here stand—however grand and wonderful, now quit it;—and take your way . . . to those vast Roman halls of Thermes; where far beneath the fantastic towers of man's upper earth, his root of grandeur, his whole awful essence sits in bearded state; an antique buried beneath antiquities, and throned on torsos!" What does Ishmael reference when he speaks of Ahab's "larger, darker, deeper part"? Does he show Ahab's "essence" to the reader before the end of the text, or do readers see only his madness, his "upper earth"?

Character

Moby-Dick provides ample material for papers that fo
and character development. As the opening section of
cates, you could examine Ishmael both as a narrator an
the narrative. Questions of voice and of development r
tive focuses for a paper on Ishmael. Quite a few of the
also provide substantive material for an essay on cha
Ahab is perhaps the most complex and compelling. Sl
to write on Ahab, you would need to hone your focus c
a paper on Ahab is a difficult task because, like *Moby-D*
whale itself, Ahab is huge, complex and contradictor
ungodly, god-like man," says Captain Peleg in chapte
Accordingly, Ahab has been seen as both tragic hero ar
has been compared to figures as diverse as Prometheus,
Lear, and Victor Frankenstein. If you were to write on
would need to decide how you view him and how the te
interpretation of his actions. How does Melville make
just a crazy, angry man bent on revenge against a "dumk
so many readers consider him, a tragic hero? Is he a villa
types of questions that you would need to consider as y
on Ahab. As you develop an essay on Ahab, or on any ch
need to consider the various insights that the novel pro\
Analyze other characters' assessments of the character a
speech and his actions.

Sample Topics:

1. **Ishmael:** In chapter 1, "Loomings," Ishmael tell:
   a great deal about his younger self and his indu
   embarking on the *Pequod*. At the chapter's end, h
   whaling journey as a kind of inward journey, say
   wild conceits that swayed me to my purpose, two ar
   floated into my inmost soul, endless processions of
   How can *Moby-Dick* be read as an inward journey
   covery? Does Ishmael grow or change as a result of
   ences with Ahab and Moby Dick? Does he learn mo
   own identity through these experiences?

aboard the whaling ships *Acushnet, Lucy Ann,* and *Charles and Henry,* affect or influence *Moby-Dick*?

While *Moby-Dick* does not draw as explicitly from the author's own experiences as *Typee* does, certainly he could not have written *Moby-Dick* without his experience at sea. Biographies of Melville should prove helpful as you shape a response to this question. Similarly, material on the whaling industry in the 19th century might add to your investigation. Mystic Seaport's Web site (www.mysticseaport.org) provides information on whaling on its page on the whaling ship *Charles W. Morgan.* Additionally, the Norton Critical Edition of *Moby-Dick* collects some information on the whaling industry in the 19th century.

2. **Melville's use of Shakespeare:** Melville was well versed in Shakespeare, and many scholars have remarked on Shakespeare's influence on *Moby-Dick.* Examine Melville's debt to Shakespeare in *Moby-Dick.*

   Obviously, some of the connections between the novel and Shakespeare derive from Melville's use of dramatic form, which the section of this chapter on form and genre addresses. In addition to Melville's use of dramatic form, *Moby-Dick* draws on the themes, language, and tensions of Shakespeare's work. Scholars have especially noted connections between *Moby-Dick* and *Macbeth, The Tempest,* and *King Lear.* You could choose to discuss Ahab's connections to one of Shakespeare's tragic heroes or you could explore thematic connections. The connections between *Moby-Dick* and *King Lear* seem especially provocative given Ahab's madness and his connection with Pip, as well as Melville's use of the theme of vision and seeing, and his use of a climactic storm scene. *The Tempest,* with its themes of civilization and savagery, community and isolation, also bears strong parallels to the themes of *Moby-Dick.*

3. **Melville's use of whaling sources, sea stories, and sea lore:** While Melville experienced life aboard a whaling ship like the *Pequod,* he supplemented his knowledge by reading about whales

and the whaling industry. Ishmael mentions some of these texts during the course of *Moby-Dick,* and the novel makes reference to the lore of the white whale and of stories about aggressive whales that attacked whaling ships. Examine Melville's use of these various accounts of whales and whaling in *Moby-Dick.* How and why does he use these sources?

Chapter 32, "Cetology," mentions a number of zoological texts that Melville was familiar with. The *Pequod*'s eventual destruction seems to mirror the fate of the whaler *Essex,* which was sunk by a whale in 1820 (which Ishmael references in Chapter 45, "The Affidavit"). Melville had heard oral accounts of the event, and he read the published account, Owen Chase's *Narrative of the Most Extraordinary and Distressing Shipwreck of the Whaleship Essex.* You can find an extract from Chase's text in the Norton Critical Edition of *Moby-Dick.* Additionally, Nathaniel Philbrick's *In the Heart of the Sea,* a recent account of the *Essex,* should prove helpful. Similarly, the Norton edition of *Moby-Dick* also includes J. N. Reynolds's "Mocha Dick," about a legendary white whale. ("Mocha Dick" is also available online at http://www.melville.org/reynolds.htm). Consideration of these sources could help you to shape an essay in a few ways. You might choose to focus on the zoological texts that Melville includes and comments upon. What function do they serve? Why does he have Ishmael reference them so overtly? How does their inclusion reflect the themes and the purposes of the novel? An essay that focuses on these texts might also examine some of the issues addressed in the Form and Genre section of this chapter. An alternative focus might be the sea stories and sea lore. Why and how does Melville include sea lore and the oral and written traditions about aggressive whales, and the white whale in particular? The interpolated tale "The Town Ho's Story" (chapter 54) might prove helpful in an investigation of this kind. While the tale seems an intrusion into the narrative line of the book, what useful purposes does it serve for Melville? How does it comment on stories, storytelling, and sea lore?

4. **Melville's use of the Bible and biblical allusion:** An attentive reader of *Moby-Dick* will quickly notice that the book is heavily laden with biblical allusion. Choose a biblical character, story, or theme that Melville uses in *Moby-Dick* and analyze its use. How and why does Melville shape it to his purpose in his novel?

If you do not know the Bible as well as Melville obviously did, you will find that footnotes and textual apparatus in a good edition of *Moby-Dick* might help you get a start with a paper that addresses this question. Character names—Ahab, Elijah, Gabriel, and Ishmael—are obvious examples of these references, and Ishmael and Captain Peleg discuss Ahab's name and its potentially prophetic nature in chapter 16, "The Ship." The connections between the *Pequod*'s captain and the biblical king who shares his name deepen when Ishmael and Queequeg encounter Elijah in the chapter titled "The Prophet." The theme of prophecy, itself, could also function as a focus for a paper on biblical allusion, for Elijah is not the only prophet in the text, nor is he the only character who believes in prophecy. In addition, *Moby-Dick* draws heavily on biblical references to whales, and these, too, could provide a good focus. Jonah is the text of Father Mapple's sermon in chapter 9, and Melville uses many other references to the story of Jonah throughout the novel. Similarly, in chapter 41, "Moby Dick," Ishmael says of Ahab: "Here, then, was this grey-headed, ungodly old man, chasing with curses a Job's whale round the world . . ." Job 41:1 speaks of the monster leviathan, "Canst thou draw leviathan with a hook? or his tongue with a chord which thou lettest down?" In many ways, this text seems to underlie the very purpose and point of *Moby-Dick*, and an exploration of this connection could result in a strong, interesting paper.

Philosophy and Ideas

Melville's voluminous reading once again lays the groundwork for his treatment of philosophical issues and concerns in *Moby-Dick*. Writing in the wake of transcendentalists such as Ralph Waldo Emerson, Melville clearly grapples with transcendentalist beliefs throughout the novel. Transcendentalism, in turn, drew much from the thinking of European romanticism. Melville was well versed in these writers, and his novel demonstrates this quite clearly. Similarly, having grown up in the Dutch Reformed Church, Melville knew both the Bible and the tenets of Calvinism, and both have a strong bearing on the novel. Once again, good biographies of Melville might prove a useful place to begin your research on Melville and philosophic issues. Similarly, the footnotes and textual apparatus in a good edition of *Moby-Dick* should prove invaluable to you as you explore some of the topic ideas that follow.

Sample Topics:

1. **Symbolism and representation:** Like the scarlet *A* in Nathaniel Hawthorne's *The Scarlet Letter*, the white whale Moby Dick serves as one of the best-known symbols in American literature. Melville's novel, like Hawthorne's, takes its central symbol as its title, and it makes symbolism and representation one of its central focuses. How might you consider *Moby-Dick* a contemplation of the nature of symbolism and representation? What does Melville say about the nature of signs and symbols and the human ability to read and to use symbols?

   In order to prepare a paper on this vast and complicated subject, you should begin by exploring how Melville presents the white whale as a symbol. How does he transform Moby Dick into something more than a "dumb brute" (chapter 36, "The Quarter-Deck")? Chapters 41 and 42, ("Moby Dick" and "The Whiteness of the Whale") should provide particular insight. What does Moby Dick represent? In addition to considering Ahab's conception of the whale as well as those of Ishmael and the crew, you might also take into account those of the other sailors and ships that the *Pequod* meets. How do the encounters in the *Pequod*'s gams help to develop Melville's contemplation of Moby Dick as a symbol? A paper that thoroughly considers *Moby-Dick* as a meditation on symbolism must also examine the function of other symbols in the book. The gold doubloon that Ahab nails to the ship's mast is especially important, and any consideration of symbols and representation in the novel must analyze its treatment in some detail. Similarly, think about the connection between this topic and some of the novel's other themes and focuses. Consider the connections between symbolism and issues of industry and the language of money. As the doubloon's central place in the novel reminds readers, money is a kind of symbol or representation, for a coin stands for or represents many other things. You might also consider the relevance of Ishmael's lengthy contemplations of whales, their nature, and their value in what are often called the novel's "cetological chapters." How are these explorations related to the novel's central concern for symbols, their function, and their meaning?

2. **Fate versus free will:** In "Loomings," Ishmael raises the question of fate versus human free will when he invokes the Fates and says, "my going on this whaling voyage formed part of the grand programme of Providence that was drawn up a long time ago." Similarly, in chapter 19, "The Prophet," Elijah ominously raises the question of human free will: "Well, well, what's signed, is signed; and what's to be, will be; and then again, perhaps it wont be, after all. Any how, it's all fixed and arranged a'ready; and some sailors or other must go with him, I suppose . . ." Consider *Moby-Dick* as an exploration of predestination versus human free will.

Moby-Dick is rife with contemplations of fate and free will, and these meditations are necessarily interwoven with the novel's contemplation of God. Underlying this consideration is the Calvinism of Melville's upbringing. You might begin by exploring the novel's treatment of God and connecting that treatment to Calvinism, along with its doctrine of predestination. Father Mapple's sermon early in the novel presents a Calvinistic worldview. In chapter 102, "A Bower in the Arsacides," Ishmael speaks of a "weaver-god," and the novel often sustains this metaphor through the imagery of weaving. How is this pattern of imagery related to the theme of fate versus free will? Clearly, the novel connects the white whale and his "predestinating head" (chapter 135, "The Chase—Third Day") to God and God's foreordained plan. Explore these connections in detail. Similarly, you should explore Ahab's assessments of Moby Dick and of his own pursuit of the whale. Ahab frequently mentions the fated nature of his hunt for Moby Dick. One especially famous example of this occurs in Chapter 132, "The Chase—First Day." How does Ahab conceive of the role of fate in his pursuit? Does he believe in a God who has foreordained his actions? If so, does he willingly submit to that God's plan? Explain.

3. **Epistemology:** Another of *Moby-Dick*'s philosophical concerns is the nature of human knowledge. What does the novel say about what we know, and how we know?

   Issues of form and symbolism provide ways to approach this very broad topic. *Moby-Dick* is filled with the language of seeing and perceiving, and through that language it explores the relationship between human perception and understanding. You might begin such an investigation through a thorough analysis of Pip's famous words in chapter 99, "The Doubloon": "I look, you look, he looks; we look, ye look, they look." How might Pip's apparently simple conjugation of the verb "to look" be important to the novel's epistemological statement? You will probably find that in approaching the topic this way you are also exploring the novel's commentary on symbolism. Ishmael's lengthy explorations of whales in the cetological chapters could also provide a way into this topic. Consider why he spends so much time discussing whale anatomy and whale behavior, as well as why he talks about different human conceptions of whales, zoological studies, art, song, and folklore. Consider, too, the elaborate metaphor of the whale as book.

4. **Transcendentalism:** Many scholars read *Moby-Dick* as Melville's assessment of the philosophy of transcendentalism expressed by such important 19th-century American writers as Ralph Waldo Emerson and Henry David Thoreau. How might you read *Moby-Dick* as a commentary on transcendentalism?

   Exploring connections between *Moby-Dick* and Emerson's philosophy could prove particularly interesting for a response to this question. In a May 1851 letter to Nathaniel Hawthorne, Melville wrote: "In reading some of Goethe's sayings . . . I came across this, 'Live in the all.' That is to say, your separate identity is but a wretched one,—good; but get out of yourself, spread and expand yourself, and bring to yourself the tinglings of life that are felt in the flowers and the woods, that are felt in the planets Saturn and Venus, and the Fixed Stars. What nonsense!" In his postscript to the letter, though, Melville returns to that concept: "N.B. This 'all' feeling, though, there is some truth in. You must often have felt it, lying on the grass on a warm summer's day. Your legs seem to send out shoots into the earth. Your hair feels like leaves upon your head. This is the *all* feeling. But what plays the mischief with the truth is that men will insist upon the universal application of a temporary feeling or opinion." Melville's description of this "all feeling" seems to share a good deal with Emerson's transcendental philosophies, especially those expressed in his work *Nature*. Literary scholars have pointed particularly to a few elements in *Nature* that seem to have a direct bearing on *Moby-Dick*, including Emerson's focus on sight and perception, his discussion of analogies, his famous passage in which he declares that in the woods he becomes "a transparent eyeball," and his assertion that "every man's condition is a solution in hieroglyphic to those inquiries he would put." A strong paper on this topic would be well-versed in Emerson's philosophies and should look at specific passages in Melville's novel that seem to comment upon the issues and beliefs that Emerson expresses.

Form and Genre

Questions of genre have haunted *Moby-Dick* from the beginning. Many contemporary reviewers panned the book because it strayed beyond the bounds of 19th-century novelistic convention. The London *Athenaeum* noted: "This is an ill-compounded mixture of romance and matter-of-fact. The idea of a connected and collected story has obviously visited and abandoned its writer again and again in the course of composition." Yet Melville's friend and editor, Evert A. Duyckinck, wrote that the book "may be pronounced a most remarkable seadish—an intellectual chowder of romance, philosophy, natural history, fine writing, good feeling, bad sayings." Since the early 20th century, though, scholars have heaped accolades on the "intellectual chowder" that is *Moby-Dick*, praising Melville's ability to challenge and to stretch traditional 19th-century conceptions of the novel as a genre and pointing the way toward the more fluid form of the modern novel. Yet even to contemporary readers, the book may appear part seafaring adventure, part philosophical treatise, part drama, part "buddy narrative," and part environmental treatise. Even the book's more traditionally narrative elements seem to draw from various sub-genres. It interweaves gothic imagery, folklore, and elements of seafaring romance. Consequently, you might craft an essay exploring genre and form in quite a few ways. You could consider early reviews of the novel, more philosophical questions of genre, *Moby-Dick*'s place in the history of the genre of the novel, or Melville's use of dramatic form. Any of these could prove provocative.

Sample Topics:

1. ***Moby-Dick* and the novel:** In modern times, it has become a critical commonplace to praise Melville for stretching and challenging the novel as a genre. Yet, many modern readers—indeed, many modern editions of the novel—prefer to dispense with the philosophy and natural history and concentrate only on the romance and the idea of a "connected and collected" story line. Construct an argument for the unity and coherence of the "intellectual chowder" that is *Moby-Dick*.

    As this chapter has already indicated, Melville strains against the conventions of 19th-century narrative in many ways in this novel. As a result, you could choose any one of Melville's narrative "sins" as a starting place for a paper on *Moby-Dick*'s form. The cetology chapters—those about whaling and whale anatomy that fall between chapters 32 and 105—are an obvious starting point. Many readers bemoan Melville's decision to interrupt his narrative with Ishmael's lengthy explanations of and meditations on whales and whaling. Consider these chapters from a thematic or a philosophical point of view. How do they add to the novel and its purposes? What relevance do they have for the story line?

Besides initial frustration with the cetology chapters, readers are often troubled by the shifting narrative voice of the novel. Drawn into the narrative by Ishmael and his engaging portrait of his meeting with Queequeg, readers soon encounter chapters where the narrative voice seems to be that of a third-person narrator who recounts events that Ishmael could not have witnessed. At other points, they are confronted with chapters that seem more like the written text of drama—complete with stage directions and soliloquies. Consider whether Ishmael remains the filtering consciousness throughout the entire novel. If that is so, what might account for his wide-ranging narrative style, including his use of dramatic form and his philosophical meditations?

Still another approach to this question might be to write a paper arguing for the relevance of the interpolated tale of the *Town-Ho*, which appears as chapter 54. This lengthy chapter was published independently in *Harper's New Monthly Magazine* just before the novel was published. Why would Melville choose to integrate this lengthy story into *Moby-Dick*? What functions does it serve within the novel? Further, what do you make of Ishmael's method of narration in this chapter, of his decision to "preserve the style in which I once narrated it at Lima, to a lounging circle of my Spanish friends"? Does this rather strange method of narration serve any apparent purpose in the novel?

Language, Symbols, and Imagery

As the section of this chapter on philosophy and ideas indicates, many readers consider *Moby-Dick* a book about symbolism. Not surprisingly, then, the text is rich with symbols and imagery. Obviously, you might write any number of essays on the white whale as a symbol. Indeed, literary scholars have made an industry of this very activity from the time the book was published. Beyond Moby Dick, though, the novel presents numerous other symbols and patterns of imagery that warrant thorough investigation. To craft a paper, begin by identifying the particular symbol or image that intrigues you. Draw some tentative conclusions about how the imagery functions in the text. How, where, and why does Melville employ it? Then you should go back over the

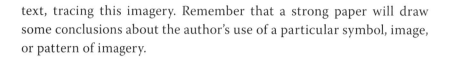

text, tracing this imagery. Remember that a strong paper will draw some conclusions about the author's use of a particular symbol, image, or pattern of imagery.

Sample Topics:

1. **Moby Dick:** Clearly Moby Dick is the novel's chief symbol. As with any well-drawn symbol, it is impossible to assign a single meaning to him. The novel clearly suggests and develops several possible interpretations of the whale. Choose one possible meaning of the white whale and explore its significance.

   As the earlier discussion of symbolism in the Philosophy and Ideas section of this chapter indicated, the white whale's indeterminacy is one of *Moby-Dick*'s central themes. While exploring Moby Dick as Melville's statement about the nature of symbols and representation seems to be the most productive way of examining the white whale, you might also craft a paper that examines the significance of one particular interpretation of the white whale and its meaning. While Starbuck claims that Moby Dick is but a "dumb brute" early in the text, readers as well as the text's characters have interpreted the whale as God, as nature, as Satan, as an embodiment of evil, and as a text or book. Nor are interpretations of the whale limited to these possibilities. The novel provides adequate material to develop these and numerous other interpretations. Certainly the text's reliance on Job 41 suggests the parallel between Moby Dick and God. If Moby Dick is, indeed, a symbol of God, how does Melville develop that symbol? What does such a reading of the whale say about the nature of the divine? Conversely, according to Ishmael, Ahab sees in Moby Dick "that intangible malignity which has been from the beginning" (chapter 41, "Moby Dick"). How can the whale encompass both an unknowable God and an "intangible malignity"? You could also consider Moby Dick as an embodiment of nature, or you could examine the novel's pursuit of the whale-as-book trope. How and why does Melville consistently develop this parallel?

2. **The imagery of ropes:** Examine the imagery of ropes throughout *Moby-Dick*. How do the novel's many cords and ropes function? How are they related to the novel's themes and purposes?

   You might begin shaping a response to this question by closely examining the chapter titles, some of which obviously announce their relevance to this investigation. Consider, too, how prevalent rope is on a whaling ship and how often Melville mentions rope, lines, cords, and ties during the course of the novel. What are their many functions on the ship and in the novel? Besides the ropes on the ship, do you see other ropes or cords in the text? Are the functions of all the novel's ropes consistent, or do they serve different purposes at different times? How might these functions reflect back on some of the novel's philosophical themes?

3. **Dreams and dream imagery:** In chapter 111, "The Pacific," Ishmael speaks of the "sweet mystery" of the sea and says, "And meet it is, that over these sea-pastures . . . the waves should rise and fall, ebb and flow unceasingly; for here, millions of mixed shades and shadows, drowned dreams, somnambulisms, reveries; all that we call lives and souls, lie dreaming, dreaming, still; tossing like slumberers in their beds; the ever-rolling waves but made so by their restlessness." Dreams and the imagery of dreams abound in *Moby-Dick*. How does Melville use dreams and the imagery of dreams?

   Quite a few of the characters in *Moby-Dick* dream, and the dreams of Ishmael, Stubb, Ahab, and Fedallah are all worth exploring in detail. How do these dreams function? What is the relationship between dreams and the conscious mind in these examples? You might also want to consider other passages in the novel that involve altered states of consciousness—how are these related to dreams? As the above passage indicates, another way to approach the imagery of dreams is to draw connections between the language of dreams and some of the text's themes and philosophical topics.

4. **Tattoos and bodily markings:** Examine the many marked bodies in *Moby-Dick*. Why does Melville repeatedly draw attention to the marks on his characters' bodies? What functions do these marks serve? How might you connect these bodily markings to the themes and philosophical issues of *Moby-Dick*?

A thorough consideration of tattoos and bodily markings must necessarily include some evaluation of Queequeg and his tattoos, but a strong paper on this question will go beyond Queequeg. Notice how many other bodies are marked in some way. Ishmael, Ahab, Moby Dick (and whales in general) all bear significant markings on their bodies. Consider how each of these characters received his marks. Consider the reactions of others to these marks. Consider, too, where else such markings occur in the novel. Queequeg, for example, reproduces his tattooed markings on his coffin. Do other characters' markings appear elsewhere in the novel? Is the imprinting on the doubloon related to these bodily markings? Why or why not? Do the tattoos and markings mean the same thing to all the characters? How are these markings related to other themes and issues in the novel, such as symbolism, texts and reading, religion, and culture? There are many directions that you might take a paper on bodily markings in *Moby-Dick*.

5. **Imagery of gender and sexuality:** *Moby-Dick* is, in many ways, a gendered novel. It seems almost exclusively masculine. All its major characters are men, and at times Melville seems to have created a rather lengthy meditation on masculinity and male symbols. Explore gendered imagery in *Moby-Dick* and draw conclusions about Melville's commentary on gender and gender roles in *Moby-Dick*.

It does not take a particularly close reading of the novel to discover just how laden it is with phallic and homoerotic imagery. It takes a bit more work, though, to consider the significance of this imagery. Why is it so prevalent in the novel? What is Melville saying about gender and about sexuality? How might this imagery be related to larger issues? How might you connect it to issues of identity or of religion? Another approach to this question is to examine the images of femininity and female sexuality in the novel. Where does this imagery appear? To what or whom is it most closely linked? What is Melville saying though his use of female imagery in this very masculine book?

6. **Imagery of fire and water:** Examine Melville's use of the contrasting imagery of fire and of water. How would you describe their significance in the novel?

Obviously, a novel set on a whaling ship is filled with water imagery, and it is possible to examine that imagery independently. You might note, for example, how frequently the sea is compared to land imagery of prairies and meadows, then craft a paper that comments on the significance of this comparison. Similarly, you can easily explore the abundance of fire imagery in this novel. Consider the traditional associations of fire with the demonic. Does Melville use fire imagery in a way that is consistent with these infernal associations? Explain. How is the fire imagery associated with some of the novel's other themes? Consider the characters consistently linked to the fire imagery. How is this significant? As the question implies, you might also construct a paper that explores the way Melville employs these two traditionally contrasting patterns of imagery.

7. **Sharks:** Besides whales, sharks are the sea creatures that make the most frequent appearances in *Moby-Dick.* Explore and explain Melville's concentration on the imagery of sharks. How do they connect to some of his other themes?

You might begin an exploration of the imagery of sharks and its related themes by examining chapter 18, "His Mark." As Captain Bildad attempts to convert Queequeg from his "pagan ways," Peleg says, "Pious harpooneers never make good voyagers—it takes the shark out of 'em; no harpooneer is worth a straw who aint pretty sharkish." This description is a telling one, and the novel provides much opportunity to pursue it. What does Melville seem to be saying about the connections between "pagans"

and sharks as the novel continues? Is Peleg correct in imply-
ing that Queequeg is sharkish? Where else do sharks appear?
How do they function? Are they related to human characters in
any other chapters? What other patterns of imagery seem to be
related to the novel's treatment of sharks?

8. **Narcissus and the imagery of reflection:** In "Looming" as
Ismael describes the lure of the sea and the connection between
meditation and water, he says, "And still deeper, the meaning
of that story of Narcissus, who because he could not grasp the
tormenting, mild image he saw in the fountain, plunged into it
and was drowned. But that same image, we ourselves see in all
rivers and oceans. It is the image of the ungraspable phantom
of life; and this is the key to it all." How might you justly call the
image of Narcissus gazing at his own image in the water "the key
to it all" in *Moby-Dick*?

You might begin shaping an essay about the imagery of Narcissus by exploring the repeated connections between meditation and the sea or water in the novel. Where else do characters
contemplate the sea or the water? What do they see and what
happens to them in these passages? The story of Narcissus is
also about reflection and self-obsession. (As Ishmael tells it, it
is about suicide.) Examine the novel for imagery of reflection.
Consider where characters find their own image reflected back
at them. How might this exploration provide a focus for your
paper? What connections can you draw between the imagery
of reflection and the themes of self-obsession and of death?
Ishmael's introductory phrase in the passage above—"And
still deeper"—also connects the story of Narcissus to depth.
Examine the novel for imagery of depth. How might this help
to develop a paper on this topic? Finally, consider Ishmael's
comment that the image Narcissus sees is "the image of the
ungraspable phantom of life." How is this statement developed
in the imagery of Narcissus in the novel? How might it provide
"the key" to some of the novel's other major themes?

Compare and Contrast Essays

Because of the breadth and the complexity of *Moby-Dick*, compare and contrast papers can often serve as useful tools. A well-shaped compare and contrast topic can allow you to break the text down into smaller parts. A thoroughly analyzed part can help you to make sense of the whole. For that reason, taking one chapter from the novel and comparing its treatment of a particular theme, character, or image with that of the whole book can help you develop a more thorough understanding of the novel. Similarly, comparing two chapters that deal with similar themes or issues can serve the same purpose. If you would like to move beyond *Moby-Dick*, you can find plenty of shared material between this text and Melville's other works as well as between this novel and the work of other authors with whom Melville was familiar. Remember, a strong compare and contrast essay addresses the significance of the similarities and differences that you note. Your paper should draw conclusions, not just point out elements for comparison.

Sample Topics:

1. **Comparing and contrasting two chapters:** One way to shape a manageable paper topic on a novel as vast as *Moby-Dick* is to compare two chapters. Choose two chapters that focus on the same theme, image, idea, or character and compare their treatment of that particular element.

   Many scholars have noted how the novel takes up the same theme or image in more than one chapter, and in so doing it creates convenient pairs of chapters for study. Some potential pairs of chapters include: chapters 41 and 42, "Moby Dick" and "The Whiteness of the Whale"; chapters 70 and 72, "The Sphynx" and "The Monkey Rope"; chapters 94 and 96, "A Squeeze of the Hand" and "The Try-Works." Similarly, you could compare the sermons of Father Mapple and Fleece in chapters 9 and 64, "The Sermon" and "Stubb's Supper," or the use of fire imagery in chapters 96 and 119, "The Try-Works" and "The Candles." You can find other chapters that you can compare fruitfully.

2. **Comparing a chapter to the novel:** Choose one chapter to focus on and compare the messages and themes of that chapter to their treatment in the novel as a whole.

Scholars often discuss the ways in which particular chapters seem to echo the philosophical themes of the book. Some, they argue, are *Moby-Dick* in miniature. You could easily craft a paper that compares the philosophical points of a chapter to those of the novel as a whole. Chapters that should prove fruitful in such an endeavor include chapter 41, "Moby Dick," chapter 42, "The Whiteness of the Whale," and chapter 99, "The Doubloon."

3. **Melville's treatment of race:** Compare Melville's treatment of race in *Moby-Dick* with that in another of his works.

Two likely works for comparison include *Typee* and *Benito Cereno.* Since *Typee* is based on Melville's own experiences in the South Seas and is, at its heart, a cultural comparison, it provides a great deal of room for comparison with *Moby-Dick.* In fact, *Moby-Dick* often seems to provide a much more mature and thoughtful meditation on some of the racial themes and issues first raised in *Typee.* Similarly, *Benito Cereno* seems to comment on racial interactions through its portrayal of the three main characters—Delano, Cereno, and Babo. It might be helpful to consider the relation between issues of race and themes of savagery and/or cannibalism in the texts you consider.

4. **Perception, knowledge, and understanding:** Compare Melville's treatment of the theme of seeing and understanding in *Moby-Dick* with that in another of his texts. What do the texts say about humans' abilities to see and understand the world?

Benito Cereno seems like the most likely text for comparison here, since that work focuses so intently on how humans see and read the world. You might compare Delano's perception and his understanding to the way some of the characters in *Moby-Dick* read the world around them. Other texts can provide material for a paper on this subject. Like *Benito Cereno,* "Bartleby, the Scrivener," for example, is concerned with what we choose to see and not to see.

Bibliography and Online Resources for *Moby-Dick*

Babb, Valerie. *Whiteness Visible: The Meaning of Whiteness in American Literature.* New York: New York UP, 1998.

Broadhead, Richard. *Hawthorne, Melville, and the Novel.* Chicago: U of Chicago P, 1973.

Bryant, John. *Melville and Repose.* New York: Oxford UP, 1993.

———, ed. *A Companion to Melville Studies.* New York: Greenwood, 1986.

Bryant, John, and Robert Milder, eds. *Melville's Evermoving Dawn.* Kent, OH: Kent State UP, 1997.

Cameron, Sharon. *The Corporeal Self: Allegories of the Body in Melville and Hawthorne.* Baltimore: Johns Hopkins UP, 1981.

Chase, Owen. *Narrative of the Most Extraordinary and Distressing Shipwreck of the Whaleship Essex . . .* New York: Corinth, 1963.

Coffler, Gail. *Melville's Allusions to Religion: A Comprehensive Index and Glossary.* New York: Praeger, 2004.

Colacurcio, Michael J. "'Excessive and Organic Ill': Melville, Evil, and the Question of Politics." *Religion and Literature* 34.3 (2002): 1–26.

Delbanco, Andrew. *Melville: His World and His Work.* New York: Knopf: 2005.

DiCurcio, Robert A. "Nantucket's Tried-Out *Moby Dick.*" The Life and Times of Herman Melville. Available online. URL: http://www.melville.org/diCurcio/tryout.htm. Downloaded on July 13, 2007.

Douglas, Ann. *The Feminization of American Culture.* New York: Knopf, 1978.

Dryden, Edgar. *Monumental Melville: The Formation of a Literary Career.* Stanford, CA: Stanford UP, 2004.

Franklin, H. Bruce. *The Wake of the Gods: Melville's Mythology.* Stanford, CA: Stanford UP, 1963.

Gilmore, Michael T. *American Romanticism and the Marketplace.* Chicago: U of Chicago P, 1985.

Gunn, Giles. *A Historical Guide to Herman Melville.* Oxford: Oxford UP, 2005.

Hayes, Kevin J. *Melville's Folk Roots.* Kent, OH: Kent State UP, 1999.

Hayford, Harrison, and Hershel Parker. *Melville's Prisoners.* Evanston, IL: Northwestern UP, 2003.

Hughes, Henry. "Fish, Sex, and Cannibalism: Appetites for Conversion in Melville's *Typee.*" *Leviathan* 6.2 (2004): 3–16.

Irwin, John. *American Hieroglyphics: The Symbol of the Egyptian Hieroglyphics in the American Renaissance.* New Haven, CT: Yale UP, 1980.

Levin, Harry. *The Power of Blackness: Hawthorne, Poe, Melville.* New York: Knopf, 1964.

Levine, Robert S. *The Cambridge Companion to Herman Melville.* Cambridge: Cambridge UP, 1998

Lewis, R. W. B. *The American Adam: Innocence, Tragedy and Tradition in the Nineteenth Century.* Chicago: U of Chicago P, 1955.

Leyda, Jay, ed. *The Melville Log: A Documentary Life of Herman Melville, 1819–1891.* New York: Gordian P, 1969.

Maroviz, Sanford E. *Melville Among the Nations: Proceedings of an International Conference,* Volos, Greece, July 2–6, 1997. Kent, OH: Kent UP, 2001.

Martin, Robert K. *Hero, Captain, and Stranger: Male Friendship, Social Critiques and Literary Form in the Novels of Herman Melville.* Chapel Hill: U of North Carolina P, 1986.

Marx, Leo. *The Machine in the Garden: Technology and the Pastoral Ideal in America.* New York: Oxford UP, 1967

Matthiessen, F. O. *American Renaissance: Art and Expression in the Age of Emerson and Whitman.* New York: Oxford UP, 1941.

Melville, Herman. *Moby-Dick.* Norton Critical Edition. Second edition. Eds. Hershel Parker and Harrison Hayford. New York: Norton, 2002.

Milder, Robert. *Exiled Royalties: Melville and the Life We Imagine.* New York: Oxford UP, 2006.

Mitchell, David. "'Too Much of a Cripple': Ahab, Dire Bodies, and the Language of Prosthesis in *Moby-Dick.*" *Leviathan* 1 (1999): 5–22.

Otter, Samuel. *Melville's Anatomies: Bodies, Discourse, and Ideology in Antebellum America.* Berkeley: U of California P, 1998.

Parker, Hershel. *Herman Melville.* 2 vols. Baltimore: Johns Hopkins UP, 1996, 2002.

Philbrick, Nathaniel. *In the Heart of the Sea.* New York: Penguin, 2001.

Reuben. Paul. PAL: Chapter 3: Herman "Melville. Perspectives in American Literature—A Research and Reference Guide—An Ongoing Project." Available online. URL: http://web.csustan.edu/english/reuben/pal/chap3/melville.html. Downloaded on October 25, 2007.

Reynolds, J. N. "Mocha Dick." *New York Knickerbocker.* 12 (1839): 377–392. Available online. The Life and Times of Herman Melville. http:// www.melville.org/reynolds.htm. Downloaded on July 13, 2007.

Rogin, Michael Paul. *Subversive Genealogy: The Politics and Art of Herman Melville.* New York: Knopf, 1983.

Samson, John. *White Lies: Melville's Narrative of Facts.* Ithaca, NY: Cornell UP, 1989.

Sandborn, Geoffrey. *The Sign of the Cannibal: Melville and the Making of a Postcolonial Reader.* Durham, NC: Duke UP, 1998.

———. "Whence Come You, Queequeg?" *American Literature* 77.2 (2005): 227–257.

Thompson, Lawrance. *Melville's Quarrel with God.* Princeton, NJ: Princeton UP, 1952.

Thompson, Shawn. *The Romantic Architecture of Melville's* Moby Dick. Cranbury, NJ: Fairleigh Dickinson UP, 2001.

Vincent, Howard P. *The Trying-Out of "Moby-Dick."* Boston: Houghton Mifflin, 1949.

Whalen-Bridge, John. *Political Fiction and the American Self.* Champaign: University of Illinois Press, 1998.

Zoellner, Robert. *The Salt-Sea Mastodon: A Reading of* Moby-Dick. Berkeley: U of California P, 1973.

"BARTLEBY,
THE SCRIVENER"

READING TO WRITE

A LTHOUGH "Bartleby, the Scrivener" is the most widely taught and accessible piece of Melville's fiction, students often complain that the story is boring. While many find Bartleby an intriguing, if aggravating, character, they find the story somewhat tedious and hard to wade through. The narrative, in other words, seems to get in the way of its most compelling aspect—Bartleby, "a scrivener the strangest I ever saw or heard of." Careful readers, though, quickly understand the reason for the story's density and tediousness. As in *Moby-Dick*, Melville creates a first-person narrator who plays an important role in the story. Without understanding the narrator, a reader has little hope of understanding Melville's tale. A close reading of the story's opening can provide a good deal of insight into the narrator, and this, in turn, should help you understand Melville's techniques, themes, and purposes.

In the opening paragraph, the narrator introduces his intent—to share "a few passages in the life of Bartleby"—and he explains that his story is largely made up of "[w]hat [his] own astonished eyes saw" of the scrivener. After this brief introduction to his topic, the narrator waits another 14 paragraphs to introduce his title character. This fact alone reveals something about his abilities as a storyteller. Clearly, neither suspense nor plot seems to be his forte. The second and third paragraphs tell readers much about both the narrator and his storytelling:

Ere introducing the scrivener, as he first appeared to me, it is fit I make some mention of myself, my *employés*, my business, my chambers, and general surroundings; because some such description is indispensable to an adequate understanding of the chief character about to be presented.

Imprimis: I am a man who, from his youth upwards, has been filled with a profound conviction that the easiest way of life is the best. Hence, though I belong to a profession proverbially energetic and nervous, even to turbulence, at times, yet nothing of that sort have I ever suffered to invade my peace. I am one of those unambitious lawyers who never addresses a jury, or in any way draws down public applause; but in the cool tranquility of a snug retreat, do a snug business among rich men's bonds and mortgages and title-deeds. All who know me, consider me an eminently *safe* man. The late John Jacob Astor, a personage little given to poetic enthusiasm, had no hesitation in pronouncing my first grand point to be prudence; my next, method. I do not speak it in vanity, but simply record the fact, that I was not unemployed in my profession by the late John Jacob Astor; a name which, I admit, I love to repeat, for it hath a rounded and orbicular sound to it, and rings like unto bullion. I will freely add, that I was not insensible to the late John Jacob Astor's good opinion.

The story's second paragraph lays out the narrator's methodology as a storyteller. Rather than allowing the story to grow organically from setting and character, he believes that he must first lay out particulars of "myself, my *employés*, my business, my chambers, and general surroundings" in order for readers to understand "the chief character." Careful readers may have already questioned the identity of the story's "chief character," noting that the narrator and his own situation, rather than Bartleby, seem to constitute his main concern. As promised, the third paragraph elaborates upon the first element in the narrator's list, himself. And the first word of the paragraph, "imprimis," meaning "in the first place," or "above all," seems to emphasize the narrator's priorities. Further, his self-portrait goes a long way to explain his methods as a storyteller: he is "safe" and "unambitious," and his "grand point[s]" are "prudence" and "method." He is, in other words, boring. No wonder, then, that it takes him 15 paragraphs to introduce his title character. No wonder that a safe, unambitious, methodical, self-centered, prudent, and elderly man should craft a meticulous narrative that many readers find dense, tedious, and boring. Apparently, this is part of Melville's larger point.

Given this initial focus on the narrator, then, careful readers should explore his self-portrait in more detail, and they should find that such a close reading of the story's initial paragraphs suggests other questions that can guide their reading of the rest of the text. You might begin by asking what else you can conclude about the narrator through a careful assessment of his self-description. In the first sentence of this paragraph, the narrator confesses that from his "youth upwards" he held the "profound conviction that the easiest way of life is best." Besides being methodical, prudent, and boring, then, the narrator might be termed lazy. And he clearly indicates that this quality has defined his professional life as a lawyer: "Hence," while other lawyers are "proverbially energetic and nervous, even to turbulence," he claims that he is "one of those unambitious lawyers who never addresses a jury . . . but in the cool tranquility of a snug retreat, [does] a snug business among rich men's bonds and mortgages and title-deeds." You might ask why the narrator's self-portrait begins with (and is ultimately confined to) his professional identity. What does this tell readers about him? Further, what does the particular nature of his legal work—his "snug business among rich men's bonds and mortgages and title-deeds"—tell about our storyteller, his values, and his worldview?

As if to amplify his description of his work "among rich mens's bonds and mortgages and title-deeds," the narrator tells of John Jacob Astor's assessment of his professional capabilities. The historical John Jacob Astor built his fortune through the fur trade and through real estate speculation on Manhattan Island. After first introducing Astor, the narrator remarks, "I do not speak it in vanity, but simply record the fact, that I was not unemployed in my profession by the late John Jacob Astor; a name which, I admit, I love to repeat, for it hath a rounded and orbicular sound to it, and rings like unto bullion." Clearly, the narrator is correct when he tells readers that he "love[s] to repeat" Astor's name, for he repeats it in three successive sentences at the paragraph's end. What do the invocations of Astor's name and the imagery the narrator uses to describe it tell us about the narrator and his values? Do you agree with the narrator's claim that his reference to Astor is not spoken "in vanity"? Similarly, do his comments about his relationship with Astor accord with his assertion that he is "unambitious"? Why or why not? Overall, what do you think about the narrator at this point? Does he seem honest, likeable, and sincere?

You might also notice that the narrator has already begun to describe the setting of his story when he says that he works in "the cool tranquility of a snug retreat." What does this description say about his office and his attitudes toward his workplace? What does this description imply about the environment of the narrator's office? You might develop the implications of this description by comparing it to modern stereotypes of Wall Street law offices. When you think of such law offices, do you think of "snug retreat[s]" and "cool tranquility"? What words come to mind when you think of Wall Street law firms? Why? It seems that this cozy environment is created by the nature of the narrator's work "among rich men's bonds and mortgages and title-deeds." Is the language that the narrator uses to describe the environment of his office in keeping with the values he expresses through his descriptions of his work and his connections to John Jacob Astor? Why or why not?

While an assessment of the narrator's character allows you to draw some logical connections between his personality and his narrative style, you may find that it also leads to other questions about the narrative. You may question the lawyer's reliability as a narrator. How might his personality, values, and worldview affect his project, a biography of the "strangest" scrivener he knows of, a scrivener who was his own employee? Are you inclined to trust his judgments of Bartleby and accept them at face value? Do you think that his assessments would be similar to those that you might draw? Why or why not?

Finally, these questions about the narrator should lead you back to Herman Melville. Why might Melville have chosen to tell Bartleby's story, this "Story of Wall-Street," through this particular narrator? How can thoughtful assessments of the narrator's personality and reliability help readers to understand Melville's points? In addition, why would Melville choose to include some historical specificity in his tale? Why, for instance, is the lawyer's office specifically located on Wall Street, and why does he mention John Jacob Astor? How can these historical details add to an understanding of "Bartleby, the Scrivener"?

Armed with a thorough assessment of the narrator, you should be well prepared to read the rest of the text closely, with some insight into Melville's themes and techniques. Such careful reading and thoughtful analysis should form the building blocks of a strong essay on "Bartleby, the Scrivener."

TOPICS AND STRATEGIES

This section of the chapter provides you with broad topic ideas that should help you develop an essay on "Bartleby, the Scrivener." Remember that these topics are just springboards for your own exploration; you will need to focus your analysis and develop your own specific thesis.

Themes

Melville subtitled "Bartleby, the Scrivener" "A Story of Wall-street," and many of the story's themes grow from this very particular setting. Even in 1853 Wall Street was the center of America's financial and business life, a point that is reinforced by the narrator's work "among rich men's bonds and mortgages and title-deeds." To write a paper about theme in "Bartleby" you should begin by identifying a theme that you discovered as you read the text and deciding what you think the story had to say about this theme. Not surprisingly, many readers see the world of business referenced in the subtitle of "Bartleby" as one of the story's central themes. If you were planning to write on this topic, you might begin by examining the relationship of each of the main characters to the world of Wall Street that surrounds them. You might also ask how the setting affects the characters and their relationships with one another. Does Melville comment on the values, beliefs, strengths, and weaknesses of Wall Street through these relationships? What does he seem to say about this world of business? Further, you could examine the story's language to see if it reflects or comments on the theme of business in "Bartleby." As these questions indicate, themes in this story are closely tied to character and to imagery and language, so a thorough examination of all these aspects of the story should help you to develop a strong paper on thematic interests in "Bartleby."

Sample Topics:

1. **Capitalism and employer/employee relations:** How might "Bartleby, the Scrivener" be read as a commentary on the rise of capitalism and its effect on the relationship between employers and employees?

A paper on capitalism and the workplace in "Bartleby" might begin with an examination of the narrator as an employer. He spends the first pages of his "biography" of Bartleby telling of his office and his other employees—Turkey, Nippers, and Ginger Nut. Are these characters good employees/workers? What do the narrator's descriptions of the atmosphere of the office and of his interactions with his other employees tell you about the narrator as an employer? What does he seem to value? How does he treat his employees? What details of the story help you to draw your conclusions? How would you describe the narrator's relationship with Bartleby? What kind of language does the narrator use when discussing Bartleby? Once Bartleby ceases to work, the narrator, at times, seems to realize that he cannot necessarily see his relationship to Bartleby as that of an employer to employee. How does he now see his relationship with the scrivener? At this point in the story, the language of religion as well as the language of law seem to creep into the narrator's meditations. How would you describe the relationship between the language of law and that of religion toward the end of the story? How does the narrator balance the two?

2. **Class relations:** Numerous elements in "Bartleby" remind readers that the narrator and his employees belong to two very different classes. While you might read the story as a comment on employer/employee relations, you might also broaden such a reading to consider it as a commentary on class relations. What does "Bartleby, the Scrivener" say about class relations in the wake of the capitalist marketplace?

This question clearly shares territory with the previous question about employer/employee relationships, although it asks you to broaden the topic a good bit. You might begin to think about this topic by considering the relationships between the narrator and his employees, for Nippers, Turkey, Ginger Nut, and Bartleby are clearly of a lower social class than the narrator. In order to focus an essay on this topic even more, you could examine the theme of charity that runs throughout the text. What acts of charity do you see in the story? What motivates the charity? At some points, the narrator actually engages in philosophical musings on the nature of charity as well as various motivations for and against charity. How do these musings help to focus the story as a commentary on the relationship between the social classes?

3. **Perception and understanding:** The language of vision, sight, and understanding runs throughout this text. How does "Bartleby, the Scrivener" focus on the human ability to see and to understand others?

The opening paragraph emphasizes that the story is built on what the narrator's "own astonished eyes saw of Bartleby," and later, when the narrator asks Bartleby why he has quit copying, the scrivener responds, "Do you not see the reason for yourself?" Consider what the narrator sees, what he does not see, and what he understands. Identify other references to the narrator's (or society's) ability to see. At one point, the narrator speculates that Bartleby has stopped copying because his vision has been "impaired" by his job. At what other points does the story comment on Bartleby's vision and his eyes? Is this theme of seeing and understanding connected to any of the other themes in the story? How is this language related to the dominant patterns of imagery in the story? What, finally, does Melville conclude about humans' abilities to see, to understand, and to know?

Character

In the opening paragraphs of the story, the narrator claims that his intent is to provide readers with "a few passages in the life of Bartleby, who was a scrivener the strangest I ever saw or heard of," and he refers to the scrivener as "the chief character about to be presented." At the same time, the narrator claims that insufficient materials exist for a full biography of Bartleby, and he calls attention to the limited scope of his account. The story is limited to "[w]hat [his] own astonished eyes saw of Bartleby." Both this paragraph and those that immediately follow focus readers' attention so firmly on the narrator that it is clear that Melville—as well as the narrator himself—wants readers to focus as much attention on the lawyer as on the scrivener. Indeed, the story line focuses on the "relationship" between these two figures. Or, perhaps it is more accurate to say that the story focuses on the effect that Bartleby has upon the narrator. Consequently, it is nearly impossible to write a paper that focuses wholly on either character. A study of the narrator must consider his interaction with and response to Bartleby. An analysis of Bartleby must be informed by an awareness that the reader sees only what the narrator "saw" of Bartleby and only what he chooses to share about Bartleby. While the relationship between these two must inform essays about either character, you still can find plenty of ways to focus essays on the behavior, attitudes, or meanings of either the narrator or Bartleby. Papers on the lawyer, for instance, might focus on his reliability as a narrator. Why do you think that he chooses to tell the story of Bartleby in the first place? Does his professed motivation (that Bartleby was "a scrivener the strangest I ever saw or heard of") seem completely honest and forthright? There is no denying that Bartleby is strange, but does that account for the narrator's desire to tell the story of their time together? Why else might the lawyer feel the need to write—and to share—an account of his encounter with Bartleby?

Sample Topics:

1. **The narrator:** As the opening section of this chapter indicates, the lawyer/narrator of "Bartleby" is an important character in the story, and some readers even consider him the "chief character." Not surprisingly, critical interpretation of the narrator has varied widely over the years, for the narrator is a conflicted character. After finally taking leave of both his office and of Bartleby, the narrator remarks:

> As soon as tranquility returned I distinctly perceived that I had now done all that I possibly could, both in respect to the demands of the landlord and his tenants, and with regard to my own desire and sense of duty, to benefit Bartleby . . . I now strove to be entirely care-free and quiescent; and my conscience justified me in the attempt; though indeed it was not so successful as I could have wished.

Does Melville seem to agree that the narrator had "done all that [he] could possibly do" and that he should therefore be "care-free and quiescent"? In an essay that seeks to analyze and evaluate the narrator's treatment of Bartleby you will need to spend a good deal of time analyzing the narrator's vacillating attitude toward his scrivener. Why does his attitude toward Bartleby change so frequently? What events and attitudes motivate or account for these changes in attitude? What principles guide the narrator's conscience? In order to answer these questions, you should evaluate the language and the imagery that the lawyer uses as he wavers between tolerating and supporting the eccentric scrivener and ridding himself of Bartleby and his strange behavior. Does his language reflect particular philosophies and beliefs that seem to guide his decisions? Such an analysis might be strengthened through a study of the lawyer's character as portrayed in the early parts of the story. What does his initial self-portrait reveal about him? How do his initial descriptions of his office and of his employees and his relationship with them inform your analysis of his dealings with Bartleby? Finally, you should consider whether you think that the narrator grows or changes as a result of his encounter with Bartleby. What do you think of his concluding exclamation, "Ah Bartleby! Ah humanity!"

2. **Bartleby:** There is no denying that Bartleby is a strange character and that he accounts for a great deal of the story's complexity. Some scholars have suggested that part of the story's difficulty involves Bartleby's status as a symbolic or allegorical character in the midst of an otherwise realistic story. If that is so, what might Bartleby be said to represent?

As with any well-drawn symbol, Bartleby cannot be reduced to any one meaning. (Indeed, that seems to be part of the story's very point.) There are myriad ways to approach this question. You might want to analyze Bartleby by focusing on the language and imagery that surrounds him. When Bartleby first appears at the office door, the narrator describes him as "a motionless young man . . . pallidly neat, pitiably respectable, incurably forlorn!" And as he begins his work, Bartleby "wrote on silently, palely, mechanically." These introductory remarks might provide you a place to begin an analysis. Even this imagery, though, is so varied that you would do well to focus on one particular pattern of imagery that is associated with the scrivener. You might, for example, choose to examine Bartleby as stationary and motionless, or you might discuss the significance of his persistent pallor. What do either of these elements suggest about Bartleby's meaning? Similarly, you might examine the language of ghostliness and death that seems to surround the scrivener. Still another approach would be to explain Bartleby's propensity for staring at walls, his "dead-wall reveries." How do they function symbolically?

Another approach to an analysis of Bartleby and his meaning might be to consider him in connection with his work as a copyist. Consider the nature of the scrivener's job. Consider, too, Bartleby's relationship with the offices at No. —— Wall Street. At one point the narrator says that Bartleby "never went anywhere." Toward the story's end, the narrator contemplates the irony of having Bartleby arrested as a vagrant (which the next tenant of the office actually does). How might such considerations help you to assess Bartleby's role in the story? In relation to the question of vagrancy, it might also be worth considering two other factors: One, instead of forcing Bartleby from the offices, the narrator himself chooses to move to new offices; two, the term *vagrancy* not only means to be idle and wandering, but, according to the Oxford English Dictionary, to be "wandering or digressing in mind, opinion, thought." Do these two facts help you to analyze Bartleby or his effect on the narrator differently?

Yet another approach to an essay analyzing Bartleby might be to examine comments on his mental health. At one point, Ginger Nut says, "I think, sir, he's a little *luny.*" Toward the story's end, the lawyer considers the scrivener "the victim of innante and incurabble disorder." Similarly, numerous scholars have persisted in trying to "diagnose" Bartleby as a "depressive." While readers might speculate on the scrivener's mental health, we certainly do not know enough about him to render a clinical diagnosis. Of course, psychoanalyzing a character or a symbol seems fundamentally unsound. You might, however, consider why the other characters—especially the narrator—choose to regard Bartleby as "luny" or "incurable."

A different kind of analysis of Bartleby might be to consider the scrivener as a kind of protester. The narrator at one point comments on Bartleby's "passive resistance." If you choose to analyze Bartleby's actions as a kind of passive resistance, you should evaluate both the form his resistance takes as well as its effect on the others around him. Why, for instance, does Bartleby persist in using the word *prefer* when he refuses to comply with commands and requests? What effect does his use of the word *prefer* have on the office? Why is that significant?

Finally, you could write an essay that considers the very fact that Bartleby is, in the words of the narrator, "unaccountable." (This is prefigured in the opening paragraph of the story, where the narrator emphasizes that he is unable to give a full biographical account of Bartleby.) Why would Melville render the title character "unaccountable"? Why would the narrator try to write an account of such a character? Is there any particular resonance to the language he uses to describe Bartleby's inscrutability?

History and Context

Melville uses a great deal of historical and geographic specificity in "Bartleby, the Scrivener," mentioning a number of real people, locations, and historical incidents. He references John Jacob Astor, Wall Street, Trinity Church, the Tombs, and the murder of Samuel Adams by John C. Colt. Exploring this historical context could provide another avenue by which to approach a paper about "Bartleby." Any good paper on history and context will necessarily be founded in some solid historical research.

Sample Topic:

1. **John Jacob Astor and "Bartleby":** Clearly something of a name-dropper, the narrator speaks of his association with John Jacob Astor in the third paragraph. He makes a point of saying that he was employed by Astor, and ends the paragraph saying

that he "love[s] to repeat" Astor's name "for it hath a rounded and orbicular sound to it, and rings like unto bullion." Does this association with Astor shape the narrator's actions in the story in any discernible way?

A paper that analyzes Astor's significance in the story will need to include some biographical and historical research, and the bibliography at the end of this chapter provides you with some sources to begin this research. Perhaps the most relevant aspects of Astor's history to explore are his real estate dealings and practices in New York City. (The owner of much of Manhattan and a good deal of the area surrounding New York City, Astor once said, "Could I begin life again, knowing what I now know, and had money to invest, I would buy every foot of land on the Island of Manhattan.")

Philosophy and Ideas

Given this story's focus on issues of the workplace, it should not be surprising that many readers apply Marxist philosophies to their analyses of "Bartleby." Still others, alert to Melville's numerous biblical references, interpret the story in light of the Christian philosophies that seem to underlie these references. Both of these approaches provide frameworks for analyzing the business practices that structure the world of Bartleby and the narrator, and either could provide you with an effective focus for a paper on "Bartleby, the Scrivener."

Sample Topics:

1. **Marxism and the alienation of labor:** Given the story's focus on the relationship between an employer and his employees, as well as the story's historical setting during the rise of American capitalism, do you think it is fair to read "Bartleby, the Scrivener" as a portrait of worker alienation?

   Unlike the maids in Melville's "The Paradise of Bachelors and The Tartarus of Maids," Bartleby is not a laborer in an industrialized setting, metaphorically chained to machinery. And yet, as many students and scholars have pointed out, law copyists were little more than human photocopy machines. In order to answer this question, you should examine the language and the imagery in the story carefully. Is there language and imagery that seems to suggest that Bartleby is somehow dehumanized by his work or by his environment? Consider, too, the relationship between the narrator and his employees. Clearly, he is not a distant or absent factory owner, nor is he a stern overseer. In fact, he sometimes seems quite knowledgeable about his employees and remarkably tolerant of their foibles. Is he at all guilty of dehumanizing the men (and the young boy) who work in his office? Think, too, about the workers, their lives, and their idiosyncrasies. How are they shaped or affected by their work and their working environment?

2. **Christian ethics:** After Bartleby refuses to leave the office at No. —— Wall Street, the narrator is at first angry and resentful, but he tells readers that he overcame these feelings by remembering Jesus' words from John 13:34: "A new commandment give I unto you, that ye love one another." He adds, "Yes, this it was that saved me." Later, after the narrator himself has quit the premises, the new tenant of the office tells the reader, "you are responsible for the man you left there." What role do Christian ethics and ideas about humans' responsibility for one another play in "Bartleby, the Scrivener"? Is the narrator "responsible" for Bartleby? Are there limits to the responsibility we bear to one another?

There are a great many other biblical references in "Bartleby" that you should consider as you shape a paper in response to this question. What other passages or incidents in the story echo biblical teachings or events? How might these passages be important? Similarly, you should reread the text closely for other language that echoes this language of responsibility— language of conscience and guilt, for example. Examine the narrator's numerous musings about how he should treat Bartleby. Similarly, you should analyze the story's rather involved treatment of charity. The narrator performs quite a few acts of charity in the story, and he frequently muses on the nature of charity. What do you think of his charitable impulses and his philosophy of charity? Does the narrator consistently act according to the "saving" words of John 13:34? If not, what kinds of principles guide his decisions? You should also consider what you think of the narrator's treatment of Bartleby. Does he, finally, bear some responsibility for Bartleby's death, or has he done everything humanly possible to assist the scrivener?

Form and Genre

Considering the form of "Bartleby" can provide you with different ways of approaching a paper topic about the story. The Read to Write section above asked why Melville might have chosen to tell Bartleby's story through this particular narrator, and this question might provide the beginnings of a thoughtful paper about Melville's strategies and his points. You could consider how a thoughtful assessment of the narrator's personality and reliability helps readers to understand Melville's ideas. Similarly, you might consider how Melville's ideas might have been affected if Bartleby had told his own story or if the story had been narrated through a third-person omniscient point of view.

Sample Topics:

1. **Narrative voice:** Why did Melville chose to tell this tale through the voice of a first-person narrator? Why does he create this particular narrator to tell Bartleby's tale?

   This question asks you to consider the narrator as a character, and it relates to the previous section on character. This question, though, asks you to consider Melville's ideas and his techniques more centrally. You should think about the reader's relationship with the lawyer-narrator of this story, for example. Early on the narrator makes it clear that he has very limited insight into Bartleby, that he knows only "[w]hat my own astonished eyes saw of Bartleby." Are you willing to trust the narrator's assessments and interpretations of Bartleby? Why or why not? Does the fact that the narrator is Bartleby's employer affect his interpretation of Bartleby and his behavior? How would you assess the narrator as a character? How willing are you to accept the narrator's assessments of his own behaviors and characteristics? What motivations—conscious or unconscious—might he have for shaping and crafting his version of the events of the story? How might the story be different if it were told through Bartleby's point of view? How might it be different if Melville had written it with a third-person omniscient narrator? What would the story lose in either of these situations? Additionally, you might want to consider questions of audience as you consider narrative voice. "Bartleby" was published in *Putnam's Monthly Magazine of American Literature, Science, and Art.* Who do you imagine was Melville's reading audience in *Putnam's*? What might they have shared with the narrator of "Bartleby"?

2. **Humor:** How and why does Melville use humor in "Bartleby, the Scrivener"?

Often readers miss Melville's humor in "Bartleby." Perhaps this is because the story's topic is, at its base, so serious. There is no denying that Bartleby is a strange character, and this strangeness creates some of the story's humor. Consider, for example, the passage where the narrator is called to the office he has vacated because he is "responsible for the man [he] left there":

> Going up stairs to my old haunt, there was Bartleby silently sitting upon the banister at the landing.
> "What are you doing here, Bartleby?" said I.
> "Sitting upon the banister," he mildly replied.

Just a page or so later the narrator desperately suggests numerous employment possibilities for Bartleby. Each one is rejected by the scrivener, who finally says, "I like to be stationary. But I am not particular." Examine these and the many other instances of humor in "Bartleby." What is their effect on the reader? How does the humor affect your assessment of Bartleby and of the narrator?

3. **"Bartleby" as ghost story:** Early in the story the narrator compares Bartleby to a ghost. After having summoned the scrivener

three times, the narrator says, "Like a very ghost, agreeable to the laws of magical invocation, at the third summons, he appeared at the entrance to his hermitage." How might "Bartleby" be read as a kind of ghost story?

A careful rereading should demonstrate just how often Bartleby is described in ways that are reminiscent of ghostliness. Where is he described as a ghost or a kind of spirit? Pay careful attention to the story's language, and consider, too, the many other ways that Bartleby seems to have ghostly qualities or tendencies. What is the significance of Bartleby's ghostliness and his haunting qualities? You might further an investigation of Bartleby's ghostliness through an investigation of other elements in the story that the narrator describes through language and imagery of insubstantiality or unreality. Do you see any significance in the elements that the narrator describes—and consequently links—through this language?

Language, Symbols, and Imagery

If Bartleby can be read as a symbolic character, he is not the only element in the story that bears symbolic weight. The story's Wall Street setting, with its many walls, is most clearly symbolic. Similarly, Melville's rich, dense prose is filled with imagery that can enhance your understanding of the story. "Bartleby" is so tightly crafted that many of the dominant images and patterns of imagery intersect and reinforce one another. You should also find that the imagery can provide a good deal of insight into the story's themes. Consider, for example, how the story's focus on eating—Bartleby's patterns of consumption—connects not only to the language that is so frequently used to describe the scrivener but to the business-oriented themes of the story. Similarly, near the story's end the narrator seems to compare Bartleby to the dead letters that he purportedly handled in the Dead Letter Office. You could easily craft a paper that examines Bartleby as a kind of dead letter. Such a paper might also draw connections between the Dead Letter Office and the many walls that populate the story. In order to write a paper about Melville's use of imagery and symbol in "Bartleby," you should reread the story and pay close attention to its language and the meanings and connotations of some of the repeated imagery.

Sample Topics:

1. **Consumption:** Many readers notice the story's focus on food and eating. When Bartleby first begins work at No. —— Wall Street, he worked incessantly, and the lawyer uses the language of eating—"famishing," "gorge," "digestion"—to describe Bartleby's work habits. Much later in the story, the narrator realizes that Bartleby never seems to leave the office; the lawyer also notes that the scrivener seems to eat nothing except ginger-nuts. By the end of the story, Bartleby "prefers" not to eat and, apparently, dies of starvation. Why does the story draw attention to Bartleby's eating habits? What other resonance might this focus on consumption have in this story?

   To write a paper on this topic, you might begin by reviewing the other imagery that is frequently used to describe Bartleby. Might any of that imagery be related to the scrivener's eating habits? How and why? Further, why would Melville draw such an explicit contrast between Bartleby's eating habits and his work habits though his use of imagery? How are the scrivener's work and his eating related? Beyond this, you might explore other meanings of consumption. How might these meanings be tied to the story's other themes and characters? How might Bartleby's eating habits be related to these other kinds of consumption?

2. **Walls:** Even a casual reader of this "Story of Wall Street" quickly notices that "Bartleby, the Scrivener" is filled with walls. What is the significance of the many walls that populate Melville's vision of Wall Street?

   A careful rereading of the story should help you note the appearance of many different types of walls. In the opening paragraphs, the lawyer claims that descriptions of his chambers and its "general surroundings" are "indispensable to the chief character about to be presented." Take particular note of the narrator's descriptions of his office. What part do walls play in the story's central setting? How might the many walls help to explain Bartleby and his behavior? You should also consider other walls in the story. How would you describe Bartleby's "relationship" with these walls? In this setting of walls, why does Bartleby spend so much time in his "dead wall reveries"? Why would he, apparently, *choose* to stare at walls? Still further, how might the story's many walls be "indispensable" to your analysis of the narrator? How might an analysis of the story's walls help to understand Melville's themes in "Bartleby"?

3. **The Dead Letter Office:** In the story's final section, the narrator mentions a rumor that Bartleby had been a clerk in the Dead Letter Office in Washington. What role does this mention of the Dead Letter Office serve?

In order to answer this question, you must have a clear understanding of just what the Dead Letter Office is. You can find good information on the Dead Letter Office online at the Smithsonian Institution's National Postal Museum. Once you have a clear understanding of the purpose of the Dead Letter Office, you can consider how this reference works in Melville's text. You might, for example, consider the reference in relation to Bartleby himself. The narrator exclaims, "Dead letters! does it not sound like dead men?" Are there ways in which Bartleby is like a dead letter? Why would Melville find the job of subordinate clerk at the Dead Letter Office symbolically appropriate for the scrivener? You might also consider if the Dead Letter Office and the narrator's description of it share any qualities with other imagery in the story. Similarly, you may want to consider whether it connects with any of the story's themes. On the other hand, you might explore why the narrator would choose to mention this rumor at the end of his narrative. Why does he choose to imagine Bartleby as a worker in the Dead Letter Office? In particular, you should analyze his descriptions of the dead letters and the intended purposes he imagines for them. Consider, too, the tone of the narrator in this final passage. How does it compare to the tone registered elsewhere in the story? Why does the narrator end with the exclamations, "Ah Bartleby! Ah humanity!"?

Compare and Contrast Essays

Bartleby's focus on labor and work provides a grounds for comparison with a great many other works—other works by Melville, works from the same period in American history, works by authors who may have influenced Melville, and more contemporary works that reflect on the nature of work in the modern world. Remember that when you write a compare and contrast essay, you need to develop a specific thesis that discusses the significance of the similarities and differences that you note. Do not allow your paper to become a mere laundry list of similarities and differences.

Sample Topics:

1. **Labor and class relations:** Many consider "Bartleby, the Scrivener" one of Melville's strongest statements about the relationship between the laboring class and the upper and middle classes. Compare Melville's comment on labor and class relations in "Bartleby" with the treatment of these themes in other works.

   Perhaps the most likely choice for this topic is "The Paradise of Bachelors and The Tartarus of Maids," which provides plenty of material for both comparison and contrast. Interestingly, the first part of the story—the Bachelor's paradise—is set in London's Inns of Court and also uses lawyers as representatives of the upper classes. You might compare the lawyers of Temple Bar and their environment to the narrator of "Bartleby" and the lifestyle he lives. The laborers that the narrator of "Paradise of Bachelors and the Tartarus of Maids" meets are the "maids" who work in the paper mill. While these women are very different from Bartleby, you should find it fruitful to compare the imagery that Melville uses to describe the maids and Bartleby. How are Bartleby and the maids similar? How does Melville see the relationship between the upper classes and the laboring classes in these two stories? Interestingly, both stories use the language of food and consumption. Do they use this imagery differently or similarly? Another approach might examine the differences between the two texts. While there are a good deal of similarities between Bartleby and the maids in the paper mill, how does Melville make some different points about the laboring class in "The Paradise of Bachelors and the Tartarus of Maids?"

Yet another approach to this topic would be to compare Melville's statements in "Bartleby" with a work by another author, and this approach offers a number of possibilities. Scholars have speculated that Melville may have had some of Charles Dickens's work in mind when he wrote "Bartleby." Perhaps the most obvious possibility for comparison is *A Christmas Carol*, published 10 years before "Bartleby" in 1843. You might consider how Melville has refigured and reseen the famous story by Dickens. A paper that analyzes these two texts might consider differences in characterization and in philosophy. Which text seems more realistic? Why? *A Christmas Carol* is well known because of Scrooge's conversion after the visits from the spirits. Do you believe that the lawyer-narrator of "Bartleby" undergoes a conversion (or is, in his own words, "saved") because of his encounter with Bartleby? Why or why not? You may want to consider the language of ghostliness that surrounds Bartleby in a paper that also analyzes *A Christmas Carol*. If you are feeling particularly ambitious, you might want to compare Dickens's treatment of the clerk Nemo in *Bleak House* to Melville's treatment of Bartleby. Yet another text that might work well for comparison with "Bartleby" is Rebecca Harding Davis's *Life in the Iron Mills*, published in *Atlantic Monthly* in 1861.

2. **Narrative voice:** Examine Melville's use of the first-person narrator in "Bartleby" and another of his works. Why does Melville use this particular narrative technique for the works in question? How does an analysis of the narrative voice clarify the points and purposes of the text?

A paper that addresses this question should consider some of the questions posed in the earlier discussion of the lawyer/

narrator of "Bartleby," especially those about his point of view, his reliability, and his relationship to Bartleby and the events he narrates. "The Paradise of Bachelors and the Tartarus of Maids" is another story that employs first-person narration, and *Moby-Dick* also provides a possible text for comparison. Given the size and complexity of Ishmael's narrative, though, you will need a strong, clear focus for a paper that examines Bartleby's employer and Ishmael as storytellers.

3. **Seeing and perception:** Examine Melville's exploration of issues of perception and understanding in "Bartleby" and compare it to his treatment of similar issues in other texts.

Any number of Melville texts could work quite well with this topic. "Benito Cereno," *Moby-Dick, Billy Budd,* and "The Paradise of Bachelors and the Tartarus of Maids" all address the limits of human perception and understanding, and all use imagery of vision and seeing. You might also think about what these texts say about the factors that often prevent humans from seeing and understanding clearly.

Bibliography and Online Resources for "Bartleby, the Scrivener"

Arvin, Newton. *Herman Melville.* New York: William Sloane, 1950.

Barnett, Louise K. "Bartleby as Alienated Worker." *Studies in Short Fiction* 11 (1974): 379–85.

Bergman, Hans. *God in the Street: New York Writing from the Penny Press to Melville.* Philadelphia: Temple UP, 1995.

———. "'Turkey on His Back': 'Bartleby' and New York Worlds." *Melville Society Extracts* 90 (1992): 16–19.

Bloom, Harold. *Herman Melville's* Billy Budd, *"Benito Cereno," "Bartleby, the Scrivener," and Other Tales.* New York: Chelsea House, 1987.

Brown, Gillian. *Domestic Individualism: Imagining Self in Nineteenth-Century America.* Berkeley: U of California P, 1990.

Bruns, James H. "Remembering the Dead." *National Postal Museum.* Smithsonian Institution. Available online. URL: http://www.postalmuseum.si.edu/resources/6a2c_deadletters.html. Downloaded May 13, 2007.

Bryant, John, ed. *A Companion to Melville Studies.* New York: Greenwood, 1986.

Campbell, Donna. "Herman Melville." *American Authors.* Washington State University. Available online. URL: http://www.wsu.edu/~campbelld/amlit/melville.htm. Downloaded May 7, 2007.

Coffler, Gail. *Melville's Allusions to Religion: A Comprehensive Index and Glossary.* New York: Praeger, 2004.

Colacurcio, Michael J. "'Excessive and Organic Ill': Melville, Evil, and the Question of Politics." *Religion and Literature* 34.3 (2002): 1–26.

Delbanco, Andrew. *Melville: His World and His Work.* New York: Knopf, 2005.

Fiene, Donald. "Bartleby the Christ." *Studies in the Minor and Later Works of Melville.* Ed. Raymona E. Hull. Hartford, CT: Transcendental Books, 1970. 18–23.

Fisher, Marvin. *Going Under: Melville's Short Fiction and the American 1850s.* Baton Rouge: Louisiana State UP, 1977.

Foley, Barbara. "From Wall Street to Astor Place: Historicizing Melville's 'Bartleby.'" *American Literature* 72.1 (2000): 87–116.

Franklin, H. Bruce. *The Victim as Criminal and Artist: Literature from the American Prison.* New York: Oxford UP, 1987.

———. *The Wake of the Gods: Melville's Mythology.* Stanford, CA: Stanford UP, 1963.

Gilmore, Michael T. *American Romanticism and the Marketplace.* Chicago: U of Chicago P, 1985.

Gunn, Giles. *A Historical Guide to Herman Melville.* Oxford: Oxford UP, 2005.

Hayes, Kevin J. *Melville's Folk Roots.* Kent, OH: Kent State UP, 1999.

Hayford, Harrison, and Hershel Parker. *Melville's Prisoners.* Evanston, IL: Northwestern UP, 2003.

Heidelbaugh, Lynn. "Dead Letter Office." *Arago: People, Postage, and the Post.* Smithsonian National Postal Museum. Available online. URL: http://www.arago.si.edu/index.asp?con=1&cmd=1&mode =&tid=2032238. Downloaded May 13, 2007.

Inge, Thomas. *Bartleby the Inscrutable: A Collections of Commentary on Herman Melville's Tale "Bartleby, the Scrivener."* Hamden, CT: Archon, 1979.

Karcher, Carolyn. *Shadow over the Promised Land: Slavery, Race, and Violence in Melville's America.* Baton Rouge: Louisiana State UP, 1980.

Kelley, Wyn. *A Companion to Herman Melville.* Oxford: Blackwell, 2006.

Levine, Robert S. *The Cambridge Companion to Herman Melville.* Cambridge: Cambridge UP, 1998.

The Life and Works of Herman Melville. Available online. URL: http://www.melville.org/melville.htm#Whois. Downloaded May 17, 2007.

McCall, Dan. *The Silence of Bartleby*. Ithaca, NY: Cornell UP, 1989.

Newman, Lea Bertani Vozar. *A Reader's Guide to the Short Stories of Herman Melville*. Boston: Hall, 1986.

Otter, Samuel. *Melville's Anatomies: Bodies, Discourse, and Ideology in Antebellum America*. Berkeley: U of California P, 1998.

Parker, Hershel. *Herman Melville*. 2 vols. Baltimore: Johns Hopkins UP, 1996, 2002.

Post-Lauria, Sheila. *Correspondent Colorings: Melville in the Marketplace*. Amherst: U of Massachusetts P, 1996.

Rogin, Michael Paul. *Subversive Genealogy: The Politics and Art of Herman Melville*. New York: Knopf, 1983.

Rowe, John Carlos. *Through the Custom-House: Nineteenth-Century American Fiction and Modern Theory*. Baltimore: Johns Hopkins UP, 1982.

Springer, Haskell. *Bartleby, the Scrivener: A Story of Wall Street*. University of Kansas. Available online. URL: http://web.ku.edu/~zeke/bartleby/index.htm. Downloaded May 17, 2007.

Stern, Milton R. "Towards 'Bartleby, the Scrivener.'" *The Stoic Strain in American Literature*. Duane J. MacMillan, ed. Toronto: U of Toronto P, 1979. 19–41.

Zelnick, Stephen. "Melville's 'Bartleby, the Scrivener': A Study in History, Ideology, and Literature." *Marxist Perspectives* 2 (1979/80): 74–92.

"THE ENCANTADAS"

READING TO WRITE

ALTHOUGH THE two works are very different, "The Encantadas" presents challenges to readers that are similar to those posed by *Typee*. As in the earlier work, Melville draws upon his own firsthand experiences in "The Encantadas," for he visited the Galápagos Islands during his whaling voyages as a young man. And once again, Melville developed his literary portrait of the islands through his reading of others' accounts of the Galápagos. The resulting work, like *Typee*, challenges traditional conceptions of genre. *Typee* is neither novel nor autobiography, and "The Encantadas" is neither short story nor memoir. Additionally, the structure of "The Encantadas"—10 short sketches linked by location—further complicates readers' attempts at interpretation. As you read this work, you should keep questions of genre, structure, and unity in mind, considering how they might affect your interpretation of Melville's themes and purposes. The first sketch, "The Isles at Large," seems to function as an introduction or overview, and in this sketch Melville paints the Encantadas as an inhospitable, earthbound hell, "looking much as the world at large might, after a penal conflagration." He emphasizes the islands' unchanging nature and their "emphatic uninhabitableness," stressing that they "refuse to harbor even the outcasts of beasts." "Little but reptile life is here found," he says, thereby introducing one of the dominant themes or "characters" of his sketch, the ancient Galápagos tortoises.

Before this first sketch is done, Melville's narrator twice meditates on these tortoises, first mentioning the superstition that "wicked sea-officers" are transformed into tortoises, and later speaking of the ways the tortoises continue to haunt him. These "introductions" to the tortoises in the first sketch indicate their importance for "The Encantadas," and they provide background and context for Melville's continued treatment of these ancient creatures throughout the work. As its title implies, "Sketch Second: Two Sides to a Tortoise," focuses upon these "mystic creatures." After capturing three tortoises with his shipmates, the narrator meditates upon "antediluvian-looking" and "really wondrous" creatures:

> As I lay in my hammock that night, overhead I heard the slow weary draggings of the three ponderous strangers along the encumbered deck. Their stupidity or their resolution was so great, that they never went aside for an impediment. One ceased his movements altogether just before midwatch. At sunrise I found him butted like a battering-ram against the immovable foot of the foremast, and still striving, tooth and nail, to force the impossible passage. That these tortoises are the victims of a penal, or malignant, or perhaps a downright diabolical enchanter, seems in nothing more likely than in that strange infatuation of hopeless toil which so often possesses them. I have known them in their jouneyings ram themselves heroically against rocks, and long abide there, nudging, wriggling, wedging, in order to displace them, and so hold on their inflexible path. Their crowning curse is their drudging impulse to straightforwardness in a belittered world.

This passage opens with an image of stratification—the narrator lying below the tortoises that move about on the deck. Just prior to this, examining the turtles and their shells, the narrator says, "I seemed an antiquary of a geologist." Coupled with his reference to geology and with his earlier reference to the tortoises as "antediluvian-looking," the image of stratification that begins this paragraph suggests Melville's familiarity with the geological theories of his time. Astute readers, then, might wonder about the effect of geological discoveries on Melville's thinking and begin to explore their relevance in "The Encantadas." In the 19th century, these scientific discoveries began to threaten the worldview of many Westerners, especially traditional Judeo-Christian beliefs about creation. Never entirely comfortable with traditional Christian beliefs, Melville seems to grapple with the Christian worldview through his portrait of the tortoises. In addition to these apparent invocations of geological advancements, just three paragraphs earlier he connected these "mystic creatures" to the Hindu god Vishnu, claiming that they "seemed newly crawled forth from beneath the foundations of the world. Yea, they seemed the identical tortoises whereon the Hindoo plants his total sphere." One might wonder, then, if the author amplifies these challenges to traditional Christian beliefs in his descriptions of the tortoises as "victims of a penal, or malignant, or perhaps a downright diabolical enchanter." Like the infernal landscape they inhabit, the tortoises seem enthralled to Satan, a "diabolical enchanter," rather than to the Christian God. Careful readers will notice, though, that "diabolical" is the narrator's last descriptor of the "enchanter" who victimizes the tortoises. The narrator seems to hold out some hope that this enchanter might not be "downright diabolical" but rather penal or malignant. Neither option sounds much better, but the suggestion of a "penal" authority may echo the Christian God who punishes Adam and Eve for their disobedience. Like Adam and Eve, the tortoises inhabit a landscape that the narrator describes in "Sketch First" as "fallen," a "Tartarus" that contrasts sharply with the "Paradise" of the South Sea Islands that lie far to the west of the Galápagos.

Is it possible, then, that you might draw some connections between these tortoises and humanity? Are humans, like these wondrous creatures, imprisoned by a "penal . . . enchanter"? Certainly, the earlier treatment of the tortoises has given readers reason to draw connections between these ancient creatures and humankind. This linkage is suggested not only by the lore that links the tortoises with the sea-officers, but by the tortoise that haunts the narrator at the end of sketch one, reminding him of his own mortality, "the ghost of a gigantic tortoise with 'Memento *****' burning in live letters upon his back." Is human life upon earth merely "hopeless toil" like that of the tortoises? Will we, like them, find that our "crowning curse is [a] drudging impulse to straightforwardness in a belittered world"? Certainly, the end of "Sketch Second" seems to suggest a reason for pessimism, for after commenting on the wondrousness of these aged "mystic creatures" who have toiled for years pursuing their "impulse to straightforwardness," the narrator and his compatriots "made a merry repast from tortoise steaks and tortoise stews." At the sketch's end, the final image that he leaves with readers is that of the tortoises' "mighty concave shells" and calipees converted into "fanciful soup-tureens and . . . gorgeous salvers," serving pieces for their own flesh. This image suggests the try-works of *Moby-Dick,* where the sailors use the whale's own charred remains to fuel the fire that renders his blubber into oil. At worst, the narrator seems to say, humans, despite their toil will wind up like the tortoises, forced into self-consumption. At best, we become animalistic predators.

This brief passage on the tortoises, then, suggests numerous possibilities for papers on "The Encantadas." You could focus on Melville's use of the Galápagos tortoises in the work, and this focus alone could yield numerous more finely honed topics for exploration. Similarly, it suggests the possibility of exploring Melville's worldview and his attitudes toward God and toward theology. In addition to evoking both God and Satan, it also suggests another of "The Encantadas" themes—enchantment. This, too, could prove a fruitful subject for a paper. Finally, this passage also asks you to consider the relationship between the 10 sketches that make up this intriguing and haunting work.

TOPICS AND STRATEGIES

This section of the chapter provides you with broad topic ideas that should help you develop an essay on "The Encantadas." Remember that these topics are just springboards for your own exploration; you will need to focus your analysis and develop your own specific thesis.

Themes

Any paper on "The Encantadas" must grapple with questions of unity and coherence, and as the Reading to Write section suggests, there are numerous themes and images that help to forge coherence among the sketches. The work's title, "The Encantadas, or Enchanted Isles," suggests the theme of enchantment, and this might serve as a solid starting place for a number of different papers. You might begin such an exploration by reviewing the work and noting all the incidences of or references to enchantment. Clearly, Melville plays with numerous connotations and meanings of the word, and you should think about the way he plays with the meaning of enchantment. "The Encantadas" provides numerous other themes to explore. The theme of the fallen world, with all its theological implications, runs like a refrain through this text, and it provides another possible focus. Whatever theme you choose to explore, be sure that you review the text carefully, noting imagery, language, characters, and other textual elements that may reflect upon your theme.

Sample Topics:

1. **The fallen world:** As readers try to account for unity in "The Encantadas," many cite the theme of the fallen world. Others comment on the infernal imagery and Melville's frequent, overt associations of the Galápagos with hell. Both interpretations seem supportable. "Sketch First: The Isles at Large" relies on imagery of fire and overtly refers to the Islands as a "Tartarus." At the same time, however, the narrator asserts, "In no world but a fallen one could such lands exist," thereby suggesting a potential contradiction. While the fallen world is not paradise, neither is it hell; it is a sort of middle ground. Construct an argument that Melville presents a "fallen world" in "The Encantadas," and explore his apparent purposes. If you agree that he presents the islands as a fallen world, why does he sketch them this way? What is his larger point behind this theme?

   A response to this question needs to grapple with the apparent doubleness of the islands. Why does this landscape of the fallen world appear so hellish? Consider, too, the theology behind the Judeo-Christian story of the fall. Adam and Eve's expulsion from paradise was a punishment for disobedience. Do the themes of disobedience and punishment appear in "The Encantadas"? If you see evidence of these themes, it would be worthwhile pursing them in more depth. Consider who is disobedient and who is responsible for punishment. Does Melville seem to refer to the Judeo-Christian God? With the fall came the possibility for redemption. Is redemption possible on the Encantadas? If so, what provides for the possibility of redemption? It is also worth noting that in "Sketch Second: Two Sides to a Tortoise," the narrator links the Galápagos tortoises to their role in Hindu mythology. An avatar of the Hindu god Vishnu, the tortoise provided stability to the newly created world by taking it upon its back. How might Hindu mythology provide a context for your investigation?

2. **Silence, speech, and storytelling:** The structure of "The Encantadas," along with its other challenges to traditional narrative genres, suggests that it is in part about storytelling. Examine

"The Encantadas" as a work about narration, storytelling, and the construction of meaning. What does it say about storytelling and its relation to truth and to reality?

As this question implies, you should consider the ways that this work challenges traditional notions of genre, and you should think about the work's unity and its structure. The section of this chapter on form and genre should prove helpful in this investigation. You might also want to explore some of the material on sources in the "History and Context" section of this chapter, since it is clear that Melville's portraits of the islands and of some of their inhabitants are drawn from the narratives of others. In some instances, he is clearly offering a retelling of events and/or a revision or reseeing of the landscape. In addition, you should find "Sketch Eighth: Norfolk Isle and the Chola Widow" a fruitful source for a paper on the theme of storytelling. Some scholars have offered the possibility that this is Melville's retelling of a story of a female Robinson Crusoe that he had read. Similarly, the narrator in the sketch tells of listening to Hunilla's story. He recounts the effects that her storytelling had on him and his shipmates, and he tells of the gaps in Hunilla's story, the events she cannot or will not speak of. These gaps, in turn, lead the narrator to contemplate his own style and his role and his responsibilities as storyteller. Here he begins to consider ethical issues. Similarly, some of the questions about Hunilla in the section of this chapter on character could be provocative for a paper that explores storytelling in this sketch. Consider, for example, how the sketch's context might affect the audience's reception. How do all the layers of narration that surround and involve Hunilla's story affect the story and its reception?

3. **Enchantment:** "Sketch First: The Islands at Large" tells how the strange currents and winds around the islands caused sailors to call the area, "The Enchanted Ground," and created the illusion that there were "two distinct clusters of isles in the parallel of the Encantadas." The narrator adds: "[T]his apparently fleetingness and unreality of the locality of the isles was most probably

one reason for the Spaniards calling them the Encantada, or Enchanted Group." This enchanted quality of the islands lends itself to Melville's portrait of the islands. Explore the theme of enchantment in "The Encantadas." How would you describe the quality of enchantment that hovers over the islands? How and why does Melville use this theme in his work?

According to the *Oxford English Dictionary, enchanted* carries four different meanings: invested with magical powers or properties; bewitched, laid under a spell; deluded, captivated as by magic; and delighted, charmed, enraptured. Melville seems to play with each of these ideas in the course of "The Encantadas"; the idea of enchantment appears, in one way or another, in nearly all of the 10 sketches. Perhaps the most obvious occurrences of this theme, though, appear at the end of "Sketch First," in the story of the "enigmatic craft" of "Sketch Fifth," and in Oberlus's assertion in "Sketch Ninth" that he is the offspring of the sorceress Sycorax (from Shakespeare's *The Tempest*). Consider whether one definition of enchantment seems to define the islands. Are they magical, bewitched, captived, delightful? Similarly, explore the connection between the quality of enchantment in "The Encantadas" and the theme of appearance and reality. Often the islands and their enchanted quality seem to throw doubt on the nature of reality. How is the interweaving of these themes significant?

4. **Nature and human nature:** Readers have long noted the movement in "The Encantadas" from nature to humanity. The early sketches focus on the landscape and the animals of the islands. The fifth sketch, "The Frigate, and the Ship Flyaway," begins the text's exploration of the relationship between the islands and humanity. This sketch shows the effects on a ship sailing among the islands. "Sketch Sixth" speaks of the Buccaneers who visit Barrington Island, while the seventh, eighth, and ninth sketches focus on human inhabitants of the islands. Finally, "Sketch Tenth, Runaways, Castaways, Solitaries, Grave-stones, etc." focuses upon the human remnants left on the islands. Explore the relationship between the landscape of

the Encantadas and the humans that inhabit them. How and why is this relationship significant?

You should begin an exploration of this issue by analyzing the view of nature and the natural world that Melville paints in "The Encantadas." Examine his imagery and his language closely. Consider, too, the various ways that humanity has envisioned and figured nature—as a garden and as a wilderness, for example. From there, you can begin to explore the relationship between the humans in "The Encantadas" and the landscape. Do the islands shape the human inhabitants or do their inhabitants shape and "civilize" the islands? Still further, consider what qualities the human inhabitants share with the islands themselves. Do they seem to be products of the same force that created the Enchanted Islands? Why or why not? You might also think about the relationship between the humans and animals that inhabit the island. How would you describe this relationship? Are humans like these natural inhabitants of the islands? Why or why not? What does Melville seem to be saying about nature and/or about humanity through these comparisons?

5. **Despair and hope:** Melville draws most of the epigrams in "The Encantadas" from Spenser's *Faerie Queene,* and many of these come from the Red Cross Knight's encounter with Despair in Book I. Examine the theme of despair in "The Encantadas," and consider what the work says about it. Does "The Encantadas" offer any cause for hope to counter the despair in this desolate landscape?

You will need to consider the related themes of changelessness and solitude that also run like a refrain through this text. How are solitariness and that "special curse," changelessness, related to the theme of despair? How and where does Melville develop the effects of solitude and of changelessness? You should find that an examination of his treatment of the tortoises, of Hunilla, and of Oberlus particularly useful here. Read closely for mentions of hope and hopelessness. What does the text seem to say about the viability of hope in "The Encantadas"? What other characteristics are linked to hope? What characteristics are linked to despair?

6. **Time:** Speaking of the age of the tortoises in "Sketch Second," the narrator says, "What other bodily being possesses such a citadel wherein to resist the assaults of Time?" A world of apparent changelessness, the Enchanted Islands confuse and challenge time. Examine Melville's treatment of the theme of time in "The Encantadas." How and why does time become important in this work?

In many ways, the islands seem removed from time. They, and the tortoises that populate them, seem both ancient and ageless. (Melville calls them "dateless," in the second sketch.) Clearly, his treatment of time is tied to the theme of enchantment and to the notion that these islands are both real and unreal. Melville plays with the metaphorical and allegorical possibilities of this middle world. While a response to this question should consider his treatment of the landscape and the tortoises, the theme of time is most relevant to Melville's treatment of humanity. Pay particular attention to the stories of Hunilla and Oberlus. How do each of these characters deal with the confusion of time on these desolate, isolated islands? What does Melville say about their attitudes and their methods? You might want to consider the relationship between humanity and time on a larger scale too. The sixth, ninth, and 10th sketches speak of the effects of time on the remnants of human life upon the island. How might these sketches be relevant to your investigation?

Character

Unlike most of Melville's other narrative works, a great deal of "The Encantadas" focuses less on character than on landscape and imagery. The latter part of the work allows some insight into the human isolates who have settled on the islands, and the eighth and ninth sketches provide lengthy portraits of the work's two fully drawn characters, Hunilla and Oberlus. While many readers see these two sketches as a kind of diptych that profiles two opposing portraits of human nature, Hunilla and Oberlus can each be considered in isolation, and each can form the basis of interesting papers on "The Encantadas."

Sample Topics:

1. **Hunilla:** The eighth sketch of "The Encantadas," "Norfolk Isle and the Chola Widow," is the best-known and most widely praised of the 10 sketches, and Hunilla, the Indian widow, receives most of the scholarly attention. Generally, readers see Hunilla as an embodiment of human virtues. Some, though, have doubted the apparent virtues of the solitary widow, reading her as yet another of the islands' deceivers. Her tale and her motives, they imply, are dubious. As you interpret the sketch and as you situate it in relation to the other sketches in "The Encantadas," do you think that Hunilla is a symbol of human virtues or of the human propensity to deceive?

   A thorough response to this question requires close analysis of sketch eight, and it requires you to consider the sketch's placement within the work as a whole. Readings that offer Hunilla as an example of human virtue often argue that Melville presents her in contrast to Oberlus in sketch nine. Similarly, readings that cast doubt on Hunilla depend a great deal on context. These readings are more likely to suggest links between sketch seven and the Chola widow sketch. In addition, they depend on an assessment of the epigraphs that Melville attaches to the sketch—an excerpt from Spenser's *Faerie Queene* (Bk. II, canto xii, stanza xxvii, ll. 5–9), Chatterton's *Mynstrelle Songe from Aella* (stanza ii), and Collins's *Dirge in Cymbeline* (stanza vi). In addition to considering the implications of the epigraphs, you will need to examine Melville's sketch in a good deal of detail. You might begin by examining Hunilla's relationships with others—her husband and brother, the narrator and his shipmates, and the other mariners and sailors she has encountered. Your conclusions are dependent on your assessment of the reliability of both the narrator and Hunilla. Are they reliable narrators? Why or why not? Further, assess Hunilla as a character. What attributes and characteristics does the narrator attribute to her? Consider, too, how this sketch engages the larger themes of "The Encantadas"—despair, hope and hopelessness, endurance, time, enchantment, and the relationship between nature and human nature. You should also analyze the imagery of sketch eight. Melville's use of the cross in this sketch should prove particularly relevant, though you might also consider the reed that Hunilla leans on and uses to keep a record of her time on the island. Once again, the Galápagos tortoises appear in this sketch, and you may wish to consider their relevance here.

2. **Oberlus:** Melville leaves little room to doubt Oberlus's evil qualities in "Sketch Ninth." The hermit is "selfish" and "misanthropic," and his "whole aspect and all his gestures were so malevolently and uselessly sinister." Often studies of Oberlus pair him with Hunilla of "Sketch Eighth," with whom he presents a clear contrast. Her endurance provides grounds against which to measure his malevolence. Rather than taking this typical approach in your analysis of his character, consider Oberlus and his colonization of Hood's Island as a metaphor for human civilization. How might you read Oberlus's story as a commentary on humanity and human civilization?

Critics often argue that Oberlus is an embodiment of Satan, "a creature who it is religion to detest." Certainly, Melville's portrait of the hermit and the imagery that is associated with him support this reading. Concomitantly, critics argue that Oberlus's misanthropy is unmotivated. Consider, however, whether the sketch provides hints about why the hermit behaves so evilly. What might be the causes of Oberlus's misanthropy? What do we know about his background? Are there any other characters in literature to whom he may be compared? Still further, you should examine how his misanthropy manifests itself. Are his methods significant? How might his background and his methods be symbolic of larger issues?

History and Context

As is the case with so many of his works, "The Encantadas" is informed not only by Melville's experience but also by his voluminous reading. Besides his use of *The Tempest,* which the Compare and Contrast section addresses, perhaps one of the most interesting ways to explore the context of "The Encantadas" is to analyze Melville's use of other writings about the Galápagos. Melville refers directly to some of his sources in the text, as he does with David Porter's *Journal of a Cruise Made to the Pacific Ocean.* Others, such as Charles Darwin's *Journal of Researches . . . during the Voyages of the H.M.S. Beagle,* seem to have a clear influence on the work even though they are not overtly mentioned in the text. The bibliography at the end of this chapter provides you with more thorough information about accessing some of these texts.

Sample Topics:

1. **Melville's sources:** Melville visited the Galápagos Islands in the 1840s while he was serving aboard whaling ships, so he had firsthand experience of the isles. "The Encantadas," though, makes clear that he was also familiar with other travelers' accounts of the islands. Examine Melville's use of these various accounts of the Galápagos Islands. How and why does he use these sources?

   "The Encantadas" allude, directly to some of Melville's sources. In a note to the ninth sketch, Melville mentions Porter's 1815 text, *Journal of a Cruise Made to the Pacific Ocean,* and he comments on the changes that he has made to Porter's version of Oberlus's story. "Sketch Fifth" lists other sources from which Melville drew: *Captain Cowley's Voyage Round the Globe* and James Colnett's *A Voyage to the South Atlantic.* At the beginning of the seventh sketch, the narrator asserts that he learned of the Dog-King's history "long ago from a shipmate." Beyond this, scholars have constructed a list of sources that Melville probably knew, including Darwin's *Journal of Researches . . . during the Voyages of the H.M.S. Beagle.* Consideration of these sources could help you to shape an essay in a few ways. The most fruitful direction might be to examine the differences between Melville's conceptions of the Enchanted Islands and those of his predecessors. How do the differences between his text and theirs help to highlight his thoughts and his purposes in "The Encantadas"?

Philosophy and Ideas

Three of the sketches explore, at least in part, human attempts to establish societies of sorts on the islands. Consequently, Melville focuses readers' attention on questions of political organization and political philosophy. Exploring his commentary on political systems could provide a fruitful way to examine "The Encantadas."

Sample Topics:

1. **Colonization and political structure:** The sixth, seventh, and ninth sketches, "Barrington Isle and the Buccaneers," "Charles's Isle and the Dog-King," and "Hood's Isle and the Hermit Oberlus," all comment on nation building and political structure. Examine these sketches and explore Melville's commentary on human political structure. Taken together, what do they say about Melville's attitudes about human abilities to create viable political and social institutions?

   A paper on this issue might explore any of these three sketches separately or it might analyze the political philosophy that emerges from all three sketches. The seventh sketch, which tells of the Creole's attempt to establish himself as the "Supreme Lord of the Island," provides the best starting place. Examine the process of colonization on the island and its movement from monarchy to republic to "permanent *Riotocracy.*" What is particularly notable about the course of the island's development? You might then compare this portrait of nation building with those presented in the other two sketches. What do the ruins of the Buccaneer's "bower of ease" tell us about these men who were "driven from Christian society"? While this sketch is less developed than the Charles's Island sketch and focuses less on civic structure, Oberlus and his rule over Hood's Island provide more room for comparison. Indeed, just a few paragraphs into this sketch, the narrator himself makes an overt comparison between the Creole and "King Oberlus." While readers are given little room to see anything but evil in Oberlus, his methods, and his purposes, you might consider why Melville develops this sketch so thoroughly. What does Oberlus and his method of colonizing the island represent? As you explore the political commentary in any of these three sketches, you should also think about the metaphorical or allegorical possibilities. What do they say about human nature? Does the setting of these experiments in colonization, the "fallen world" of the Encantadas, have any bearing on the commentary that Melville provides? Could any of the sketches be brought to bear upon American history or American society?

2. **Geology and Darwin:** "The Encantadas" was published in 1854, just five years before Charles Darwin's *On the Origin of Species* and five years after the publication of Darwin's journal from his own journey to the Galápagos. Scholarship has demonstrated that Melville knew of geologic theories of his time and that he had read Darwin's account of the HMS *Beagle*'s journey to the Galápagos. How do the imagery and the language of "The Encantadas" demonstrate Melville's awareness of geological theories of that time? How does this awareness shape Melville's vision of the islands and their inhabitants?

A thorough answer to this question must grapple with Melville's animal imagery as well as with his treatment of the theme of time. In the Galápagos tortoises that populate this work, these two focuses converge. The tortoises are notable for their age, and as the narrator explores their shells, he says, "I seemed an antiquary of a geologist, studying the bird-tracks and ciphers upon the exhumed slates trod by incredible creatures whose very ghosts are now defunct." Besides their age, what else is remarkable about these creatures? Examine Melville's treatment of these aged creatures; how does it reflect his thinking about geology and natural selection? This investigation should also lead you down other paths. You might examine the work for other images that suggest or reflect the geological discoveries of the time. And you should consider how all these images relate to or reflect upon the humans that populate this work. What is the relationship between humanity and the tortoises and other creatures of these harsh and barren islands? What implications do the geological theories of his time have upon Melville's conception of his own race? How might these theories have affected his worldview and his treatment of religion and of God?

Form and Genre

As the Reading to Write section of the chapter indicated, generic classification presents one of "The Encantadas'"s most difficult puzzles. While it is certainly not a short story, it does not quite seem to be actual travel literature or memoir. Questions of structure and unity are necessarily linked to issues of genre, and both structure and genre can provide fodder for thoughtful papers on "The Encantadas."

Sample Topics:

1. **Melville's use of epigraphs:** Melville begins each of his sketches with epigraphs drawn from other texts. While Melville does not identify his sources, scholars have identified them and have drawn numerous connections between the epigraphs and the individual sketches. Choose one sketch and explore the relevance of the epigraphs that Melville appends at its opening. How do they help or hinder an analysis of the sketch?

   Leon Howard and Russell Thomas first identified the epigraphs in the 1930s, and you will find full references to their articles in the bibliography for this chapter. Not surprisingly, though, readers have varied in their assessments of the epigraphs' relevance and relation to the individual sketches. If you find the relationship between one sketch and its epigraph (or epigraphs) particularly intriguing, you should begin by learning more about the epigraph and the work that it is drawn from. If your edition of "The Encantadas" does not provide you with the source, Thomas's article will provide the necessary reference. You will also need to familiarize yourself with the work from which the epigraph is drawn. Many are from Spenser's *Fairie Queene.* Once you have read from the cited work and once you know something about its background and its themes and purposes, you can begin to assess its relationship to "The Encantadas." Do the epigraphs reinforce the ideas and the themes of the sketch, or does Melville seem to use them ironically? Your analysis should move beyond this, though, and should grapple with the significance of these relationships. Why would Melville choose to use these epigraphs from these particular texts in these particular ways? How do they enhance your understanding of the sketch?

2. **Genre:** Many of Melville's works seem to challenge traditional genre classifications, and "The Encantadas" is no exception. A piece of short fiction, first published in *Putnam's* in 1854 and later collected in *The Piazza Tales*, "The Encantadas," unlike "Bartleby, the Scrivener" or "The Paradise of Bachelors and the Tartarus of Maids," lacks a coherent narrative and clearly cannot be aptly called a tale or a short story. Like *Typee*, which is also drawn from Melville's experience in the South Seas, "The Encantadas" is hard to classify. Over the years, readers have been drawn to "The Encantadas" but have reached no conclusions about how to classify the work. Some readers have linked it, like *Typee* before it, to travel writing, and others have remarked on the poetic qualities of its language. Like *Typee*, it blends personal experience and observation with fictional elements, and it draws upon and references other texts. It seems to blend narrative, character, memoir, and travel writing. Construct a paper that classifies "The Encantadas" as a particular genre of writing. Is it a tale, a short story, a long prose poem, a piece of travel literature, or something altogether different?

This question obviously requires that you familiarize yourself with the characteristics of different genres of writing. You might look at a good handbook of literary terms in order to find precise definitions. Also bear in mind that this question cannot be answered definitively. Your job is to make the most coherent argument that you can, while demonstrating your knowledge of the various genres and of "The Encantadas." One

approach that might prove particularly fruitful is to explore
the relevance of more modern genres for "The Encantadas."
You might find that, as a piece of 19th-century magazine fiction, it shares more with contemporary journalism than it
does with genres like the short story. Do you think that "The
Encantadas" could be defined as "literary journalism" or as
"creative nonfiction"? Explore current ideas and philosophies
about those genres and evaluate their relevance for an understanding of "The Encantadas."

3. **Structure and unity:** Perhaps as an outgrowth of the work's
   resistance to traditional genre classifications, scholars have
   proposed numerous strategies to explain the unity, structure,
   and coherence of "The Encantadas." Some scholars see in it a
   number of paired sketches; many remark on an overall bipartite structure, noting that it first explores the natural world and
   then examines the human inhabitants of that world; its connections to Dante's *Inferno* provide others with a kind of structural
   coherence, and still others find a unity of theme or of imagery.
   Construct an argument that explains how Melville shapes these
   10 separate sketches into a unified whole. What elements or
   strategies account for the coherence of the text as a whole?

   Your own experience of the text could be a good starting place
   for a response to this question. As you first read "The Encantadas," did you see connections among the sketches? Did they
   seem one coherent work, or did they seem like 10 different
   works randomly collected under one title? Did the sketches
   seem to share anything beyond their setting? If you see connections between the sketches, are they linked by imagery,
   theme, philosophy, or by some other factor? Still further, are
   those connections sufficient to shape the work into a coherent whole? You might also want to explore the very notion of
   disconnectedness as a unifying feature. In other words, might
   Melville's choice of form—10 independent sketches—reflect,
   echo, or embody a thematic or philosophical principle that
   underlies the whole of the text?

Language, Symbols, and Imagery

Some scholars have commented on the poetic quality of "The Encantadas," especially the early sketches, which have no human characters. This poetic quality is built largely from the dense description and evocative imagery of this text. Some of the imagery here is familiar to readers of Melville's other fiction; "The Encantadas" is full of fire and infernal imagery. Similarly, many scholars have drawn comparisons between Moby Dick and the Galápagos tortoises that populate this work. A strong paper on language or imagery will grow from a careful, close reading of the text.

Sample Topics:

1. **Imagery of hell:** Only the most obtuse reader can miss the infernal imagery within "The Encantadas." Even in its first paragraph, sketch one makes quite clear the associations between hell and the Enchanted Isles: The Encantadas look "much as the world at large might, after a penal conflagration." Less obvious is why Melville draws so many connections between the Enchanted Isles and hell. With this question in mind, explore and analyze the many ways that Melville draws connections between the Encantadas and hell. What patterns of imagery allow Melville to create this hell on earth? Why does he seem so insistent on creating this effect? What his purpose in portraying the islands as an earthly inferno?

   A response to this question must be based in a close reading of Melville's figurative language. Take note of how often he uses imagery associated with fire. Beyond this, consider other patterns of imagery that convey this effect. Consider, too, how he applies this imagery. If he compares the islands themselves to a kind of hell on earth, how does he present their inhabitants—both human and nonhuman? How would you describe the relationship between the Encantadas and their inhabitants? You may want to think about the allegorical possibilities of the islands. Does Melville present a kind of realistic sketch of the Galápagos Islands as a travel writer would, or is it possible that he offers them as a kind of allegorical representation? If so, what do they represent or embody? If you read the landscape allegorically, what does the work tell us about Melville's worldview?

2. **Animal imagery:** Explore Melville's use of animal imagery in "The Encantadas," and construct an argument about how and why he uses animal imagery in this piece.

This is a particularly broad question, and you will need to focus your response considerably. Melville spends a great deal of time cataloging and describing the nonhuman inhabitants of the isles. In addition, he frequently uses animal imagery to enhance his description of the islands and their inhabitants. Each of these two techniques could provide an entry to this question. You may wish to focus on Melville's fascination with identifying and cataloging the animal life in and around the Encantadas. Why does he spend so much time describing the birds, fish, and reptiles that populate this world? You might also draw connections between this question and that posed in the Philosophy and Ideas section about geology and evolution. Consider the potential implications that scientific advancements in geology and animal science may have for Melville's use of animal imagery in this piece. Another related approach would explore the connections between the humans and the animals.

Rather than focusing more generally on the animal imagery, you could focus entirely on Melville's use of the Galápagos tortoises. This focus could, in turn, lead in a number of different directions. Quite clearly, Sketch Second, "Two Sides to a Tortoise," presents the narrator's longest meditation on the tortoises, and you might focus on this sketch alone. You should think about the qualities that the narrator attributes to the tortoises and his attitudes toward them. Examine the figurative language that describes them. How is it significant? What symbolic value does the narrator find in these ancient creatures? You might find it helpful to evaluate the narrator's tone in this sketch as well. Does he seem fairly forthright, or do you sense any irony in his tone? What bearing does his tone have on your interpretation? Tortoises play notable roles in other sketches, so you could move beyond this sketch to consider Melville's use of the tortoises more generally. In what other sketches do they seem significant? How would you describe their roles and their qualities there?

Another species that plays a significant role in "The Encantadas" is the dog. Unlike the tortoises, the dogs in Sketch Seventh: "Charles's Isle and the Dog-King" and "Sketch Eighth: Norfolk Isle and the Chola Widow" are not native to the islands, and they are domesticated. Similarly, unlike tortoises, dogs carry well-defined symbolic value in Western culture. Consider how and why Melville used dogs so prominently in "The Encantadas."

3. **Cross imagery:** The eighth sketch, "Norfolk Isle and the Chola Widow" is one of the best-known segments of "The Encantadas," and many see in Hunilla a sign of redemption. These readings place a good deal of weight on the image of the cross that appears in the final paragraph. Hunilla rides into Payta on "a small gray ass: and before her on the ass's shoulders, she eyed the jointed workings of the beast's armorial cross." Yet this final cross is not the only one that appears in the sketch. Explore Melville's use of cross imagery here and draw some conclusions about its function.

This question relates to the discussion of the character of Hunilla on page 176, and you may want to think about the questions posed there. Examine the story carefully. Where, and in what forms, do crosses appear? Describing Hunilla's rites for her dead husband and brother, the narrator speaks of "the strong persuasions of her Romish faith." What connections do you see between Hunilla's Catholicism and the cross imagery? Similarly, you might want to consider the question of faith more broadly. How might the cross imagery relate to more abstract treatments of faith? As you examine this imagery, does it give you any insight into Melville's attitudes toward religion and toward faith?

Compare and Contrast Essays

"The Encantadas" should provide you with plenty of material for compare and contrast papers. You might choose to compare elements within this text, perhaps studying the relationship between two paired sketches, or you might wish to compare themes and characters in this work with those in another of Melville's work. Melville's island setting provides a few opportunities for developing compare and contrast papers. Remember that your thesis should make a clear, specific point about the relevance or the significance of the comparisons you draw. An effective compare and contrast paper does much more than just point out similarities and differences. You need to tell your readers why your comparisons are significant.

Sample Topics:

1. **Paired sketches:** Readers have identified numerous structural patterns in "The Encantadas." For example, Melville develops the work through paired sketches (though readers have not always agreed about which sketches should be regarded as pairs). Choose two sketches that could be compared as companion pieces, and explore what each has to say about a particular theme or issue in "The Encantadas." How does this pair of sketches help you to understand the work as a whole?

   Most frequently, readers see connections between the eighth and ninth sketch, seeing Hunilla and Oberlus as examples of starkly different human responses to the various hardships of the islands. And yet, some readers have contradicted such interpretations, seeing more connections between Hunilla and the renegade sailors of the seventh sketch. Still others have spoken of similarities between Hunilla and Oberlus. There are numerous other possibilities for pairings among the sketches depending on the particular theme, image, or issue that you wish to explore.

2. **Melville and gender:** Men populate much of Melville's fiction, but "The Encantadas" provides readers with one of his most affecting female characters. Compare Hunilla and her suffering

to that of the maids in "The Paradise of Bachelors and the Tartarus of Maids." What possibilities for comparison exist between this solitary woman on Norfolk Island and the young women living and working at the New England paper mill?

Despite the differences in their situations, Hunilla and the maids provide a good deal of material for comparison. As you explore the portraits presented in their individual sketches, be sure not to ignore their contexts. Both Hunilla and the maids appear in works that are composed of multiple sketches. Further, consider whether Melville seems to be making any broader statements about gender and about women's roles in these two works.

3. **Revolution and social order:** Explore Melville's commentary on social order, political structure, and revolution in "The Encantadas" with his treatment of these themes in another of his works. Or compare his treatment here with that of another American writer.

   This question asks you to focus on the seventh and the ninth sketches in "The Encantadas." Both *Benito Cereno* and *Billy Budd* provide possible texts for comparison since each examines issues of social order along with the threat of revolution or revolt. Similarly, you could look to some of Nathaniel Hawthorne's works to find similar themes. "My Kinsman, Major Molineux" and "The Maypole of Merry Mount" could be useful in a paper on this topic.

4. **Melville's enchanted isles:** Melville treats the idea of enchantment in both *Typee* and "The Encantadas," and he figures both the Galápagos and Nukuheva as enchanted isles. Compare his treatment of the theme of enchantment in both works.

   "Sketch First: The Isles at Large" makes overt reference to the South Sea Islands when the narrator speaks of the "charming palm isles to the westward and southward." Clearly, he intends to contrast these islands with the Galápagos. What renders the quality of enchantment so different on the Galápagos? Is the enchantment simply a matter of location and setting, or does Melville use this theme to amplify or support other themes or issues in these two texts?

5. **Melville's foundlings:** Another of Melville's foundling characters, Oberlus, speaks of himself as "fatherless," and claims descent from Sycorax, the sorceress who appears in Shakespeare's *The Tempest*. Choose another of Melville's foundlings and compare him to Oberlus. What accounts for the similarities and/or the differences in their portrayal?

Orphans and characters of obscure heritage abound in Melville's works: Ishmael, Ahab, Pip, Billy Budd, Claggart, Bartleby. Nearly all of these characters share something with Oberlus. While you may find it difficult to draw many parallels between Billy Budd and Oberlus, you may be surprised to find how many connections you can draw between an apparently harmless character like Bartleby and the misanthropic Oberlus.

6. **Silence and speech:** Examine Melville's treatment of silence and speech in "The Encantadas" and another of his works.

The eighth sketch deals most overtly with silence and speech in the narrator's methods of retelling Hunilla's story. Consider the connections between the issues raised in this sketch and those of "Bartleby, the Scrivener," *Benito Cereno,* and *Billy Budd, Sailor.*

7. **"The Encantadas" and Shakespeare's *The Tempest*:** In the ninth sketch, Oberlus claims, "This island's mine by Sycorax my mother." Here he quotes Caliban from *The Tempest*. In light of this connection, argue whether or not you believe that the themes, issues, and characters of Shakepeare's play influenced Melville's ideas and purposes in "The Encantadas."

Melville read and admired Shakespeare, and there is a good deal of room to compare Oberlus and Caliban. *The Tempest,* though, provides other possible starting places for compare and contrast papers. Both works are set on islands. Both examine the relationship between humanity and the natural world. Intriguingly, sailors abandon both Hunilla and Sycorax on their respective islands. Any of these connections might prove a basis for an interesting comparative study.

Bibliography and Online Resources for "The Encantadas"

Arvin, Newton. *Herman Melville.* New York: William Sloane, 1950.

Beecher, Jonathan. "Variations on a Dystopian Theme: Melville's 'Encantadas.'" *Utopian Studies* 11 (2000): 88–95.

Bickley, R. Bruce. *The Method of Melville's Short Fiction.* Durham, NC: Duke UP, 1955.

Bryant, John, "Toning Down the Green: Melville's Picturesque." In *Savage Eye: Melville and the Visual Arts.* Christopher Sten, ed. Kent, OH: Kent State UP, 1991. 145–61.

Bryant, John and Robert Milder, eds. *Melville's Evermoving Dawn.* Kent, OH: Kent State UP, 1997.

Colnett, James. *A Voyage to the South Atlantic.* Available online. URL: http://www.galapagos.to/TEXTS/COLNETT.HTM. Downloaded on November 4, 2007.

Cowley, William Ambrosia. *Cowley's Voyage Round the World.* Available online. URL: http://www.galapagos.to/TEXTS/COWLEY-MS.HTM. Downloaded on November 4, 2007.

Darwin, Charles. *Journal of Researches . . . during the Voyages of the H.M.S. Beagle. The Complete Works of Charles Darwin Online.* Available online. URL: http://darwin-online.org.uk/content/frameset?itemID=F10.3&viewtype=text&pageseq=1. Downloaded on November 4, 2007.

———. Journal of Researches . . . during the Voyages of the H.M.S. Beagle. (Galápagos chapter only). Available online. URL: http://www.galapagos.to/TEXTS/J-OF-R-G.HTM. Downloaded on November 4, 2007.

Delano, Amasa. *A Narrative of Voyage and Travels.* Available online. URL: http://www.galapagos.to/TEXTS/DELANO.HTM. Downloaded on November 4, 2007.

Delbanco, Andrew. *Melville: His World and His Work.* New York: Knopf: 2005.

Dillingham, William B. *Melville's Short Fiction, 1853–1856.* Athens: U of Georgia P, 1977.

Dryden, Edgar A. "From the Piazza to the Enchanted Isles: Melville's Textual Rovings." In *After Strange Texts: The Role of Theory in the Study of Literature.* Ed. David L. Miller. University: U of Alabama P, 1985.

———. *Monumental Melville: The Formation of a Literary Career.* Stanford, CA: Stanford UP, 2004.

Fogle, Richard Harter. *Melville's Shorter Tales.* Norman: U of Oklahoma P, 1960.

Howard, Leon. "Melville and Spenser—A Note on Criticism," *Modern Language Notes* 46 (1931): 291–92.

Karcher, Carolyn. *Shadow over the Promised Land: Slavery, Race, and Violence in Melville's America.* Baton Rouge: Louisiana State UP, 1980.

Liquete, Maria. "When Silence Speaks: The Chola Widow." In *Melville and Women.* Eds. Elizabeth Schultz and Haskell S. Springer. Kent: Ohio State UP, 2006. 213–28.

Moses, Carole. "Hunilla and Oberlus: Ambiguous Companions." *Studies in Short Fiction* 22 (1985): 339–42.

Newberry, Ilse. "'The Encantadas': Melville's Inferno." *American Literature* 38 (1966): 49–68.

Newman, Lea Bertani Vozar. *A Reader's Guide to the Short Stories of Herman Melville.* Boston: Hall, 1986.

Porter, David. *Journal of a Cruise Made to the Pacific Ocean.* Available online. URL: http://www.galapagos.to/TEXTS/PORTER-1.HTM. Downloaded on November 4, 2007.

Robertson-Lorant, Laurie. *Melville: A Biography.* New York: Clarkson Potter, 1996.

Seelye, John. *Melville: The Ironic Diagram.* Evanston, IL: Northwestern UP, 1970.

Thomas, Russell. "Melville's use of Some Sources in 'The Encantadas.'" *American Literature* 3 (1932): 432–56.

Wertheimer, Eric. *Imagined Empires: Incas, Aztecs, and the New World of American Literature, 1771–1876.* Cambridge: Cambridge UP, 1999.

"THE PARADISE OF BACHELORS AND THE TARTARUS OF MAIDS"

READING TO WRITE

TO READERS familiar with Melville's prior work, it should come as no surprise that "The Paradise of Bachelors and the Tartarus of Maids"—published in *Harper's* in 1855—defies traditional genric classification. While this piece seems more like a short story than "The Encantadas," Melville challenges readers through a bipartite, or diptych, structure. At first glance, the two parts of the story seem to have few connections to each other. "Paradise" feels more like a sketch than a short story, while "Tartarus" comes a bit closer to meeting readers' expectations for a short story. Few would argue that "Tartarus" is the richer of the work's two halves, and some scholars have argued that it could—and should—stand independently. For the modern student of Melville, finding the connections between the work's two parts and understanding how the relationship informs the story's meaning are likely to be the first tasks at hand. Perhaps the most obvious connection between "Paradise" and "Tartarus" is the narrator. He visits both Elm Court, Temple and the paper mill at Devil's Dungeon, and he recounts these visits for the reader. His experiences in the paper mill allow him to draw the connections between the world of the bachelors in London and that of the girls who work in the New England mill. Early in "Tartarus" the narrator reintroduces himself and tells the reader a good deal about himself and the purpose of his journey to Devil's Dungeon. Consider how his introduction provides questions, issues, and themes to pursue as you continue reading. Having described the landscape around the mill, he tells of his reason for traveling through this bleak, cold "Plutonian" landscape:

> Having embarked on a large scale in the seedsman's business (so extensively and broadcast, indeed, that at length my seeds were distributed through all the Eastern and Northern States, and even fell into the far soil of Missouri and the Carolinas), the demand for paper at my place became so great, that the expenditure soon amounted to a most important item in the general account. It need hardly be hinted how paper comes into use with seedsmen, as envelopes. These are mostly made of yellowish paper, folded square; and when filled, are all but flat, and being stamped, and superscribed with the nature of the seeds contained, assume not a little appearance of business-letters ready for the mail. Of these small envelopes I used an incredible quantity—several hundreds of thousands in a year. For a time I had purchased my paper from the wholesale dealers in a neighboring town. For economy's sake, and partly for the adventure of the trip, I now resolved to cross the mountains, some sixty miles, and order my future paper at the Devil's Dungeon paper-mill.

The narrator's line of work is likely to be the first thing you notice about this paragraph, for it is surely a unique sort of work. In the body of Melville's fiction, readers have met sailors, sea captains, lawyers, and office clerks, but never the proprietor of a seed business. You might wonder, then, at Melville's choice of occupation. Why does he assign his narrator the role of "seedsman"? What resonances are there to that job and to that title? Is the fact that the narrator describes himself as sewing and broadcasting seed significant?

Careful readers will also consider the nature of the narrator's journey. While his visit to the Inns of Court in "Paradise" seems to be a pleasure trip, is it significant that here he embarks on a business trip? Further, you might explore his motivations for this trip. The "demand for paper," he says, created an "expenditure [that] soon amounted to a most important item in the general account." In an attempt to control expenses, the narrator resolves "to order my future paper at the Devil's Dungeon paper-mill" rather than continuing to buy from the nearby wholesaler with whom he had been doing business. He has, in other words, resolved to cut out the middleman and go straight to the source. The narrator indicates that he decided to travel 60 miles in the cold and snow "for economy's sake, and partly for the adventure of the trip." Some readers might legitimately wonder about the veracity of the latter purpose. Although the narrator claims in the next paragraph that "the sleighing [was] uncommonly good," a 60-mile sleigh trip in the "bitter cold" of January over the mountains of New England hardly sounds like a promising adventure. As you continue to read, then, you might be curious about whether the trip fulfilled both of his purposes. Is this a successful business trip? Does it provide him with an "adventure," and if so, of what kind? Still further, you might want to explore the relationship between the two purposes. Does the business affect the pleasure? Does the pleasure affect the business?

Explaining why a seedsman would need so much paper that it might necessitate a trip to the paper mill, the narrator describes the envelopes in which he packages his seeds, and claims that he uses "several hundreds of thousands in a year." He compares the envelopes, which are "stamped" and "superscribed," to "business-letters ready for the mail." This comparison of the seed envelopes with business letters suggest the idea of circulation, as letters circulate in the mail, and circulation also has an economic meaning, as coins, bills, and goods are put into circulation. This meaning is echoed by the idea of the narrator's seeds being "broadcast." You might wonder, then, if the economic connotations of these circulating seeds/business letters is significant to Melville's larger ideas and purposes in this text. Certainly these references, coupled with the economic factors that motivated the narrator's trip, suggest that business and economics are in the forefront of the narrator's mind and may also be in the forefront of his creator's mind.

A reader who knows something of Melville's biography might also want to explore other connections between Melville and his narrator. It is likely that "The Paradise of Bachelors and the Tartarus of Maids" was suggested by Melville's own experiences—a trip to the Inns of Court in 1849 and an 1851 journey to Carson's Mill in Dalton, Massachusetts, to buy paper for his writing. As an author, Melville depended on paper, and his texts, like the seeds and envelopes of his seedsman narrator, were broadcast and circulated. Or so he hoped; Melville was acutely aware of the influence that business and economic concerns had upon the dissemination of his texts and his ideas. His books did not sell well, and in 1851 just five months after his journey to the Dalton paper mill, Melville wrote Nathaniel Hawthorne of his artistic and economic frustration: "Dollars damn me; and the malicious Devil is forever grinning in upon me, holding the door ajar. My dear Sir, a presentiment is on me,—I shall at last be worn out and perish, like an old nutmeg-grater, grated to pieces by the constant attrition of the wood, that is, the nutmeg. What I feel most moved to write, that is banned,—it will not pay. Yet, altogether, write the *other* way I cannot." You might wonder, if this story that seems to focus on economics, work, and business reflects the author's concerns about his own life and livelihood. Like his narrator, he was pressured and pressed by economics, and like his narrator he traveled to a New England paper mill in January. Yet Melville's assertion that he is like "an old nutmeg grater" suggests another parallel. Between his work and the economic pressure of the "dollars," he feels that he will "at last be worn out," "grated to pieces" by the action of the grater and the "constant attrition of the wood." The destructive mechanical action of the grinder anticipates the imagery of "Tartarus," where the machinery of the mill seems to wear the life out of the maids. As you read, you may be able to draw parallels not only between Melville and his narrator but also between the author and the young women of the factory.

A piece of magazine fiction, "The Paradise of Bachelors and the Tartarus of Maids," was dependent on the circulation of *Harper's*. As you continue to read this text, you should reflect on the ideas that Melville hoped to convey through this work. If you read attentively, exploring the relationship between "Paradise" and "Tartarus," considering the importance of business and economics to the story and its author, and analyzing the language and the motivations of the narrator, you should easily find a suitable focus for a paper on this work.

TOPICS AND STRATEGIES

This section of the chapter provides you with broad topic ideas that should help you develop an essay on "The Paradise of Bachelors and the Tartarus of Maids." Remember that these topics are just springboards for your own exploration; you will need to focus your analysis and develop your own specific thesis.

Themes

Quite clearly, Melville takes up the theme of industrialization in this short work, but "The Paradise of Bachelors and the Tartarus of Maids" also addresses other themes and issues. To write a paper about thematic concerns in this piece, you should begin by identifying a theme that you found intriguing. From there, you should go back over the text carefully and attempt to draw some conclusions about Melville's treatment of that theme. If you want to discuss Melville's commentary on industrialization, for example, begin by exploring the imagery and the language associated with the paper mill and the effects of work on the maids. Such an exploration will help you draw conclusions about Melville's ideas about industry and work. Additionally, you should move beyond "Tartarus" and analyze the relation between "Paradise" and "Tartarus" in order to gain a fuller understanding of Melville's ideas. The narrator's role should also prove suggestive in such a study.

Sample Topics:

1. **Industrialization:** Clearly, one of Melville's interests in "The Paradise of Bachelors and the Tartarus of Maids" is industrialization. Perhaps more difficult, though, is to determine precisely what the work says about industrialism. Examine "The Paradise of Bachelors and the Tartarus of Maids" as a study of 19th-century industrialism. What does Melville argue about industry?

   The setting and imagery of "Tartarus" provide an obvious starting place for a paper on industrialization, and clearly Melville does not paint a rosy picture of industry in the 19th century. And yet, your biggest challenge in a paper on this topic might be moving beyond a broad and rather obvious statement that Melville critiques industrialism. A strong thesis should comment more specifically upon why or how Melville renders this critique. Still further, consider whether he proposes solutions to the problems he presents. A paper on this theme, then, will clearly need to examine the imagery of the second part of the work. What kinds of imagery dominate the portrait of the paper mill? How and why is that imagery important? What arguments does Melville's imagery make about industrialization and its effects on humanity and on society? Such an investigation should also grapple with the narrator and his role in the sketch. Why does he travel to the paper mill in the first place, and how is his reaction to the mill significant? Still further, you need to move beyond an exploration of the second part of the work. The first section that chronicles the narrator's visit to the bachelor's paradise seems far removed from the misery of "Tartarus," but Melville deliberately yokes these two apparently disparate sketches together in one work. Is there a relationship between the paradise and the Tartarus? What devices and techniques does Melville use to communicate these connections? How does the relationship between the two parts of the text reflect upon Melville's commentary on industrialism? Does Melville bring issues of social class to bear on his portrait of industrialism?

2. **Gender:** In the largely masculine world of Melville's prose, "The Paradise of Bachelors and the Tartarus of Maids" provides a rare glimpse at women. Given that the world of Melville's prose seems largely centered on men and masculinity, do you believe that "The Paradise of Bachelors and the Tartarus of Maids" can be fairly assessed as a commentary on women and their place in the world?

So many of Melville's prose works are set at sea in a world that seems almost exclusively male; generally women seem peripheral to his concerns. *Typee*'s Fayaway, Hunilla from "The Encantadas," Lucy and Isabel from *Pierre,* and the undifferentiated "maids" from "Tartarus" are perhaps the only notable exceptions (and Fayaway, Lucy, and Isabel themselves play supporting roles). Does this fact alone render suspect any argument for "The Paradise of Bachelors and the Tartarus of Maids" as a sympathetic commentary on women's plight? Some readers have read this work as a sympathetic look at the burdens—both biological and industrial—of women. Others have interpreted the work as a rejection of women and female sexuality. Do you think it is significant that all the women in this work—the maids—are undifferentiated? Why? Obviously, you will need to explore the narrator's portrait of these maids. His description is laden with symbolism and figurative language, and to explore its treatment of gender you will need to explore the language and imagery closely. Similarly, you will need to think about the narrator's reactions to both the maids and the bachelors in some detail. Explore his reactions to the women in the mill. Does he seem to react sympathetically? Still further, how does he respond to "Old Bach" and to Cupid, the two males he meets at the mill? Consider, too, his reactions to the bachelors in the first sketch as well as any relationship between these bachelors and the maids.

3. **Production and reproduction:** Examine "The Paradise of Bachelors and the Tartarus of Maids" as a commentary on the related themes of production and reproduction. How might you read the work as a commentary on reproduction, production, or the relationship between the two?

Clearly, related to both gender and industry, this topic reflects upon those two themes, and it provides still other directions for a thematic study. The title of the work, with its emphasis on both the maids and bachelors, seems to bespeak a certain sterility, a failure to reproduce. Do you think that "The Paradise of Bachelors and the Tartarus of Maids" is a commentary on sterility? If so, how and why does Melville develop the idea of sterility? While the title obviously suggests the importance of characterization for such an investigation, you should also examine the imagery and language. How does the figurative language develop or enhance Melville's meditation on sterility? Through its apparent contrast of bachelors and maids and of paradise and Tartarus, the title of the work also suggests a focus on opposites or opposition. Does the work contain suggestions of abundance, reproduction, or fertility that oppose the suggestions of sterility? Where do you see imagery suggestive of reproduction or of fertility? How and why is this imagery suggestive? How does it allow Melville to expand on this theme? Be sure to think of the resonance of the word *reproduction*. What connotations or meanings does it carry besides

its biological meaning? Who and what reproduces (or is reproduced) in this work? How and why is this suggestive?

4. **Writing and authorship:** Some readers have read "The Paradise
of Bachelors and the Tartarus of Maids" as a meditation on publishing and authorship. How might you develop such a reading
of the work?

Analyzing "The Paradise of Bachelors and the Tartarus of
Maids" as a commentary on authorship is more difficult than
exploring its treatment of gender or industry, but some of the
work's imagery is, indeed, suggestive for such a study. You
could begin by examining the importance of paper for the
second part of the work. Paper was a necessary commodity for
Melville, and he might have included his own prose among the
"sorts of writings" that would be "writ on those now vacant"
sheets of paper that are produced in the mill. Explore the
treatment of the blank paper in this part of the work. What
resonance does it have for an examination of writing and publishing? Still further, publishing, like papermaking, was an
industry in Melville's day, and there is ample biographical evidence that Melville's relationship with the publishing industry was never an easy one. (Research into Melville's biography
could help you develop a paper on this theme.) Does Melville's
analysis of the means and the ends of industry have any relevance for an exploration of "The Paradise of Bachelors and
the Tartarus of Maids" as commentary on authorship? Still
further, you should think about possible connections between
Melville and his narrator. How might you relate the two? How
might this relation be suggestive for a paper on the theme of
authorship?

Character

Unlike much of Melville's fiction, "The Paradise of Bachelors and the
Tartarus of Maids" provides few fully developed characters. That fact,
though, could provide a potential focus for a paper. If you examine
Melville's treatment of the maids or his treatment of the bachelors, you
could explore the reasons why Melville deviates from his usual pattern of

character development. Does it make sense that both the maids and the bachelors appear as corporate characters, two groups comprising undifferentiated individuals? This approach to character could form the basis of a thoughtful paper. Similarly, more in keeping with Melville's style, he draws a narrator who invites exploration and analysis, and you could focus an interesting paper around this figure.

Sample Topics:

1. **The narrator:** There is some evidence that Melville developed "The Paradise of Bachelors and the Tartarus of Maids" from two of his own experiences: an 1849 meal held in his honor in Elm Court, Temple, while he was in London promoting his work *White-Jacket,* and his 1851 trip to Carson's Mill in Dalton, Massachusetts, to buy paper for his writing. Despite the work's basis in biography, Melville creates a narrative persona in "The Paradise of Bachelors and the Tartarus of Maids." Analyze Melville's narrator as a character. How and why does Melville create this narrative persona rather than speaking in his own voice or writing in the voice of a third-person narrator?

    A reader well versed in Melville knows he enjoyed crafting first-person narrators—such as Ishmael and the lawyer-narrator of "Bartleby"—who are worthy of study and analysis. The discussion of the sexual imagery in the Language, Symbols, and Imagery section of this chapter suggests that one way to analyze the narrator is to explore his attitudes toward sexuality. While his "seedsman's business" is suggestive for such an exploration, it also underscores his reason for visiting the mill in the first place—he hopes to cut out the middle man in his business dealings and purchase his paper directly from the manufacturer "for economy's sake, and partly for the adventure of the trip." How is the nature of his business significant? How are his motivations significant? Further, you might consider the effect of the adventure on the man and on his business. Does the trip affect him? What evidence does the story provide to support your assertion? Does the emotional impression of his experiences have any bearing on his business decisions? Explain. Still further, explore the potential connections between Melville and his narrator, between the narrator and the bachelors, between the narrator and the maids, and between the narrator and Melville's readers. Might these relationships tell you anything about the author's apparent purposes behind his portrayal of the narrator?

2. **The maids:** Besides the narrator, few of the characters in this sketch are fully drawn. Old Bach and Cupid seem to be the only other characters who are individualized. Both the maids and the bachelors, though, could be analyzed collectively. Examine Melville's portrayal of the maids in the second half of the sketch. How does he characterize them? Why, finally, does he choose not to characterize any of the maids individually? How does his portrayal of these women advance his themes and his purposes?

An examination of Melville's portrayal of the "girls" who work in the paper factory will likely bring you back to questions about gender or of industrialization, so you might find the questions posed in the Themes section of this chapter helpful in this exploration. You should analyze the imagery associated with the maids. Pay particular attention to the various patterns of imagery Melville employs. How are these patterns of imagery related to one another? How do they deepen or broaden the characterization of the maids? Remember that you should draw conclusions about how or why Melville characterizes the girls as he does.

3. **The bachelors:** Most readers respond more to the second half of this work than the first, rightly arguing that "Tartarus" is richer and more fully developed than "Paradise." Some argue that "Tartarus" could stand on its own, while "Paradise" depends on the second half of the sketch for its meaning. With these arguments in mind, analyze Melville's characterization of the bachelors in the first half of the work. How would you describe Melville's attitude toward the bachelors? How and why is this attitude significant or important? Are the bachelors important in and of themselves, or does their characterization take on

more resonance once they are contrasted with the maids in the second part of the work?

This question asks you to explore issues of characterization and of structure. A close, careful analysis of the bachelors themselves provides a good beginning for this topic. Examine the language and the imagery associated with the bachelors. How is their "paradise" described? How and why is this description significant? Explain the significance of the narrator's lengthy parallel between the Knights Templar and the "modern Templar." How does the narrator describe the modern Templars' work and their lives? Pay close attention to the lengthy description of the bachelors' meal in the first half of the sketch. How would you describe the language the narrator uses here? How does this language help define his tone? You will likely be able to develop and enhance the conclusions you draw from these questions when you broaden your analysis to include "Tartarus." Examine the connections between the sketches. How do these connections help to develop the characterization of the bachelors? Still further, can you draw any connections between the proprietor of the paper mill and the bachelors or between Cupid and the bachelors?

History and Context

Melville's own biography provides the richest context for your study of the context of this work, since it is likely based on two of his own journeys. Still further, some critics argue that the imagery of gestation in the piece reflects Melville's own family situation. You may find it interesting to explore the working conditions in factories of Melville's time. This, too, could provide a useful lens through which to analyze the text.

Sample Topics:

1. **Melville's biography:** As the Reading to Write section of this chapter indicated, Melville built "The Paradise of Bachelors and the Tartarus of Maids" out of his own experiences: a trip to the Inns of Court in 1849 and an 1851 journey to Carson's Mill in

Dalton, Massachusetts, to buy paper for his writing. Scholars have suggested that this story's focus on business and economics might derive from the economic pressures that Melville felt trying to support his family through his writing. Examine "The Paradise of Bachelors and the Tartarus of Maids" as Melville's commentary on his own experiences with writing, economics, and family.

Biographies of Melville should give you more background about his life and his livelihood. Consider the relevance of paper and of circulation/distribution for a discussion of this topic. You might also consider the potential parallels between Melville and his narrator and between Melville and the maids as well as the bachelors. Additionally, does the language of sexuality and gestation have any relevance to your investigation? Some scholars tie this story to the difficult pregnancy that Lizzie Melville was going through at the time her husband was drafting this story. Does this biographical fact seem germane? Finally, you may want to think about the literary trope of a book as offspring or child. Might that be applicable to your investigation?

2. **Factory conditions during Melville's time:** Learn something about the conditions in factories of Melville's time. Does he base his work in historical accuracy? How might these conditions have affected the meaning of this work?

In addition to exploring the working conditions in factories, specifically consider the conditions of women working in these factories in Melville's day. How were women in industry treated differently from men? Further, you might wish to learn more about 19th-century ideas about domesticity and women's roles. How would women's work affect attitudes toward women and domesticity? The article by Barbara Welter listed in the bibliography should provide good background on domesticity in the 19th century, and Foner's book should provide useful information on women's work.

Philosophy and Ideas

Melville's narrator makes explicit mention of John Locke's theory of the tabula rasa during his tour through the paper mill, and this remark allows Melville to comment upon the idea that experience writes upon the human mind. An exploration of his use of Locke's theory should provide you with another angle through which to view Melville's social critique in this piece.

Sample Topics:

1. **John Locke and the tabula rasa:** Watching the paper dropping from the "great machine" near the end of his tour, the narrator thinks of the "sorts of writings that would be writ on those now vacant things." He adds: "I could not but bethink me of that celebrated comparison of John Locke who, in demonstration of his theory that man had no innate ideas, compared the human mind at birth to a sheet of blank paper; something destined to be scribbled on . . ." Examine the relevance of Locke's idea of the tabula rasa for "The Paradise of Bachelors and the Tartarus of Maids." How does Melville use this theory in the work?

   You should begin by learning a bit more about Locke's belief and his philosophy. From there, you should think about the relevance of his analogy comparing the human mind to a blank sheet of paper. Does the narrator's experience with the paper and the people in the paper factory seem to provide good "evidence" for the validity of Locke's theory? Why or why not? Is there evidence that Melville is using Locke's theory to prove another point? Explain. Quite clearly, you need to examine the characterization of the maids in the second part of this sketch, for they are overtly paralleled to the paper that they produce. How apt is this analogy? Are there other places where Melville uses similar imagery? How is this relevant for your exploration? You might also examine the narrator's portrayal of Cupid, who also seems a product of the paper factory. How is this character related to the belief that worldly experience "scribble[s]" upon human beings?

Form and Genre

Like so much of Melville's work, "The Paradise of Bachelors and the Tartarus of Maids" challenges traditional genre classifications. The two-part structure of this work and the nature of the relationship between the two apparently disparate parts provide starting places for a paper about form and genre. In some ways, "The Paradise of Bachelors and the Tartarus of Maids" partakes of two genres—story and sketch. In addition to exploring the work's form, you may find that exploring the work's relationship to the gothic tradition in literature proves suggestive. Certainly, Melville uses imagery and language common to gothic literature, and an analysis of the way he uses this imagery might provide a suggestive starting place for another paper on genre.

Sample Topics:

1. **Gothic literature and the female gothic:** Many readers have noted Melville's frequent use of gothic imagery and gothic elements. "The Paradise of Bachelors and the Tartarus of Maids," along with *Moby-Dick, Benito Cereno,* and *Pierre,* clearly draws on the gothic tradition. Unlike the other works, though, "The Paradise of Bachelors and the Tartarus of Maids," with its strongly gendered themes, seems closely related to what is now known as the "female gothic" tradition. Explore "The Paradise of Bachelors and the Tartarus of Maids" as a gothic work that is strongly aligned with the female gothic tradition.

   You should begin by familiarizing yourself with the gothic tradition in literature as well as with scholarship on the female gothic. The latter, as defined by Ellen Moers, who coined the term, is "the work that women writers have done in the literary mode that, since the eighteenth century, we have called the Gothic." Clearly, then, "The Paradise of Bachelors and the Tartarus of Maids" cannot rightly be called "female gothic," and yet the work shares the concerns, aims, and the imagery of the female gothic. Focusing on the imagery of the text and the points it seems to make about the maids, as well as examining the women's position in society and their relationships with men, could help you to develop a thoughtful response to this question.

2. **Diptych structure:** Most readers respond more to the second half of this work than the first, rightly arguing that "Tartarus" is richer and more fully developed than "Paradise." Some argue that "Tartarus" could—and should—stand on its own and that Melville's use of the diptych structure creates a difficult—and ultimately unsuccessful—work. Other readers see the diptych structure as integral to the unity and the meaning of "The Paradise of Bachelors and the Tartarus of Maids." Construct a paper that argues for or against the effectiveness of Melville's two-part, diptych structure in this work.

"The Paradise of Bachelors and the Tartarus of Maids" is just one of the bipartite, diptych tales that Melville published during this phase of his career. Most readers argue that this work is his most successful use of this structure. Clearly, you must analyze the links and the connections between the two parts of this work before you construct an argument about its unity. What links do you see between the two apparently disparate parts of this work? Your list of links should begin with the narrator. What other elements might you add to that list? No matter what your initial opinion about the work's structure, think about how you might argue in favor of its coherence, and then evaluate the strength of your argument. Any analysis of the unity of "The Paradise of Bachelors and the Tartarus of Maids" must also consider the work's themes and apparent purposes. Given Melville's ideas in the work, would he have any legitimate reasons for structuring the text as he does? Examining the text in light of these questions should provide you with a solid ground on which to build a paper about the unity and the structure of "The Paradise of Bachelors and the Tartarus of Maids."

Language, Symbols, and Imagery

Particularly rich in imagery, "The Paradise of Bachelors and the Tartarus of Maids" provides ample material for papers on figurative language. While much of the imagery of "Tartarus" makes clear the dehumanization of the women, you should find that stronger papers on Melville's use of imagery move beyond Melville's rather obvious argument about dehumanization and consider this imagery in conjunction with either the larger patterns of imagery or the larger purposes of the work as a whole. Clearly, though, you should begin any investigation into Melville's use of imagery through a close rereading that focuses upon the figurative language in the text.

Sample Topics:

1. **Economic language:** The larger ideas of "The Paradise of Bachelors and the Tartarus of Maids" involve industrialism and capitalism. How does Melville use the language of economics to develop the social critique of this work?

   This question allows you to work with some of the basic principles of capitalism and industrialism. Consider the relevance of economic terms such as *production, circulation,* and *consumption* for "The Paradise of Bachelors and the Tartarus of Maids." Explore the process of production in the paper mill, and think about the products of this industry as Melville portrays it. How does the imagery of the work help to develop Melville's notions of products and production? How is the economic process of consumption presented in this work? Pay particular attention to the imagery and the narrative tone as you analyze Melville's treatment of consumption. Consider, too, what other resonance a word like *consumption* carries. Finally, Melville plays with the idea of circulation in a number of different ways. Examine his treatment of the circulation of commodities. Besides the circulation of commodities or products, what other kinds of circulation does he explore here? How are these various types of circulation related? How are they related to his treatment of consumption and production?

2. **Sexual imagery:** Even though it is interwoven into the complex layers of figurative language, the sexual imagery in "The Paradise of Bachelors and the Tartarus of Maids" is hard to miss. Reread the work carefully and take note of how abundant the imagery of sexuality and reproduction is. How does Melville use this language to comment upon or develop the themes and issues of the work?

The density of this imagery would allow you to focus a paper on this topic in quite a few ways. In a work whose title seems to speak of gender and celibacy, you might find this imagery reflective of Melville's treatment of gender issues. Even this approach, though, would need to be more tightly focused, and a good beginning tactic might be to explore the work's treatment of male sexuality and female sexuality separately. Ironically, in this work that seems to segregate the genders so explicitly, language and imagery suggestive of male sexuality appear in both the bachelors' sketch and the maids' sketch. You may find it suggestive to compare the treatment of male sexuality in the two "halves" of the work. Melville treats female sexuality exclusively in "Tartarus." What does this sketch suggest about women and sexuality? A related approach would explore the relationship between the sexual imagery in the story and the theme of reproduction. How does this imagery help to develop Melville's exploration of that theme? How is the language and imagery of gestation related to this inquiry? A psychoanalytic study of the narrator provides yet another way to shape a response to this question. Remember that the same narrator tells of his journeys to the bachelors' paradise and to the paper mill. The imagery, then, is his as well as Melville's. What does his use of sexually charged language tell us about his own attitudes toward sexuality, gender, and reproduction?

Compare and Contrast Essays

In "The Paradise of Bachelors and the Tartarus of Maids," Melville addresses some issues that are familiar to readers of his fiction. Similarly, he uses narrative strategies that he had used in his earlier works. These connections should provide you with many suggestive parallels to develop into a compare and contrast paper. Whatever your subject, be sure that you forge a thoughtful, analytical thesis that does more than just point toward similarities and differences in the texts. Your paper should present an argument about the significance of the similarities and differences that you have discovered.

Sample Topics:

1. **Melville, women, and gender:** Many readers see "The Paradise of Bachelors and the Tartarus of Maids" as a surprisingly powerful and sympathetic comment on women and their position in society, and many read Melville's portrait of Hunilla from "Sketch Eighth" of "The Encantadas" the same way. Compare Melville's treatment of women in the two works. What do these pieces say about Melville's attitudes toward women, their place in society, and their relationship with men?

   This question builds from some of the issues addressed in previous sections of this chapter. Analyze the maids' characterization, the language and the imagery that describes the women, their work, and their environment. Consider their relation to the men (and the boy) in the work. As you examine Hunilla, think about the imagery associated with her. Similarly, like the maids, Hunilla exists in a world that is isolated and separated from others (and each of their worlds is described as a Tartarus); examine her relation to the other people who enter her world. How are these interactions significant?

2. **Social class:** Analyze "The Paradise of Bachelors and the Tartarus of Maids" and "Bartleby, the Scrivener" as Melville's commentary on social class. What do the two works say about class relations in the Melville's America?

   Characters and imagery should provide you with plenty of material to address this question. What similarities do you see between Bartleby and the young women who work in the paper mill? How is their work similar? Pay particular attention to the language and imagery that Melville uses to describe both the maids and the scrivener. What similarities do you note? Why do you think they share the qualities that they do? Further, you might explore their relationships with their bosses. Is the lawyer-narrator of "Bartleby" at all like Old Bach? Do you see any connections between Bartleby's employer and any other elements of "The Paradise of Bachelors and the Tartarus of Maids"? You might want to compare Melville's use of economic language in the two texts and consider how his treatment of this language develops his commentary on class.

Should you wish to compare Melville's treatment of social class with that of another writer, Rebecca Harding Davis's *Life in the Iron Mills* would be an excellent choice. Both works deal with questions of gender, and both use imagery of entrapment and enclosure.

3. **Melville's bachelors:** Melville populates his fiction with bachelors, many of whom seem to share a great many characteristics. Using "The Paradise of Bachelors and the Tartarus of Maids" and at least one other Melville work, analyze his use of the bachelor figure. What do these men represent for Melville? Why do they appear so frequently in his work?

You have a number of possibilities for comparison here. Perhaps the most obvious choice is the lawyer who narrates "Bartleby, the Scrivener," but quite a few of Melville's sailors could prove useful here, too. Captain Vere presents one possibility. Additionally, you may find it suggestive that Captain Delano's ship in *Benito Cereno* is called *The Bachelor's Delight*.

4. **The law:** In "Paradise," the narrator tells the reader that "the Templar, is to-day a Lawyer," and his sketch of Elm Court, Temple is to some degree a commentary on lawyers and the law. Compare Melville's treatment of the law in "The Paradise of Bachelors and the Tartarus of Maids" with that in another of his works.

Billy Budd provides Melville's most extended study of the law, and that work should provide you with plenty of material for a paper on this topic. *Benito Cereno* is another work that comments on the law and its role in society. "Bartleby, the Scrivener" is another possibility for comparison, though it focuses more on the lawyer-narrator than on issues of law.

5. **Hell:** Both "The Paradise of Bachelors and the Tartarus of Maids" and "The Encantadas" furnish readers with portraits of hell. But these two versions of hell look quite different. Examine the imagery and the inhabitants of these two Melvillean hells. What do they share? How do they present a similar picture of Melville's conception of hell on Earth?

You will probably find the differences between these two portraits of hell most striking. Melville fills "The Encantadas" with images of fire, heat, and dryness, while the narrator of "Tartarus" travels in a world of snow, ice, and "white vapors." You will have to work with more abstract ideas in order to draw the connections here. What abstract qualities do Melville's landscapes conjure? You should think about the human inhabitants of these two hells. Do they share anything? You might also find it suggestive to think about the structure of the two works. Do they share any structural similarities, and, if so, how might these similarities be suggestive?

Bibliography and Online Resources for "The Paradise of Bachelors and the Tartarus of Maids"

Arvin, Newton. *Herman Melville.* New York: William Sloane, 1950.

Bickley, R. Bruce. *The Method of Melville's Short Fiction.* Durham, NC: Duke UP, 1955.

Browne, Ray B. *Melville's Drive to Humanism.* Layfayette, IN: Purdue U Studies, 1971.

Bryant, John, and Robert Milder, eds. *Melville's Evermoving Dawn.* Kent, OH: Kent State UP, 1997.

Chase, Richard. *Herman Melville: A Critical Study.* New York: Macmillan, 1949.

Delbanco, Andrew. *Melville: His World and His Work.* New York: Knopf: 2005.

Dillingham, William B. *Melville's Short Fiction, 1853–1856.* Athens: U of Georgia P, 1977.

Fisher, Marvin. *Going Under: Melville's Short Fiction and the American 1850s.* Baton Rouge: Louisiana State UP, 1977.

Fogle, Richard Harter. *Melville's Shorter Tales.* Norman: U of Oklahoma P, 1960.

Foner, Philip S. *The Factory Girls.* Urbana: U of Illinois P, 1977.

Gilmore, Michael T. *American Romanticism and the Marketplace.* Chicago: U of Chicago P, 1985.

Martin, Robert K. *Hero, Captain, and Stranger: Male Friendship, Social Critiques and Literary Form in the Novels of Herman Melville.* Chapel Hill: U of North Carolina P, 1986.

Moers, Ellen. *Literary Women.* New York: Doubleday, 1976.

Newman, Lea Bertani Vozar. *A Reader's Guide to the Short Stories of Herman Melville.* Boston: Hall, 1986.

Oates, Joyce Carol. Introduction. *American Gothic Tales.* New York: Plume, 1996. 1–9.

Parker, Hershel. *Herman Melville.* 2 vols. Baltimore: Johns Hopkins UP, 1996, 2002.

Rogin, Michael Paul. *Subversive Genealogy: The Politics and Art of Herman Melville.* New York: Knopf, 1983.

Seelye, John. *Melville: The Ironic Diagram.* Evanston, IL: Northwestern UP, 1970.

Welter, Barbara. "The Cult of True Womanhood: 1820–1860." *American Quarterly* 18 (Summer 1966): 151–74.

BENITO CERENO

READING TO WRITE

L IKE THE sailor's knot that functions as one of its most memorable symbols, *Benito Cereno* is a dense and intricate work. With its complex narrative voice and structure, its difficult subject matter, and its sources found in historical incidents and texts, the work has spawned a complicated and often contradictory critical history. Early in the 20th century, prominent literary critic F. O. Matthiessen called the novella "comparatively superficial," charging that it did not sufficiently address the issue of slavery. And yet, over the years *Benito Cereno* has come to be accepted as one of Melville's best works. Even today, though, while many modern critics argue that it directly addresses the evils of slavery and racism and critiques slaveholding societies, others maintain that the work is steeped in and reflective of the racism of Melville's antebellum America. This background should give you a taste of some of the difficulties that you might encounter as you begin a paper about *Benito Cereno*. But even in the opening paragraphs of the narrative, attentive readers will recognize that this convoluted critical history is a natural outgrowth of Melville's ideas. Human perception and understanding, the story seems to argue, are nearly always mediated. Our cultural values and beliefs are lenses though which we view the world, and sometimes these lenses cloud our vision.

Consider how the third and fourth paragraphs of *Benito Cereno*, where Captain Delano first views the *San Dominick*, pose questions of how we perceive and interpret the world around us:

> The morning was one peculiar to that coast. Everything was mute and
> calm; everything gray. The sea, though undulated into long roods of

swells, seemed fixed, and was sleeked at the surface like waved lead that has cooled and set in the smelter's mould. The sky seemed a gray surtout. Flights of troubled gray fowl, kith and kin with flights of troubled gray vapors among which they were mixed, skimmed low and fitfully over the waters, as swallows over meadows before storms. Shadows present, foreshadowing deeper shadows to come.

To Captain Delano's surprise, the stranger, viewed through the glass, showed no colors; though to do so upon entering a haven, however uninhabited in its shores, where but a single other ship might be lying, was the custom among peaceful seamen of all nations. Considering the lawlessness and loneliness of the spot, and the sort of stories, at that day, associated with those seas, Captain Delano's surprise might have deepened into some uneasiness had he not been a person of a singularly undistrustful good nature, not liable, except on extraordinary and repeated incentives, and hardly then, to indulge in personal alarms, any way involving the imputation of malign evil in man. Whether, in view of what humanity is capable, such a trait implies, along with a benevolent heart, more than ordinary quickness and accuracy of intellectual perception, may be left to the wise to determine.

The first of these paragraphs clearly acts to set the scene, building as it does on the first two paragraphs of the story that introduce Delano, his ship, their position off the coast of Chile, and the early morning announcement that "a strange sail was coming into the bay." Perhaps the first thing that readers are apt to notice about this third paragraph is the repetition of the word *gray*. After informing readers that "Everything was mute and calm; everything gray," the narrator remarks on the "sky [that] seemed a gray surtout," the "troubled gray fowl," and the "troubled gray vapors." Even the sea, "like waved lead that has cooled and set in the smelter's mould," contributes to the monochromatic scene. This overwhelming grayness should raise a number of questions, which should lead the reader in two directions. Modern readers might first gravitate to moral connotations so often linked with the color gray. When we speak of "shades of gray," we speak figuratively of moral ambiguity, where clear distinctions—black and white—have disappeared. Does Melville's setting where "everything [is] gray" prefigure some moral ambiguity in the story? This preponderance of gray is especially provocative in a text that grapples so explicitly with issues of race and the interaction of "whites and blacks."

Secondly, this morning scene of gray on gray should lead to questions about perspective and perception. If everything is gray—the sea, the sky, the birds, and the vapors—how clearly could an observer of this gray morning differentiate between sea, sky, and vapors? How could a viewer make out the "troubled gray fowl" flying within the "troubled gray vapors among which they were mixed"? In fact, if the morning is marked by vapors, do they alone not cloud the viewer's vision? Already, the text seems to encourage readers to think about the accuracy and clarity of human perception. And, indeed, as the sixth paragraph begins, the narrator remarks, "It might have been but a deception of the vapors, but the longer the stranger was watched, the more singular appeared her maneuvers."

Still further, a careful reader might notice interpretation mingled with this descriptive paragraph. Labeling the birds and the vapors "troubled" certainly entails some personification and, hence, some interpretation of both elements. Similarly, you might notice a contradiction inherent to the paragraph. For "troubled" birds and vapors seem to belie the earlier claim that "everything was mute and calm." Questions like these should, in turn, cause you to question the point of view of the story. Whose point of view are readers privy to in this paragraph? Who sees the birds and vapors as "troubled"? While a third-person narrator clearly tells the story, you might notice just how quickly the narrator's perspective seems to coincide with Delano's. The story's second paragraph begins with the ship's mate informing Delano of the "strange sail" coming into view, and as the paragraph ends Delano "rose, dressed, and went on deck." Immediately following these words, the reader is introduced to the gray morning that met Delano as he stood on the deck of the *Bachelor's Delight.* Are the descriptions of the birds and the vapors as "troubled" those of Delano or those of the narrator? What of the final, more ominous images that close the paragraph—to whom do they belong? How can readers distinguish between the perceptions of the narrator and those of the captain, whose perspective the voice seems largely limited to? Further, how reliable is a perspective that views a scene as simultaneously "calm" and "troubled"?

As if to cut though the clouded air and to focus the reader's perspective both through Captain Delano and on him, the next paragraph begins with the American captain examining the ship "through the glass," thereby linking readers' view of the ship with Delano's. What the captain and the reader see is a ship that "showed no colors; though to do so upon entering a haven . . . was the custom among peaceful seamen of all nations." Having learned this fact, you might immediately wonder if the strange ship is not peaceful. And yet, the narrative does not pursue this question, but instead reverts its focus back to the American captain. At this point, the narrator seems to separate the reader's perspective from Delano's. Like most readers, Delano might have felt some apprehension at the sight of the ship, the narrator says, "had he not been a person of singularly undistrustful good nature, not liable, except on extraordinary and repeated incentives, and hardly then, to indulge in personal alarms, any way involving the imputation of malign evil in man." In the sentence that follows, the narrator clearly asks readers to focus on Delano: "Whether, in view of what humanity is capable, such a trait implies, along with a benevolent heart, more than ordinary quickness and accuracy of intellectual perception, may be left to the wise to determine." These final two sentences invite readers to question Delano's perspective and his wisdom—his "good nature," "his benevolent heart" and his "intellectual perception." At the same time, the narrator's comments might lead you to frame other questions about the strange ship that Delano is about to encounter. In contrast to Delano's expectations, might this ship that "show[s] no colors" harbor "malign evil"? Might it show readers "of what humanity is capable"?

A thoughtful analysis of the opening of *Benito Cereno* should provide guideposts for your continued reading of this difficult text. Already, the story's point of view, its color imagery, Captain Delano and his perceptions, and the human capacity for evil have emerged as issues to explore as you continue to read. Any of these concerns could provide a basis for a thoughtful paper, and a close reading of the whole work should easily provide you with more potential topics for papers on this complex, intricately crafted novella.

TOPICS AND STRATEGIES

This section of the chapter provides you with broad topic ideas that should help you develop an essay on *Benito Cereno.* Remember that these topics are just springboards for your own exploration; you will need to focus your analysis and develop your own specific thesis.

Themes

As the preceding paragraphs indicate, perception and understanding constitute a major theme in *Benito Cereno*. This work is so complex, though, that you could easily identify quite a few other themes to discuss in an essay. The nature of evil is clearly another of Melville's main focuses, and in more recent years slavery has received a good deal of attention in scholarly works on the text. Whatever theme you find compelling, you should prepare to write a paper on that theme by deciding the relevant aims of the novella. If you are writing about perception and understanding, you should think about why Melville writes about that theme. Why is it important? What does he say about it? What conclusions does he reach? How does he use narrative style, imagery, or character development to shape his ideas about human perception and understanding?

Sample Topics:

1. **Perceiving and understanding:** From the opening paragraphs that focus on Captain Delano's observations of the "strange sail" through the gray vapors, the theme of perceiving and understanding clearly takes center stage in *Benito Cereno*. Most of the novella concerns Delano's attempts to make sense of the strange scene on the *San Dominick* that "challenged his eye." What does *Benito Cereno* say about humans' ability to understand the "true character" of the world that surrounds us?

   In your response to this question, you might begin by examining the language of vision and seeing. You will also need to examine Captain Delano, his perceptions, and his attempts to understand the strange world of the *San Dominick*. You could begin this analysis by examining the metaphors and analogies that describe the ship even before Delano boards. What do these suggest about the American captain and his values, beliefs, ideals, and prejudices? Similarly, look at his vacillating interpretations of the *San Dominick* and its situation once he is on board. Examine his interpretations of the scenes, events, and characters he witnesses. Why does he interpret these sights as he does? Ironically, at times when he seems closest to figuring out what has occurred on the *San Dominick* he is quick to dismiss his misgivings. Why? As you analyze Delano and his "intellectual perceptions," you should also compare his reactions to your own. Most readers separate their perspective and their interpretation of the events from Delano's as the story progresses. How does Melville's narrative technique allow this separation? Why does Delano still fail to recognize the truth of the situation? Does knowing Delano's background and his character help you to understand why it takes so long until the "scales dropped from his eyes"?

2. **Acting and masks:** Scholars have frequently remarked that *Benito Cereno* presents a series of tableaux for interpretation. Indeed, much of what Delano and the reader see on the *San Dominick* is acting or pretense that masks the truth of the situation. Examine these themes in *Benito Cereno*. What is Melville saying though his use of these themes?

A paper that examines acting and masks in *Benito Cereno* might also consider some of the same issues addressed in the discussion of perception and understanding. After all, Delano watches an elaborate act on board the *San Dominick* in which every character—white or black—has a specific role to play. And unlike a drama presented in the theater, the point of this drama is deception. Take note of how frequently Melville uses the language of the stage in the story. Consider why the American captain is taken in by the acting. You should examine the roles that the various characters play in the drama on the slave ship. You might focus on Babo particularly. He seems a particularly successful actor. Why? What do we learn about him through the roles he plays? As you consider this theme, a number of individual scenes or tableaux might be examined in detail, particularly the staged appearances of Atufal in chains and the shaving scene. Additionally, you might consider the relevance of the ship's "shield-like stern-piece" for your analysis. Finally, you might think about these themes in connection with questions of identity and truth that are so prevalent in *Benito Cereno.*

3. **Storytelling, truth, and silence:** Having boarded the *San Dominick* and learned the "true character" of the ship, Captain Delano listens as "with one voice, all poured out a common tale of suffering." Soon he presses Don Benito to "favor him with the whole story." Throughout the novella, he listens to Don Benito as he recounts the fabricated story of the events that happened on board the slave ship. By the end of the novella, through Benito Cereno's deposition, readers hear Don Benito tell another version of the events that happened on his vessel. Consider *Benito Cereno* as a comment on storytelling and truth telling.

A paper that focuses on storytelling and truth in *Benito Cereno* must take the narrative structure of the tale into account. Early critics complained that Melville ruined the dramatic tension of the novella by continuing the story after its logical climax, Delano's revelation and the retaking of the *San Dominick.* Consider why Melville chose to continue his story beyond what many readers would clearly see as its logical conclusion. Why would he append excerpts from Benito Cereno's legal deposition? Why would he include the concluding conversation between the two captains? Do you believe that readers have heard the "whole story" by the end of the work? Why or why not? As you think about storytelling and its relation to truth, you should also consider the text's use of silences. Frequently, Don Benito's coughing fits render him silent as Delano pushes to hear more details of his story. Clearly, there is much he longs to tell Delano, but Babo, who never leaves Benito's side, acts as a censor. What other gaps or silences occur in *Benito Cereno?* What other forces censor speech in this story? Why does Melville draw so much attention to gaps in narratives and to characters who do not speak?

4. **Slavery and racism:** As the Reading to Write section of this chapter pointed out, early critics of *Benito Cereno* thought that the story was diminished because it did not grapple overtly with

the issue of slavery. Modern scholars, though, see slavery and racism as one of the novella's main themes, though they are divided as to what it says about slavery. Do you think that *Benito Cereno* can be read as a critique of slavery and racism?

An investigation of Melville's treatment of slavery and racism would refer to some of the themes already discussed. Clearly, the text does not give us a thorough glimpse into the lives of the slaves nor does the third-person narrator provide insight into the workings of their minds. Like Delano, readers must extrapolate from what they "see." Do the happenings on the *San Dominick* provide readers with any insight into the conditions of slavery? What techniques does Melville use to provide these insights? Consider the power relations on the ship. Who is master, and who is slave? Consider, too, the characterizations of Cereno, Delano, and Babo. Examine the language used in descriptions of the African characters. Does this language provide any evidence of racism? Explain. It is especially important to determine whose attitudes this language reflects. Does it reflect Melville's attitude, that of his narrator, or of Delano? You must think very explicitly about Melville's narrative techniques in order to answer these questions thoroughly. Similarly, you might think about the attitudes toward the Africans expressed in the deposition and in Babo's punishment. Why do you think Babo refuses to speak after he is captured? How might this be relevant to the treatment of slavery in the text? To adequately develop a paper on the text's treatment of slavery, consider some of the historical context discussed in the History and Context section of this chapter.

5. **The human capacity for evil:** The third paragraph of the text states that Captain Delano, because of his "undistrustful" nature, is not predisposed to see "malign evil in man." The narrator immediately questions the wisdom of such a tendency "in view of what humanity is capable." Consider *Benito Cereno* as a text about the nature of human evil.

While you could focus this topic in quite a few ways, you will need to consider character development. A fairly traditional reading of this text interprets Babo as an embodiment of primitive human evil. Do you think this is valid? Why or why not? Does such a reading leave Melville open to charges of racism? Do any of the white characters act according to evil or primitive impulses? Further, you might also consider whether the linkage of primitivism and evil is valid. In exploring the ambiguity of humanity's moral nature, you would do well to examine the color imagery in the work, especially the use of black, white, and gray. Further, it might be worthwhile to examine the use of animal imagery.

6. *Benito Cereno* **as an allegory of New World innocence:** If you consider the two ship captains, Captain Delano and Don Benito, as representatives of the "new world" of America and the "old world" of Europe, what does *Benito Cereno* assert about America and its place in the world order in the 19th century?

An essay on this topic should consider some of the shaping myths of American culture, including the belief in new world innocence, in an American culture that would break from the traditions and the corruptions of Europe. How might you read Delano as a new world "innocent"? Consider, too, how Delano is particularly American in his attitudes, beliefs, and his worldview. What particularly American values does he represent? Remember that in 1855, when *Benito Cereno* was being serialized in *Putnam's Monthly*, America was drifting toward the Civil War. You should also analyze Delano's attitudes about and his responses to Don Benito and Babo. Examining the imagery associated with both characters might prove helpful, too. (And you should think about whether the imagery is linked to Delano's perspective or to the narrator's.) Still further, consider the role that the Africans (particularly Babo) and slavery play in this allegory. You might also examine the *San Dominick*'s figurehead and the chalked phrase underneath it. How might these be significant for such an allegorical reading of the text?

Character

The title of the novella, *Benito Cereno,* seems to indicate that the work is a character study of the Spanish captain. But readers soon find that they learn far less about Cereno than they do about Delano. In fact, while Cereno is the object of Delano's study, Delano quickly becomes the focus of readers' scrutiny. You could craft an effective paper about any of the three major characters in the text—Delano, Cereno, and Babo. Additionally, even Atufal, who makes relatively few appearances in the text, could serve as an effective topic for a paper. As a result of Melville's narrative techniques, though, you must be careful in your assessment of characters. Be sure to discern and analyze the particular point of view that provides individual glimpses of the characters. It is important that you know when particular images or insinuations about characters are filtered through Delano's consciousness. At other points, readers seem to hear the opinions of the third-person narrator. Whose perception are you witness to? Sometimes this can be a hard question to answer, yet analyzing the characters in *Benito Cereno* can help you to develop thoughtful papers about characterization and its relation to some of the story's themes.

Sample Topics:

1. **Captain Delano:** The American captain spends a good deal of the text metaphorically "in the dark" about the "real nature" of the events that play out before him. As Babo jumps into Delano's boat at the end of the novella, the narrator remarks, "[t]hat moment, across the long-benighted mind of Captain Delano, a flash of revelation swept, illuminating in unanticipated clearness his host's whole mysterious demeanor, with every enigmatic event of the day, as well as the entire past voyage of the *San Dominick.*" By the end of the novel, do you agree that Delano has experienced revelation and illumination?

   An essay on this topic would have to examine the ending of the text—the deposition and the conversation between the two captains—in order to evaluate what the American captain learns.

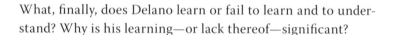

What, finally, does Delano learn or fail to learn and to understand? Why is his learning—or lack thereof—significant?

2. **Benito Cereno:** Don Benito seems never to recover from his experiences on the *San Dominick*. In the final conversation between the two captains, Delano urges the Spaniard to "forget" the past and he asks, "What has cast such a shadow on you." Cereno's response is short and provocative: "The negro." Why is Don Benito unable to recover from his experiences? What does he mean by his reply to Delano's question?

As with the previous question about Delano, an essay about Cereno would have to examine the final passages of the novella in detail. Consider whether Cereno learns anything through his experiences with the slave revolt. What does he mean when he tells Delano that "the negro" has cast a shadow on him? Still further, you might consider the significance of Cereno's silences at the end of the text. How are they different from his earlier silences and the gaps in his story? Why are there topics about which he refuses to speak? You might also think about the meaning of the story's last paragraph, with its concluding words, "Benito Cereno, borne on the bier, did, indeed, follow his leader." What insight does this line provide into Cereno's experiences?

3. **Babo:** In the final conversation between Delano and Cereno, the Spanish captain remarks on how profoundly Delano misjudged him, concluding, "So far may even the best man err, in judging the conduct of one with the recesses of whose condition he is not acquainted." How does this comment serve as a key to understanding Babo and his role in *Benito Cereno*?

Perhaps the most fundamental issue you would need to think about is how much Cereno, Delano, and the reader learn about Babo. Think about each of the two ship captains. What does each know of Babo's identity, his experiences, and his "condition"? Similarly, how much does the reader actually learn about Babo? Thinking about speech and silence would probably be helpful here. We hear Babo's voice frequently during the elaborate ruse on the ship, but after his capture, he refuses to speak. What do we learn about him through his dialogue and through his silences? You will probably also find it useful to examine the imagery associated with Babo throughout the text. Consider whose perspective this imagery represents. Examine the novella's concluding paragraph carefully. Does the final image of Babo's head provide any insight into Babo's character and/or his role in Melville's work? Why does Melville choose this final image? What relevance does it have for any of the story's themes?

4. **Atufal:** Examine the symbolic value of the character of Atufal in *Benito Cereno.* What does he represent?

There are a number of important points to consider in response to this question, and, obviously, the theme of slavery has particular relevance. To begin, you should think about the very image of Atufal appearing in chains. Beyond this, analyze this image in relation to the fact that these appearances are part of the "performance" staged by Babo and Atufal. Why would Babo and Atufal have planned this particular ritual for Delano's viewing? Similarly, the imagery of the lock and the key should prove suggestive.

History and Context

Benito Cereno was inspired by historical events and texts, and, because of Melville's narrative technique, parts of the text seem to masquerade as history. Knowing something of American attitudes toward slavery in the 1850s and knowing about the slave revolts that happened aboard the ships *Amistad* and *Creole* should prove helpful to any study of the novella. Beyond that, these historical sources and the relationship between Melville's fiction and true events can provide some particularly interesting topics. Remember, though, that your project is to understand and illuminate the text, not just report on the historical events that lay behind it. Effective papers dealing with the history and context of *Benito Cereno* should draw conclusions about the work based on a study of its context.

Sample Topics:

1. **Amasa Delano's *A Narrative of Voyages and Travels* . . . :**
   Scholars have long noted that Melville used one chapter from
   Captain Amasa Delano's 1817 work, *A Narrative of Voyages and
   Travels, in the Northern and Southern Hemispheres: Compris-
   ing Three Voyages Round the World, Together with a Voyage
   of Survey and Discovery in the Pacific Ocean and the Oriental
   Islands* as a source for *Benito Cereno.* How does an examination
   of chapter 18 of Amasa Delano's narrative help to shed light on
   Melville's themes and purposes?

   Chapter 18 of Amasa Delano's *Narrative* is reproduced in the
   Bedford College Edition of *Benito Cereno,* and Lea Newman's *A
   Reader's Guide to the Short Stories of Herman Melville* should
   prove helpful to your analysis of the text, as should the California Polytechnic State University site "Herman Melville's
   Benito Cereno." Comparing the historical Delano's account of
   the events with Melville's fictional account should prove interesting. Look for any changes that Melville makes. Examine his
   changes in characters, setting, names, and action. What are the
   effects of these changes? How do they help develop his themes
   and/or purposes?

2. **The slave revolts on the *Amistad* and the *Creole*:** There is good
   reason to believe that Melville used other historical events to
   help him shape *Benito Cereno.* In the 1840s, there were highly
   publicized insurrections aboard two slave ships, the *Amistad*
   and the *Creole.* How does an understanding of these revolts,
   along with an awareness that Melville's reading public was probably quite familiar with them, provide insight into Melville's
   purposes in *Benito Cereno*?

   The connection between *Benito Cereno* and the *Amistad* incident has received a good deal of attention, and there are a
   number of sources in the bibliography at the end of this chapter that can provide good background on both the events on
   board the ship and what happened in the wake of these events.

See, for example, Karcher's "Riddle of the Spinx" (in Burkholder's *Critical Essays on Melville's "Benito Cereno"*), Osagie, and Sale (who also discusses the *Creole*). You might also explore Mystic Seaport's Web page entitled Exploring *Amistad* at Mystic Seaport, which includes an article by Mary K. Bercaw Edwards that examines the connections between the *Amistad* and *Benito Cereno*. The case of the *Amistad* is particularly relevant because of the legal case that it spawned. You might think of the legal deposition at the end of *Benito Cereno* in light of this history. Many modern readers are particularly aware of the *Amistad* because of Steven Spielberg's 1997 film *Amistad*. While you should not depend on the film's complete historical accuracy, you may find that viewing it lends a good deal of immediacy and interest to the historical events it presents.

3. **The slavery debate in antebellum America:** How does an awareness of the debate about slavery that took place in antebellum America provide insight into Melville's ideas in *Benito Cereno*?

Besides the events on the *Amistad* and the *Creole*, the growing debate over slavery in America provides a very important context for *Benito Cereno*. The year 1850 saw the passage of the Fugitive Slave Law. Melville's own father-in-law, Justice Lemuel Shaw, though he was resolutely opposed to slavery, presided over the Sims case in 1851 and ruled that Thomas Sims should be returned to slavery. And, as Melville's biographer Andrew Delbanco writes, "By the 1850s, pro- and anti-slavery polemics had become fierce and frequent," and there were growing fears of slave rebellion. Additionally, Melville wrote *Benito Cereno* in the wake of such antislavery texts as Harriet Beecher Stowe's *Uncle Tom's Cabin* and Frederick Douglass's *Narrative of the Life of Frederick Douglass, an American Slave*. Numerous sources in the bibliography at the end of this chapter, including Delbanco and Yellin, should help provide historical context on the slavery debate. Consider whether this background causes you to read Melville's text as a critique of slavery or as a work that fed fears of slave violence and revolt.

4. ***Putnam's Magazine****:* Just as modern-day magazines frequently have identifiable political leanings, so, too, did those published in Melville's time. *Benito Cereno* was serialized in *Putnam's Monthly Magazine* in November and December 1855. How does *Putnam's Magazine* provide context for understanding the ideas expressed in *Benito Cereno*?

You can browse through, read, and search the 1853, 1854, and 1855 issues of *Putnam's* (along with later issues) online at Cornell University's Making of America Web site. A thorough examination of these issues should allow you to draw conclusions about *Putnam's* perspective on political issues of the day, including the question of slavery. It should be fruitful to examine *Benito Cereno* as a political statement based on its publication context.

Form and Genre

Apparently, many early readers relished *Benito Cereno* as a kind of mystery story. They were anxious to read the "clues" in the text in order to solve the mystery of the *San Dominick*. Clearly, the dreamlike atmosphere of Melville's work, coupled with the fairly apparent indications that all is not as it seems, provide a basis for classifying *Benito Cereno* this way. And yet, attentive readers are often quick to decipher the true situation aboard the ship, and analysis of Melville's narrative style indicates that this was his intent. Readers should, in fact, figure out the puzzle long before Delano does. Melville's narrative style helps to draw readers' attention away from Cereno, the object of Delano's study and the title character, turning their attention instead toward Delano himself. Through reflective analysis of the American captain, readers are led to some of the most important themes of the text. Thoughtful examination of Melville's methods and techniques can, consequently, provide effective focuses for papers on *Benito Cereno*.

Sample Topics:

1. **Narration and point of view:** As the Reading to Write section of this chapter indicated, Melville employs a complicated narrative style in *Benito Cereno*. While the story is told by a third-person narrator, the narrator's perspective often seems to

merge with Delano's, showing or telling us only what Delano sees. Why would Melville have chosen such a complicated narrative style to tell this story to his particular audience?

This question relates to the previous topic about "perceiving and understanding." You will need to evaluate Delano's powers as an observer and an interpreter, but this question also asks you to think more pointedly about the difference between the reader's interpretation and Delano's. Consider the irony that this difference in perception creates. Given what you know of the historical situations that this text is rooted in, why would Melville want the readers of *Putnam's* to focus more on Delano and his "intellectual perception" than on the title character, Cereno? Are there qualities that Melville's audience might share with Delano?

2. **Narrative structure and history:** Why does Melville rely so heavily on historical narratives in his construction of *Benito Cereno,* and why does he interrupt the dramatic tension of his story line by appending the deposition and the conversation between the captains to the logical conclusion of the narrative of Delano's experiences on the *San Dominick*? Consider the structure of *Benito Cereno* as a commentary on the way that history is constructed.

The previous discussion of storytelling relates to this question, though this topic asks you to focus more specifically on the construction of history. By the end of Melville's narrative, the reader has read a few different versions of the *San Dominick*'s history. Does one version seem more "truthful" or more complete than the others? Which is likely to be recorded as a historical account of the event? Why? How might a consideration of these issues lead you to an exploration of issues of power and morality? What relation does this issue have to the questions of law that might arise as a result of Melville's inclusion of the deposition in the story?

3. ***Benito Cereno* as a gothic narrative:** Scholars have long commented on the nightmarish, unreal feel to this text. How might
   you read *Benito Cereno* as a gothic text?

   Melville borrows quite a few images and themes from the
   gothic tradition—the language of dream, enchantment, death,
   decay, sleepwalking, and madness. Even the early comparison of the *San Dominick* to a monastery echoes the setting of
   many gothic novels. Perhaps the most fruitful way to develop
   a paper on this topic would be to research the methods and
   aims of gothic fiction in the 18th and 19th centuries and decide
   whether *Benito Cereno* shares more with the gothic tradition
   than just imagery and setting.

Language, Symbols, and Imagery

Benito Cereno is rife with provocative images. Melville develops patterns
of imagery—such as the gothic imagery of death and decay or the color
imagery of black and white—and he sometimes uses singular, striking
images. Both the patterns of imagery and the more isolated images can
provide effective lenses though which to view his themes, characters,
and his purposes. If you choose to write about Melville's use of imagery,
you should go back over the text and pay particular attention to the repetition of the language or imagery that you find compelling. Think about
how this imagery functions, and consider its relevance to issues of theme
or character.

1. **Color imagery:** Examine Melville's use of color imagery in
   Benito Cereno, particularly his use of black, white, and gray.
   How is this imagery tied to the novella's major themes? How
   does it help to develop his ideas?

   The Reading to Write section discussed the use of the color
   gray in the third paragraph of *Benito Cereno,* and it noted
   its connection to issues of morality. Do you think that Melville uses the imagery of black and white in ways traditional to
   Western culture, where black signifies evil and white signifies

goodness or purity? How does his use of gray support or complicate an analysis of the black and white imagery in the text? How does this imagery function in a text primarily about a struggle between white men and black men?

2. **Animal imagery:** Animal imagery pervades *Benito Cereno.* What is Melville saying about human nature through his use of this imagery?

In order to shape an essay on Melville's use of animal imagery, you will need to identify any patterns in the use of this imagery. Is this language frequently used to describe characters? Which characters are described through this language? Further, consider the connotations associated with certain animals. Comparing someone to a fox is certainly different from describing him through references to a dog or to a bear. Are the connotations of the animal imagery consistent throughout the story? If not, when does the imagery change? Why? You must also consider whose point of view the imagery reflects. Are particular usages reflective of the narrator's thinking? Of Delano's perspective? Of Cereno's or Babo's? What do these references tell us about the particular consciousness to which they are linked?

3. **The "shield-like stern-piece" of the *San Dominick:*** As Delano observes the strange ship that approaches the *Bachelor's Delight,* the narrative notes the "shield-like stern-piece" of the ship. How is this stern-piece emblematic of the novella and its themes?

In order to develop a paper on this topic, be alert to the way this one image incorporates the imagery and the themes that are prevalent throughout the novella (and it incorporates quite a few). Similarly, you will need to consider both the significance and the repetition of this image at other points in the narrative.

4. **The figurehead of the *San Dominick* and the chalked sentence, "Follow your leader":** What is the relevance of the ship's

figurehead and the sentence "Follow your leader," that is written in chalk below it?

You might begin by remembering that the "figure-head" (or the skeleton that has replaced it) is covered throughout most of the text. How is this fact alone reflective of the story's themes? You must consider Babo's original purpose in affixing Aranda's skeleton to the ship's beak and think about the revelation of the skeleton during the narration. Analyze the significance of the skeleton and the figure that it replaced. Think, too, about its connection to other patterns of imagery throughout *Benito Cereno.* How does the figurehead help to develop the story's themes? Are there other images in the story that seem to echo or reflect this image? You might also consider the significance and the repetition of the phrase "Follow your leader" in some detail. Is there any ambivalence in the meaning of that sentence? Why does Melville use a modified version of that sentence as the closing words of the novella? What do they mean in this final context, and how are they tied to the image of Aranda's skeleton?

5. **The knot:** Write a paper analyzing the knot that the old sailor throws to Delano during his time on the *San Dominick.* How does it serve as a metaphor for *Benito Cereno*?

The narrator very clearly compares the knot to Delano's thought process, though there are a number of other, more productive ways to analyze the knot as a metaphor. You might find it most relevant to questions of narrative style, narrative structure, and storytelling. Think about the knot in relation to the reader's task as well as to Delano's task.

6. **Keys and locks:** Images of keys and locks also figure prominently in *Benito Cereno.* How is Melville using them? How do they reflect the text's themes and purposes?

Quite clearly, keys and locks are particularly relevant to the theme of slavery. Interestingly, though, you might also find it

fruitful to analyze this imagery in relation to questions of storytelling, truth, and understanding.

7. **Religious imagery:** Early in the narrative, Delano compares the
San Dominick to a monastery. Trace the use of religious imag-
ery in *Benito Cereno*. How would you characterize this imagery?
How is it relevant to the story's major themes?

In order to write a response to this question, you will need
to think about any patterns in the novella's use of religious
imagery. Is the imagery applied to anyone or anything in particular? Is the imagery associated with any particular religion?
Why might this be relevant? To whose perspective is that
imagery linked? Can your analysis of this imagery tell you
anything about the attitudes or perspectives of the character
that is linked to that imagery? You might also consider the
importance of the name of the slave ship, the *San Dominick*.

Compare and Contrast Essays

Benito Cereno should provide you with plenty of material for compare
and contrast papers. You might choose to compare elements within this
text, such as the two captains, or you might wish to compare themes and
characters in this work with those in another of Melville's work. Given
the text's concern with slavery, you might also find it fruitful to examine
it in relation to other 19th-century texts that comment on the institution of slavery. Whichever approach you take, remember that your thesis
should make a clear, specific point about the relevance or the significance
of the comparisons you draw. An effective compare and contrast paper
does much more than just point out similarities and differences. Remember, you need to tell your readers why your comparisons are significant.

Sample Topics:

1. **Delano and Benito Cereno:** Write a paper that compares the
two ship captains in *Benito Cereno*. How are they alike? How are
they different? Why would Melville invite a comparison of these
two characters? How does such a comparison work to support
or develop the work's themes and concerns?

The contrasts between Delano and Don Benito are clearly more evident and striking, and your paper should work to evaluate the significance of these differences. At the same time, you would do well to remember that both are captains and both of their lives are at stake on the *San Dominick* (though Delano is apparently unaware of the latter fact). Any effective paper on this topic needs to take into account the conversation that takes place between the two men at the end of the novella. Similarly, you may find it helpful to think about Babo's relation to each man. What do their relations to and attitudes toward Babo tell us about these two characters, their similarities and their differences?

2. **Slavery:** *Benito Cereno* was published during a time of heated debate about the institution of slavery in America. Examine this text in light of other 19th-century literary treatments of slavery.

   Stowe's *Uncle Tom's Cabin* and Douglass's *Narrative of the Life of Frederick Douglass, an American Slave* provide two possibilities for comparison. Some scholars have suggested that each of these influenced Melville and his ideas in *Benito Cereno*. Published after *Benito Cereno*, Harriet Jacobs's *Incidents in the Life of a Slave Girl* might also prove a good choice. In focusing your paper, you should think carefully about the statements your chosen texts make about slavery and their methods of communicating these ideas. If you work with Jacobs or Douglass, you should also consider questions of genre. Finally, keeping in mind the intended audiences of your texts might prove useful in a comparison of the authors' literary techniques and strategies.

3. **Charity:** Examine the theme of charity in *Benito Cereno* and "Bartleby, the Scrivener." What attitude do these works express about motivations and the value of charity?

   The narrator of "Bartleby" takes up the theme of charity quite often, and he sees himself as benevolent and charitable in his dealings with his employees. How do his beliefs about charity and his charitable impulses compare to those of Delano? You might want to think about what motivates the charity of each of these men. How effective are their charitable efforts?

4. **Babo and Bartleby:** By the end of their stories, both Bartleby and Babo refuse to speak. Compare the silence of Babo and Bartleby. What is the significance of the silence of each of these characters? Why do you think that each finally chooses not to speak?

   In order to address this question you should remember that each character chooses silence, and you should speculate about the reasons for this choice. Further, you might question whether Babo and Bartleby, in many ways so different, share any other characteristics or concerns. Despite their obvious differences, there is much that these two share.

5. **Imagery of illness:** *Benito Cereno* is filled with suggestions and images of illness. Examine Melville's treatment of the theme of illness in this and another of his works. What does the author say through his use of this theme? How does it connect to other thematic concerns in his works?

   Perplexed and offended by the Spainish captain's erratic behavior, Delano speculates that Cereno suffers from both physical and mental illness. In this, he could be fruitfully compared to the narrator of "Bartleby, the Scrivener" and his employees who view Bartleby as "luny." Additionally, the abundant imagery of decay and death in *Benito Cereno* might prove useful to you in a paper on this topic. "The Paradise of Bachelors and the Tartarus of Maids" and *Moby-Dick* could also work well in a compare and contrast paper on the theme of illness.

   If you would like to move beyond Melville's own work, you could also craft a strong paper comparing Melville's use of this theme to Nathaniel Hawthorne's imagery of illness.

Hawthorne was a strong influence on Melville, and the two men developed a close friendship. "My Kinsman, Major Molineux," which also explores the theme of revolt, would provide an excellent source for comparison in a paper about the imagery of illness.

6. **Melville's bachelors:** Melville named Captain Delano's ship *The Bachelor's Delight,* and the name connects Delano to the other bachelors in the author's work. What qualities does the American captain share with the other bachelors that figure prominently in Melville's work? Why do you think Melville ascribes these particular qualities to bachelors?

Perhaps the most likely candidates for this question are the numerous bachelors that appear in "The Paradise of Bachelors and the Tartarus of Maids." The qualities of the bachelors are one of the chief focuses of that work. Similarly, you might also draw comparisons between the narrator of "Bartleby, the Scrivener" and Delano. Examining the connections between these bachelor characters and the other characters with whom they interact should help you to develop a strong focus for this paper.

Bibliography and Online Resources for *Benito Cereno*

Amistad. Dir. Steven Speilberg. DreamWorks, 1997.

Barber, Benjamin. *Fear's Empire: War, Terrorism and Democracy.* New York: Norton, 2003.

Bickley, R. Bruce. *The Method of Melville's Short Fiction.* Durham, NC: Duke UP, 1975.

Bloom, Harold. *Herman Melville's* Billy Budd, *"Benito Cereno," "Bartleby, the Scrivener," and Other Tales.* New York: Chelsea House, 1987.

Bryant, John, ed. *A Companion to Melville Studies.* New York: Greenwood, 1986.

Bryant, John, and Robert Milder, eds. *Melville's Evermoving Dawn.* Kent, OH: Kent State UP, 1997.

Burkholder, Robert E. *Critical Essays on Herman Melville's "Benito Cereno."* New York: G. K. Hall: 1992.

Cassuto, Leonard. *The Inhuman Race: The Racial Grotesque in American Literature and Culture.* New York: Columbia UP, 2006.

Coffler, Gail. *Melville's Allusions to Religion: A Comprehensive Index and Glossary.* New York: Praeger, 2004.

Delbanco, Andrew. *Melville: His World and His Work.* New York: Knopf, 2005.

Edwards, Mary K. Bercaw. "The *Amistad Incident*: A Source of Herman Melville's *Benito Cereno* or Not?" "Exploring Amistad at Mystic Seaport." Mystic Seaport: The Museum of America and the Sea. Available online. URL: http://amistad.mysticseaport.org/discovery/themes/bercaw.benito.cereno.html. Downloaded June 1, 2007.

"Exploring *Amistad* at Mystic Seaport." Mystic Seaport: The Museum of America and the Sea. Available online. URL: http://amistad.mysticseaport.org/main/overview.html. June 1, 2007.

Fisher, Marvin. *Going Under: Melville's Short Fiction and the American 1850s.* Baton Rouge: Louisiana State UP, 1977.

Fogle, Richard Harter. *Melville's Shorter Tales.* Norman: U of Oklahoma P, 1960.

Franchot, Jenny. *Roads to Rome: The Antebellum Protestant Encounter with Catholicism.* Berkeley: U of California P, 1994.

Franklin, H. Bruce. "Slavery and Empire: 'Benito Cereno," *Melville's Evermoving Dawn.* Eds. John Bryant and Robert Milder. Kent, OH: Kent State UP, 1997. 147–161.

Gross, Seymour L. *A Benito Cereno Handbook.* Belmont, CA: Wadsworth, 1965.

Gunn, Giles. *A Historical Guide to Herman Melville.* Oxford: Oxford UP, 2005.

Hayes, Kevin J. *Melville's Folk Roots.* Kent, OH: Kent State UP, 1999.

Hayford, Harrison, and Hershel Parker. *Melville's Prisoners.* Evanston, IL: Northwestern UP, 2003.

"Herman Melville's *Benito Cereno.*" California Polytechnic State University. Available online. URL: http://cla.calpoly.edu/~jbattenb/benitocereno/home-bc.htm. Downloaded June 1, 2007.

Karcher, Carolyn. *Shadow Over the Promised Land: Slavery, Race and Violence in Melville's America.* Baton Rouge: Louisiana State UP, 1980.

———. "The Riddle of the Sphinx: Melville's 'Benito Cereno' and the *Amistad* Case." *Critical Essays on Herman Melville's "Benito Cereno."* Ed. Robert E. Burkholder. New York: G. K. Hall, 1992. 196–229.

Kavanagh, James H. "That Hive of Subtlety: 'Benito Cereno' and the Liberal Hero." *Ideology and Classic American Literature.* Ed. Sacvan Bercovitch and Myra Jehlen. Cambridge: Cambridge UP, 1986. 352–383.

Kelley, Wyn. *A Companion to Herman Melville.* Oxford: Blackwell, 2006.

Levine, Robert S. *The Cambridge Companion to Herman Melville.* Cambridge: Cambridge UP, 1998.

———. *Conspiracy and Romance: Studies in Brockden Brown, Cooper, Hawthorne, and Melville.* New York: Cambridge UP, 1989.

The Life and Works of Herman Melville. Available online. URL: http://www.melville.org/melville.htm#Whois. Downloaded May 17, 2007.

The Making of America. Cornell University. Available online. URL: http://cdl.library.cornell.edu/moa. Downloaded June 1, 2007.

Martin, Robert K. *Hero, Captain, and Stranger: Male Friendship, Social Critiques and Literary Form in the Novels of Herman Melville.* Chapel Hill: U of North Carolina P, 1986.

Matthiessen, F. O. *American Renaissance: Art and Expression in the Age of Emerson and Whitman.* New York: Oxford UP, 1941.

Melville, Herman. *Benito Cereno.* Bedford College Editons. Ed. Wyn Kelley. New York: Bedford/St. Martin's, 2008.

Newman, Lea Bertani Vozar. *A Reader's Guide to the Short Stories of Herman Melville.* Boston: Hall, 1986.

Osagie, Iyunolu Folayan. *The* Amistad *Revolt: Memory, Slavery, and the Politics of Identity in the United States and Sierra Leone.* Athens: U of Georgia P, 2000.

Otter, Samuel. *Melville's Anatomies: Bodies, Discourse, and Ideology in Antebellum America.* Berkeley: U of California P, 1998.

Parker, Hershel. *Herman Melville.* 2 vols. Baltimore: Johns Hopkins UP, 1996, 2002.

Post-Lauria, Sheila. *Correspondent Colorings: Melville in the Marketplace.* Amherst: U of Massachusetts P, 1996.

Rogin, Michael Paul. *Subversive Genealogy: The Politics and Art of Herman Melville.* New York: Knopf, 1983.

Sale, Maggie Montesinos. *The Slumbering Volcano: American Slave Ship Revolts and the Production of Rebellious Masculinity.* Durham, NC: Duke UP, 1997.

Sandborn, Geoffrey. *The Sign of the Cannibal: Melville and the Making of a Postcolonial Reader.* Durham, NC: Duke UP, 1998.

Stuckey, Sterling. *Going through the Storm: The Influence of African American Art in History.* New York: Oxford UP, 1994.

Sundquist, Eric. *To Wake Nations: Race in the Making of American Literature.* Cambridge: Belknap P of Harvard UP, 1993.

———. "*Benito Cereno* and New World Slavery." *Reconstructing American Literary History.* Ed. Sacvan Bercovitch. Cambridge: Harvard UP, 1986. 146–167.

Wallace, Robert K. *Douglass and Melville: Anchored Together in Neighborly Style.* New York: Spinner, 2005.

Yellin, Jean Fagan. *The Intricate Knot: Black Figures in American Literature, 1776–1863.* New York: New York UP, 1972.

BATTLE-PIECES

READING TO WRITE

MELVILLE TURNED to poetry later in his life. After the commercial failure of his novel *The Confidence Man: His Masquerade* in 1857, he traveled through Europe and the Holy Land. Upon his return to the United States, he embarked on a lecture tour, speaking about the art-work he had seen abroad. It seems clear that Melville was writing poetry during his travels around the United States, though his first published volume of poetry, *Battle-Pieces and Aspects of the War*, did not appear until 1866. While the American Civil War constitutes the major focus of the volume, Melville's brief prose preface to the volume, along with the prose supplement that functions as a kind of afterword, provides insight into the volume's purposes and concerns. In the preface, Melville states that most of the "pieces" in the collection "originated in an impulse imparted by the fall of Richmond." In other words, they originated in the waning days of the war. (Richmond fell on April 3, 1865.) And though he claimed that the poems "were composed without reference to collective arrangement," he found in retrospect that they "naturally fall into the order assumed." Many—though not all—of the poems comment upon specific battles, events, or personages, and Melville ordered the volume chronologically. The retrospective nature of both the composition of the poetry and the arrangement of the collection suggest that although Melville's subject was the war, his interest in the volume was more forward-looking. The supplement to the volume seems to confirm this suspicion. "It is more than a year since the memorable surrender, but events have not yet rounded themselves into completion," he notes, and the rest of the supplement concerns the country's future. Writing about slavery, he notes, "for the future of the freed slaves we may well be concerned; but the future of the whole country, involving the future of the blacks, urges a paramount claim upon our anxiety." The effect of the Civil War upon the nation and the prospects for reunification, then, seem not only the paramount anxiety of the supplement but also of the poetry. The whole of the volume registers anxiety about the state of the nation, and that sense of anxiety reverberates even in the poems that begin the volume.

Consider how fundamental this anxiety is to the second poem of the collection, "Misgivings." This short piece is often considered one of the introductory poems of the volume:

> **Misgivings**
> **(1860)**
> When ocean-clouds over inland hills
> Sweep storming in late autumn brown,
> And horror the sodden valley fills,
> And the spire falls crashing in the town,
> I muse upon my country's ills—
> The tempest bursting from the waste of Time
> On the world's fairest hope linked with man's foulest crime.
> Nature's dark side is heeded now—
> (Ah! Optimist-cheer disheartened flown)—
> A child may read the moody brow
> Of yon black mountain lone.
> With shouts the torrents down the gorges go,
> And storms are formed behind the storm we feel:
> The hemlock shakes in the rafters, the oak in the driving keel.

"Misgivings" bears the date 1860, so it is set before the advent of the war. To analyze the poem's purposes, you should first make sense of its literal meaning; note that the first stanza comprises just one sentence. The subject of that sentence, "I," does not appear until the fifth line. This line, "I muse upon my country's ills—" also provides the focus of the poem: "my country's ills." A dependent clause opens the sentence, introducing the event that spurs the poet's meditation, a storm. And yet, an alert reader will take note of Melville's diction. Melville first mentions the clouds rather than the storm that they betoken. Further, the contrast between the "*ocean* clouds" and the "*inland* hills" that they threaten emphasizes the disparate nature of these two elements. The ocean realm seems to intrude upon dry land. Further, the poet's words seems convoluted in the next line, which keeps the reader's focus on the clouds. Rather than focusing on the storm and indicating that it "sweeps" onto land, Melville's rather convoluted diction insists that the clouds "sweep storming" over the landscape. By centering on the clouds in these opening lines, Melville creates a sense of anticipation, for often clouds signal a coming storm.

The third and fourth lines begin to chart the storm's effect. It brings fear and destruction. It fills the "sodden" valley with horror, and it brings the church spire "crashing" down. An alert reader will wonder at the specific image of destruction that Melville sketches in these lines. Is it significant that it is the church spire that crashes to the ground in the wake of the storm? Does the poet point toward a failure of faith, of religion, or of values through this image?

In the lines that follow, the speaker makes explicit the analogy between the ocean storm that motivates his meditation and the "country's ills" that are the subject of that meditation. These ills are a "tempest bursting from the waste of Time." This phrase should raise a few questions. First, you might wonder what the poet means by "the waste of Time," and still further, you might wonder why "Time" is capitalized. Certainly the "waste of Time" seems a reference to the past. Adding resonance to this reading, scholars have noted literary echoes in this image, citing both Shakespeare and Milton. Critic Robert Milder notes that the passage echoes Milton's description of Satan approaching Eden in *Paradise Lost,* who comes from "emptier waste, resembling air." Given this Miltonic echo, readers might wonder if Melville, working with a common conception of America, is figuring the country as a prelapsarian Eden. The next line of "Misgivings" encourages such a reading, for the tempest descends upon "the world's fairest hope linked with man's foulest crime." It seems that Melville figures the coming war as a fall from grace. This line also encourages you to explore "man's foulest crime." Does Melville refer to revolution, slavery, fratricide, or the coming fracture of the union? Still further, what is the relationship between tempest, "fairest hope," and "foulest crime"? Is there a causal relationship between the coming tempest and the crime?

The poet's contemplation of the country's ills continues in the second stanza, which begins, "Nature's dark side is heeded now." The passive phrasing of this line suggests that it is not just the speaker, but also the country as a whole that heeds "Nature's dark side." Is Melville suggesting that "man's foulest crime" is the outgrowth of "Nature's dark side"? Even readers unfamiliar with Melville's earlier works should wonder at the metaphysical import of this phrase. Is Melville painting a picture of an indifferent or a hostile universe? Readers familiar with *Moby-Dick* might think of Ahab's belief in the "dark hindoo half of nature." Is this suggestion of dark nature related to the fallen church spire of stanza one?

The poem ends, as it began, with images of storms, and once again the speaker's diction is almost painfully convoluted: "With shouts the torrents down the gorges go." Is this difficult diction purposeful? If so, what purpose does it serve? Like the concluding lines of the first stanza, the last two lines of this stanza consider the storm in relation to time. Instead of looking backward at the "waste of Time" as he had done in the first stanza, here the poet suggests that the nation will face a series of future storms: "And storms are formed behind the storm we feel." The final images of the poem suggest the destructive power of the ensuing storms, for in response "The hemlock shakes in the rafter, the oak in the driving keel." While describing hemlock and oak trees threatened by the violence of the storm, Melville also suggests the peril that the storm poses for humanity, for the structures of land and sea—the rafter of the house and the keel of the ship—are threatened by the tempest. Clearly, the future that Melville foresees in "Misgivings" is one in which the structures of American society are assaulted by "Nature's dark side." An alert reader who analyzes "Misgivings" closely will be prepared to read the other poems in *Battle-Pieces* with an eye toward many of Melville's themes, and the state of the American union should be the foremost among these.

TOPICS AND STRATEGIES

This section of the chapter provides you with broad topic ideas that should help you develop an essay on *Battle-Pieces*. Remember that these topics are just springboards for your own exploration; you will need to focus your analysis and develop your own specific thesis.

Themes

Since *Battle-Pieces* comprises numerous individual poems, you will find a multitude of themes that you could examine in a paper. Some of the more important themes—America, union, and war, for example—run throughout numerous poems in the volume. Other topics, though, such as time, could provide effective subjects for an essay on *Battle-Pieces*.

Sample Topics:

1. **America and democracy:** Though the most obvious topic of *Battle-Pieces* is the Civil War, the volume also demonstrates an interest in the relationship between the past and the present. One of Melville's interests was the effect of the war upon the future of America. In the supplement that concludes the volume, he writes, "The years of the war tried our devotion to the Union; the time of peace may test the sincerity of our faith in democracy." Examine *Battle-Pieces* as a work concerned with the identity of America and the role of democracy in American identity.

   Many of the poems in the volume prove to be forward-looking, concerned with America's future. "The Portent" and "Misgivings" provide a good starting place for this exploration, as do "The Conflict of Convictions" and "Apathy and Enthusiasm." You could also choose to examine "America," which uses a female figure to represent America and which charts the course of American history. "The Apparition" also shows an interest in the course of history. What does Melville argue is necessary for democracy to succeed? What should the country learn from the Civil War?

2. **Union and reunification:** In the prose supplement appended to *Battle-Pieces*, Melville shows how profoundly he is interested in the idea of the Union and in the work of reunification. He argues that, "It is enough, for all practical purposes, if the south have been taught by the terrors of civil war to feel that Secession, like Slavery, is against Destiny; that both now lie buried in one grave; that her fate is linked with ours; and that together we

comprise the Nation." Examine *Battle-Pieces* as a meditation on union and the difficulties of reunification.

One approach to this question would consider the idea of union and unity from a more abstract and philosophical perspective. Explore the poetry for images of fracture, disintegration, and dissolution. Look also for images of unity and healing. What does Melville say about these two disparate movements? What causes does he attribute to dissolution? What qualities are necessary for union and reunion?

You could also approach this question from a more political perspective and explore the importance of union for America. Why does Melville place such importance on the idea of union and nationhood? Why is succession against "Destiny"? Does he imply that America has a foreordained place and function?

3. **War:** While *Battle-Pieces* is clearly a contemplation of the Civil War and its effects on America, it is also a more abstract contemplation on war and its effects on humanity. What arguments does Melville make about war?

You might approach this question by considering Melville's references to other wars. "The Battle of Stone River, Tennessee," compares the war to the War of the Roses in Britain. Similarly, the volume makes numerous references to the French Revolution. Melville's clear reliance on John Milton's *Paradise Lost*, with its descriptions of the war in heaven, might also be relevant for your examination. Consider, too, Melville's treatment of soldiers and of scenes of battle. How graphic are his descriptions? Does he see war as glorious or noble? Why or why not?

4. **Law and civil authority:** In the prose supplement, Melville warns that the North should avoid "measures of dubious constitutional rightfulness." In "DuPont's Round Fight," he tells of a union victory brought about by right rule and the application of law. Examine Melville's treatment of law and civil authority in *Battle-Pieces.* Where does he contemplate the role of law?

What does he say, finally, about law and its role and position in American society?

You might find it helpful to read the prose supplement at the end of the volume carefully in order to gain a fuller understanding of Melville's philosophy about law and social order. A number of the poems near the end of the collection should prove fruitful for an investigation of this subject, including "Lee at the Capital" and "The Martyr." Similarly, you might think about what the opening poem, "The Portent," states about the law and its application.

5. **Slavery:** In modern popular consciousness, the American Civil War was fought over slavery, and yet slavery does not seem to be the focal point of Melville's volume. Indeed, in the supplement he states, "For the future of the freed slaves we may well be concerned; but the future of the whole country, involving the future of the blacks, urges a paramount claim on our anxiety." Examine *Battle-Pieces* as a commentary on slavery. Does the volume reflect Melville's statement in the supplement that slavery was "an athestical iniquity"?

You should examine the poetry for statements about slavery, and you should also look closely at Melville's portrayals of slaves and freed slaves. Similarly, images of blackness could also prove suggestive for your study. "Misgivings," "The Swamp Angel," and "Formerly a Slave" are among the poems that you might use in a paper on Melville's treatment of slavery.

6. **Time:** A concern with time—its pressures and its patterns—runs throughout *Battle-Pieces.* Melville composed most of *Battle-Pieces* in the wake of the Civil War. The poetry is retrospective, but Melville's concerns are largely for the future. Indeed, Melville states in his short preface that most of the works "were composed without reference to collective arrangement," but chronology became the ordering principle of the volume, and many of the poems note the dates of the historical events Melville describes. Examine Melville's treatment of time in *Battle-Pieces,* and draw

some conclusions about his philosophy and attitudes toward time or about his use of time in this work.

A paper on time in *Battle-Pieces* might take one of any number of approaches to this topic. You could focus on Melville's pre-occupation with the future. Despite the retrospective focus, he clearly indicates his concern with the future in the prose supplement at the end of the work. "It is more than a year since the memorable surrender," he says, "but events have not yet rounded themselves into completion." The rest of the supplement clearly demonstrates his fears for the future of the nation. Explore how that concern for the future of the nation is manifest in the poetry. How does the poetry show itself to be future oriented and not merely retrospective? Another approach is to explore Melville's treatment of history. In "The Conflict of Convictions," one of the introductory poems to *Battle-Pieces*, Melville writes, "The generations are inured to pains, / And strong Necessity / Surges, and heaps Time's strand with wrecks." Melville seems to fear that without resolution and reunification America could become another of the "wrecks" along "Time's strand." What does Melville say about history and its relation with the present time? Still another focus might be *Battle-Pieces'* concern with prophecy and prediction. The volume begins with a poem entitled "The Portent" and frequently considers the validity of portents, prophecy, and prediction.

7. **The Fall:** Early in "The Conflict of Convictions," Melville writes, "Return, return, O eager Hope,/ And face man's latter fall." Explore Melville's references to the Fall in *Battle-Pieces.* How and why does Melville see the Civil War as "man's latter fall"?

The volume is full of references to the Fall, and to explore this theme thoroughly, you would do well to consider the various myths of America that had shaped American identity until the Civil War. One such myth was the notion of America as an Eden, a promised land. Think about the metaphorical possibilities of such a myth. To antebellum Americans, what aspects of their country were Edenic? According to Melville, how does the war destroy these Edenic ideals? A related theme, the movement from innocence to experience, is also worth exploring. How does Melville portray innocence in *Battle-Pieces*? Who, or what, is associated with innocence? Conversely, how does Melville portray experience? Adam and Eve fell when they ate of the tree of knowledge. Does Melville see this "latter fall" as a result of knowledge? Explore and explain. Still further, you might consider whether the idea of the fortunate fall is a notion that Melville explores in this collection. Is America better off as a result of this fall from "innocence"? Why or why not?

8. **God, nature, and fate:** During the Civil War many Americans invoked their faith and their religion to assure themselves of the justness of their cause. Like Shakespeare's Henry V, they were assured that "God fought for us." And yet, the horrors and the devastation of the Civil War challenged the religious faith of many Americans. "The Conflict of Convictions," invoking Milton's *Paradise Lost,* seems to align the South with Satan, and clearly Melville saw the North's cause as a just one. Examine the worldview that he expresses in *Battle-Pieces.* Does the poetry portray a God who supports and guides the Northern cause? Explore and explain.

For this very broad topic, many, if not most, of the poems in the collection are potentially useful for your argument. You might, for example, choose to examine the plethora of biblical references in the text as well as the abundant Christ imagery. Consider how Melville employs these references. Is he consistent in his application? You may find that considering some of these references in relation to Milton's *Paradise Lost* lends more resonance to their use. Poems such as "The Swamp Angel" and "The Martyr" could provide potential starting places for such an examination, as could "Apathy and Enthusiasm" and "The Conflict of Convictions."

You could take a broader approach to this question, examining Melville's use of natural imagery and its relationship to God and God's plan. Is God manifest in nature (as such transcendentalists as Ralph Waldo Emerson claimed), or does Melville see nature as hostile or even indifferent to humanity and human struggles? Once again, many poems in the volume should prove fruitful for your investigation, and you would do well to limit your examination to just a few. Some potential starting places include "Misgivings," "The Conflict of Convictions," "Shiloh" (the name means "Peace with God"), "Apathy and Enthusiasm," "The Swamp Angel," "The March to the Sea," "A Scout Toward Aldie," and "Commemorative of a Naval Victory."

9. **Youth and age:** Melville's contemplation of the Civil War and its aftermath also allowed him to explore human nature, and in *Battle-Pieces* he presents a study of youth and old age. In "The March into Virginia" Melville argues, "All wars are boyish, and are fought by boys, / The champions and enthusiasts of the state." Explore Melville's treatment of youth and age in *Battle-Pieces*. What does he say about them and about the relationship between them?

In a response to this question, you may wish to focus particularly on his portraits of youth and youthfulness. That study, though, could be greatly enhanced by an examination of the relationship between youth and age. Clearly, this question asks you to explore questions of innocence and experience that were posed in the question about Melville's treatment of the Fall. Still further, you might note that "The March into Virginia" draws distinct connections between youthfulness, or boyishness, and war. What does he imply when he calls boys "The champions and enthusiasts of the state"? Analyze other poems in the collection that examine the relationship between youthfulness and war or youthfulness and "the state." Are the views expressed in this early poem consistent throughout the collection? Does Melville develop or modify this argument over the course of *Battle-Pieces*? "The College Colonel," "Apathy and Enthusiasm," "Commemorative of a Naval Victory," "On the Slain Collegians," and "In the Turret," are among the poems that may be useful to your study.

History and Context

While the Civil War battles and combatants provide obvious historical context for the whole of this volume, Melville's copious reading also provides contextual background. His use of Milton's *Paradise Lost* and *The Rebellion Record* could prove interesting foundations for strong papers on *Battle-Pieces.*

Sample Topics:

1. **Melville and Milton:** In one of the introductory poems in *Battle-Pieces,* "The Conflict of Convictions," Melville refers to the American Civil War as "man's latter fall." While he is clearly echoing Judeo-Christian mythology, he is also echoing *Paradise Lost.* Examine Melville's use of Milton's epic poem in *Battle-Pieces.* How and why does he rely on or echo Milton's treatment of the Fall? How does his use of the earlier work help to support or shape his ideas in *Battle-Pieces*?

   To address this question, you must be familiar with Milton and *Paradise Lost.* You might find it helpful to focus this question through thematic issues. For example, you could explore Melville's use of or reaction to Milton's treatment of Satan. Similarly, you might focus your paper through the larger theme of the Fall. No matter what your specific approach, you should try to draw some conclusions about how Melville uses Milton to advance some of his own ideological concerns in *Battle-Pieces.* To help develop your own argument about the text, you might also explore some scholarly works that examine Melville's dept to Milton.

2. **Melville's portraits of historical events and people:** Many of the poems in *Battle-Pieces* portray individual battles, events, and people. Choose one such event or person and, after some historical research, compare the portrait Melville draws to that which emerges from your research. Construct an argument about the significance of the differences you note between Melville's portrayal and the historical accounts. You may find it helpful, too, to consider how Melville focuses his portrait. In other words, while his portrait might reflect historical facts,

does he choose to focus on certain aspects of the person or the event? How and why are his choices significant?

This investigation is related to the question below about Melville's use of *The Rebellion Record,* and you might want to begin your historical research with that text. Melville's knowledge of the Civil War, though, was not limited to the information in *The Rebellion Record,* so your historical research for this question should go beyond that source. Read modern histories, too. Consider how Melville's choices about his poetic portrayal of historical events help to further his ideological agenda.

3. **Melville's use of *The Rebellion Record*:** Not an actual participant in battle, Melville drew a great deal from *The Rebellion Record,* which chronicled the war through newspaper and personal accounts. You can read *The Rebellion Record* online. Explore the text and consider it as Melville's source for the "facts" about individuals, battles, and other events. Draw conclusions about how Melville used the accounts he found in *The Rebellion Record.* Does Melville aim for a journalistic quality in his poetry, or does he shape the more journalistic aspects of *The Rebellion Record* for his own purposes?

Once again, you should base your examination on the ideological underpinnings of *Battle-Pieces.* Does Melville make an argument about the Civil War, the process of Reconstruction, or about war in general through his poetry? If so, how does his use of the sources provided in *The Rebellion Record* demonstrate or help to support your argument? Depending on the particular focus of your paper, you may find some of the questions posed in the section of this chapter on "Themes" helpful or suggestive. Also, consider whether the form of *Battle-Pieces* as a whole reflects the form of *The Rebellion Record.*

Philosophy and Ideas

One of the most consistent philosophical threads running through *Battle-Pieces* is Melville's concern with the ability of the written word to portray the experience of war. He returns to this issue throughout the volume, and these references may provide the building blocks of an interesting paper.

Sample Topics:

1. **Writing and portraying experience:** In a number of the poems in *Battle-Pieces,* Melville's subject seems to be his own art, for he explores the relationship between experience and its retelling. Choose some of the poems that comment on the relationship between experience and the retelling of that experience. What argument does Melville make about art's capacity to portray the reality of experience? How does he make that argument?

   You might focus on any number of poems to address this question. "A Utilitarian View of the *Monitor*'s Fight" and "DuPont's Round Fight" both make very overt—and quite different—arguments about the relationship between war and poetry, and either of these could form the focus of a strong paper. Other potential focuses include "Armies of the Wilderness" and "The March into Virginia."

Form and Genre

Melville's brief preface emphasizes the fragmentary nature of *Battle-Pieces.* The poems are "Pieces," composed individually, "without reference to collective arrangement." The poems present "aspects" that are "as manifold as are the moods of involuntary meditation." Despite the apparently fragmentary nature of the pieces, Melville states that they "naturally fall into the order assumed." This very tension, then, between fragmentary pieces and collective unit provides a starting place for papers examining questions of form and genre. You might analyze the coherence of the volume as a whole. Does Melville make any clear, consistent points or arguments over the course of the volume, or do his poems stand as unrelated fragments or pieces of the war? Issues of unity and coherence in this volume should provide interesting material for papers on form and genre.

Sample Topics:

1. **Unity:** Melville's brief prose introduction to *Battle-Pieces* claims, "With few exceptions, the Pieces in this volume originated in an

impulse imparted by the fall of Richmond. They were composed without reference to collective arrangement, but being brought together in review, naturally fall into the order assumed." Given this claim, do you believe that it is possible to examine and construct arguments about *Battle-Pieces* as a whole, or is this volume more correctly viewed as individual poetic units only loosely related because of their broad topic, the Civil War?

Clearly, the title of the volume, *Battle-Pieces and Aspects of the War,* emphasizes the fragmentary nature of the book, as does Melville's claim about the composition of the poems and his assertion that the "aspects which the strife as a memory assumes" are "manifold," "variable, and at times widely at variance." Yet his claim that the poems "naturally fall into the order assumed" attributes a coherent order to the collection. You might think about any ordering principles that hold the collection together. Clearly, Melville considered chronology as he put the work together. Further, he also claims some thematic coherence—"but a few themes have been taken" from the "events and incidents of the conflict." Scholars have argued for various unifying principles. Many take note of the particular appearance of the first edition, which used blank pages to separate certain groups of poems. Consequently, many readers see the first four—or five—poems as "introductory." Others explore thematic unity. William H. Shurr, for example, argues that *Battle-Pieces* is held together by two thematic cycles, which he calls "the cycle of law" and "the cycle of evil." You should consider these arguments as you make your own decisions about the work's coherence (or lack thereof).

2. **Voice:** Examine Melville's use of voice in *Battle-Pieces,* and draw some conclusions about how his use of voice affects the unity of the volume or how it reflects upon or develops one of the themes of the work.

In his prose introduction to *Battle-Pieces,* Melville states that the "aspects" of war to which the title refers "are as manifold as are the moods of involuntary meditation—moods variable, and at times widely at variance." Subsequently, the voices of the poems, like the moods of meditation, are variable. While some of the poems seem to emanate from distinct moods or attitudes, some, such as "Apathy and Enthusiasm," seem to make use of more than one distinct voice. Some critics have tried to identify distinct voices, or speakers, within the work. Robert Milder speaks of "two voices, those of the 'enthusiast' and the 'mediator,' that will coexist with the battle-pieces themselves." No matter how you choose to focus your paper, you will need to grapple with the variable moods and voices of the poems. Are there other elements of the poems, besides the "moods" or attitudes, that help to develop or suggest different speakers? Does language, tone, or diction have any bearing on your assessment of Melville's use of voice?

3. **Irony:** Many readers see irony as a driving force behind *Battle-Pieces*, and they argue that readers must recognize the irony in order to understand Melville's attitudes and purposes. Construct an argument about how and why Melville uses irony in *Battle-Pieces* to make a particular point about war, human nature, or the Union.

   In order to examine Melville's irony in *Battle-Pieces*, you must grapple with the issue of voice addressed above. Similarly, you should look for thematic tension within the collection and within individual works themselves. You may find it helpful to consider Melville's poetry in relation to the attitudes and the rhetoric about the Civil War that were common in Melville's time. How do Melville's language and his attitudes compare with these other commentaries on war? Is it possible to read his work as a reaction to some of his contemporaries' representations of and attitudes toward the war?

4. **Poetic form and meaning:** In "DuPont's Round Fight," Melville parallels the rules of war with the rules or laws of poetry: "In time and measure perfect moves / All Art whose aim is sure." If you understand elements of poetic structure, rhyme, meter, and diction, examine the interaction of structure and meaning in

Battle-Pieces. How does Melville use these elements to develop or enhance his ideas in *Battle-Pieces?*

This is a very broad topic that requires you to focus your approach. Since a topic like this requires you to work very closely with some of the more technical aspects of the poetry, you could easily focus an entire paper on just one or two poems. "DuPont's Round Fight" could prove a starting place, though the volume offers numerous possibilities.

Language, Symbols, and Imagery

Melville is known for the poetic qualities of his prose, and his poetry, written late in his life, uses many of the same images he employed throughout his career. His images of darkness, in particular, seem appropriate for his subject—war—and yet they also seem closely akin to imagery that Melville used years before in *Moby-Dick.* Symbols and images are the building blocks of poetry, and *Battle-Pieces* should provide you with plenty of potential topics on language, symbols, and imagery.

Sample Topics:

1. **Darkness:** In "Misgivings" Melville writes, "Nature's dark side is heeded now," invoking a familiar pattern of imagery, the contrast of darkness and light. Explore his use of dark and light throughout *Battle-Pieces* and construct an argument about how and why he uses this imagery.

   Numerous readers have noted that the imagery of darkness marks the prevailing tone and movement of the volume. In order to narrow your focus, you should begin by rereading and noting Melville's many uses of darkness. Think about how and why he is using this imagery. Clearly, in a volume written about—and in the wake of—the Civil War, this imagery hardly seems surprising or out of place. You should move beyond this realization, though. Note what Melville links to this darkness. What does the darkness represent? Why is the imagery of darkness so prevalent throughout this text, and what does this indicate about Melville's worldview? What does it suggest about his attitude toward the war, toward the North, toward the South, and toward the restored Union? Further, what is the relationship between darkness and light, and does that relationship remain consistent? How might your assessment of this relationship help to develop your argument about Melville's use of the imagery of darkness?

2. **Nature:** Examine the natural imagery in *Battle-Pieces*, then draw some conclusions about how and why Melville uses this imagery. Do his images of nature develop the thematic purposes in his work?

While there are many ways that you could shape a paper about Melville's use of natural imagery, one particularly intriguing approach might be to examine the way he renders the landscape. In his attempt to paint battle "pieces," and render "aspects" of the war, Melville often sketches verbal pictures of the American landscape. Some of these landscapes are part of his portraits of particular characters, events, and battles, and some are more abstract and seem to bespeak his ideology. The introductory poem, "The Portent," while re-creating John Brown's hanging, provides a brief glimpse of the landscape: "Gaunt the shadow on your green, / Shenandoah!" The beautiful and elegiac "Shiloh" focuses on the view of the battlefield of Shiloh, effectively sketching a kind of landscape. Melville provides many more glimpses of the American landscape throughout the collection, and you could construct a strong paper by analyzing Melville's portrait of that landscape.

Another more traditional way of approaching this topic would be to consider what Melville's presentation of nature says about his worldview, his philosophical beliefs about the nature of the universe. You might consider the natural imagery that Melville uses by analyzing the early poems in the volume—"The Portent," "Misgivings," and "Apathy and Enthusiasm." "Misgivings," especially, focuses on the natural world and seems to do so in order to delineate a specific worldview. Working from this poem's treatment of "The tempest bursting from the waste of Time," you might find it suggestive to trace the imagery of storms and tempests throughout *Battle-Pieces*.

"The Apparition" is just one of many poems that should prove useful in such an investigation. Conversely, you could choose to examine calmer, more pacific images of nature. "Shiloh," for instance, begins and ends with the images of swallows "skimming lightly" over the "hushed" fields. What do these more pacific images of nature suggest about Melville's worldview? Do they contradict his stormier views? Why or why not? In yet another approach, you might find that even in this poetry written in his latter years, Melville still turned to the imagery of the sea. This, too, might prove an interesting focus for a paper on his use of natural imagery.

3. **Language of industrialism:** Reread *Battle-Pieces* paying particular attention to Melville's use of mechanical imagery or the language of industrialism. Why does he use this imagery so frequently in a volume about the Civil War and its aftermath? How does it reflect his attitudes toward America and American values in his own time?

You may be surprised to discover just how prevalent this imagery is in *Battle-Pieces*, and it is particularly suggestive about Melville's attitudes toward war, toward humanity, and toward human attitudes about one another. As its title suggests, "A Utilitarian View of the *Monitor's* Fight" might provide a good starting place for your investigation, but there are numerous other poems that could help you develop a strong paper on this subject, including "The Swamp Angel," "DuPont's Round Fight," "The Temeraire," "At the Cannon's Mouth," and even the pastoral "Shiloh."

Compare and Contrast Essays

Battle-Pieces shares numerous concerns with Melville's fiction. *Billy Budd* provides a particularly rich text to mine for comparisons, for both works were written toward the end of Melville's career. Whatever your approach or topic, remember that your thesis should make a clear, specific point about the relevance or the significance of the comparisons you draw. An effective compare and contrast paper does much more than just point out similarities and differences. Remember, you need to tell your readers why your comparisons are significant.

Sample Topics:

1. **Law:** The first poem in *Battle-Pieces*, "The Portent," introduces the theme of law and justice in its opening lines: "Hanging from the beam, / Slowly swaying (such the law), Gaunt the shadow on your green, / Shenandoah!" One possible implication of this opening is that "the law" is responsible for casting the shadow of war upon the country. Melville's examination of law and justice continues throughout the collection. Compare his treatment of law in *Battle-Pieces* to his treatment of the law in another text.

   Billy Budd presents one of the most suggestive possibilities for a paper on Melville and the law. Like *Battle-Pieces*, it was written in the wake of the Civil War. Its exploration of Billy's trial and execution raises complex questions about the rights of the individual and the rightness of civil law. *Billy Budd*, like *Battle-Pieces*, also addresses related issues of revolution and revolt and explores their relationship with the law and justice. *Benito Cereno* is yet another text that shares all of these concerns, especially when the voice of the law enters the text in the form of Don Benito's deposition. Finally, "Bartleby, the Scrivener" presents another possibility for comparison.

2. **War:** The horror of war is one of Melville's major themes in *Battle-Pieces*. Examine his treatment of war in this collection and compare it to statements about war found elsewhere in his work.

   Once again, *Billy Budd* presents the most likely possibility for comparison. In fact, *Billy Budd*'s treatment of war is closely related to the questions of law that it explores. You might think about the effect that war has on law and on other elements of civil society. This should prove a fruitful way to begin a compare and contrast paper about Melville and war.

3. **Democracy:** Much of Melville's concern in *Battle-Pieces* focuses on questions of democracy and the viability of reunification. Explore his treatment of democracy in this and another of his works.

   American democracy and questions of civil order are themes that run throughout Melville's work. "Hawthorne and His Mosses," *Billy Budd*, "The Encantadas," and *Moby-Dick* all present possibilities for comparison. The specific focus of your paper will differ according to the texts you choose to work with.

4. **Nature:** Compare Melville's use of natural imagery in this text to that in another of his works. Does his use of nature imagery in the two works reflect similar issues and concerns?

   Melville's natural imagery tells readers something of his worldview. In order to work with this question productively, you should narrow your topic a great deal. You might, for instance, want to examine Melville's use of storm imagery or imagery of the sea. For either of these topics, *Moby-Dick* might prove an effective text for comparison. There are, of course, numerous other focuses for a comparative paper on imagery. Clearly, the bleakness and darkness of the warring world that Melville sketches in his war poetry might be easily compared to the landscape of "The Encantadas," especially given his insistence that both of these landscapes are those of fallen worlds. Similarly, "The Paradise of Bachelors and the Tartarus of Maids" also presents a bleak, sterile, fallen world.

5. *Battle-Pieces* **and other literature of the Civil War:** Compare Melville's portrayal of the Civil War to other Civil War poetry. How do they compare? Does Melville view the war in the same way as the other poets whose work you have examined? Does he seek to make similar points about the war, the country, or the soldiers?

Walt Whitman's *Drum Taps* is probably the best known and the most suggestive text to compare to *Battle-Pieces*. Both authors shape a series of poems about the war, and yet their styles and their apparent purposes are quite different. How would you describe and account for the differences in their works?

Bibliography and Online Resources for *Battle-Pieces*

Aaron, Daniel. *The Unwritten War: American Writers and the Civil War.* New York: Knopf, 1973.

Buell, Lawrence. "Melville the Poet." *The Cambridge Companion to Herman Melville.* Ed. Robert S. Levine. Cambridge: Cambridge UP, 1998. 135–36.

Cohen, Hennig, ed. *The Battle-Pieces of Herman Melville.* New York: Thomas Yoseloff, 1963.

Dawes, James. *The Language of War: Literature and Culture in the US from the Civil War Through WWII.* Cambridge, MA: Harvard UP, 2002.

Delbanco, Andrew. *Melville: His World and His Work.* New York: Knopf, 2005.

Dillingham, William B. *Melville and His Circle: The Last Years.* Athens: U of Georgia P, 1996.

Dryden, Edgar. *Monumental Melville: The Formation of a Literary Career.* Stanford, CA: Stanford UP, 2004.

Garner, Stanton. *The Civil War World of Herman Melville.* Lawrence: UP of Kansas, 1993.

Karcher, Carolyn. *Shadow over the Promised Land: Slavery, Race, and Violence in Melville's America.* Baton Rouge: Louisiana State UP, 1980.

Milder, Robert. *Exiled Royalties: Melville and the Life We Imagine.* New York: Oxford UP, 2006.

Parker, Hershel. *Herman Melville.* 2 vols. Baltimore: Johns Hopkins UP, 1996, 2002.

Pommer, Henry F. *Milton and Melville.* Pittsburgh, PA: U of Pittsburgh P, 1950.

The Rebellion Record: A diary of American Events (1861–1863). Internet Archive. Available online. URL: http://www.archive.org/details/rebellrecord06 moorrich. Downloaded November 29, 2007.

Rogin, Michael Paul. *Subversive Genealogy: The Politics and Art of Herman Melville.* New York: Knopf, 1983.

Shurr, William H. *The Mystery of Iniquity: Melville as Poet, 1857–1891.* Lexington: U of Kentucky P, 1972.

Stein, William B. *The Poetry of Melville's Late Years: Time, Myth, and Religion.* Albany: State U of New York P, 1970.

Sten, Christopher, ed. *Savage Eye: Melville and the Visual Arts.* Kent, OH: Kent State UP, 1991.

Sweet, Timothy. *Traces of War: Poetry, Photography, and the Crisis of the Union.* Baltimore: Johns Hopkins UP, 1990.

Warren, Robert Penn. "Melville the Poet." *Melville: A Collection of Critical Essays.* Ed. Richard Chase. Englewood Cliffs, NJ: Prentice Hall, 1962.

BILLY BUDD, SAILOR

READING TO WRITE

ELVILLE'S LAST work has generated a large body of widely varied, and often contradictory, critical responses. Writing in 1955, R. W. B. Lewis stated that *Billy Budd* "is, of course, unmistakably the product of aged serenity; its author has unmistakably got beyond his anger or discovered the key to it; and it would be pointless to deny that it is a testament of acceptance." Despite Lewis's confident assertions, many critics see great pessimism in *Billy Budd.* Robert K. Martin, for example, argues that Melville "gave expression in *Billy Budd* to his gravest doubt about man's ability to survive in more than a state of animal-like acceptance." In fact, *Billy Budd* remains the subject of heated scholarly disagreement. This lack of critical consensus about the novella likely stems from its complicated genesis, Melville's protracted revision of the text, and from the fact that it remained unfinished at his death in 1891. The work of scholars Harrison Hayford and Merton M. Sealts has shown that Melville's tale grew from the ballad or poem "Billy in the Darbies," which concludes contemporary versions of the text. From that start, Melville developed the work in stages. Early on, he developed the poem into a narrative work that centered on the innocent, young Billy, who is sentenced to hang as a result of Claggart's lie. The work continued to grow and develop, and near his death Melville began to develop his portrait of Captain Vere. These last stages of revision added a new dimension—an interest in law and justice—to the text. These revisions were incomplete at Melville's death, and it was not until 1962 that Hayford and Sealts published an edition of the work now considered by scholars to be the authoritative text of the novella.

As you begin *Billy Budd*, though, it seems a relatively straightforward text. Chapter 1 begins with Melville's description of the "Handsome Sailor," whose "moral nature was seldom out of keeping with the physical make," and Billy is summarily introduced: "Such a cynosure, at least in aspect, and something such too in nature, though with important variations made apparent as the story proceeds, was the welkin-eyed Billy Budd—or Baby Budd, as more familiarly . . . he at last came to be called." Clearly, Billy is well made, both physically and morally. Just after this introduction, readers learn that the narrative will center upon events that occurred just after "he had entered the King's service, having been impressed on the Narrow Seas from a homeward-bound English merchantman into a seventy-four outward bound, H.M.S. Bellipotent." In other words, in accord with British law at the time, Billy was taken from a civilian ship and "drafted" into the British navy. Beyond this introduction, the reader's first insight into Billy's character comes through the voice of the merchant ship's captain as he speaks with the *Bellipotent's* lieutenant. For careful readers, this interchange tells much about the direction that the novella will take and the issues that it will address. Consider what you might glean from the following passage that begins with the captain's description of Billy's presence aboard his ship:

> Before I shipped that young fellow, my forecastle was a rat-pit of quarrels. It was black times, I tell you, aboard the *Rights* here. I was worried to that degree my pipe had no comfort for me. But Billy came and it was like a Catholic priest striking peace in an Irish shindy. Not that he preached to them or said or did anything in particular; but a virtue went out of him, sugaring the sour ones. They took to him like hornets to treacle; all but the buffer of the gang, the big shaggy chap with the fire-red whiskers. He indeed, out of envy, perhaps, of the newcomer, and thinking such a "sweet and pleasant fellow," as he mockingly designated him to the others, could hardly have the spirit of a gamecock, must needs bestir himself in trying to get up an ugly row with him. Billy forebore with him and reasoned with him in a pleasant way—he is something like myself, Lieutenant, to whom aught like a quarrel is hateful—but nothing served. So, in the second dogwatch one day, the Red Whiskers in the presence of the others, under pretense of showing Billy just whence a sirloin steak was cut—for the fellow had once been a butcher—insultingly gave him a dig

under the ribs. Quick as lightning Billy let fly his arm. I dare say he never meant to do quite so much as he did, but anyhow he gave the burly fool a terrible drubbing. It took about a half a minute, I should think. And lord bless you, the lubber was astonished at the celerity. And will you believe it, Lieutenant, the Red Whiskers now really loves Billy—loves him, or is the biggest hypocrite that ever I heard of. But they all love him. . . . But Lieutenant if that young fellow goes—I know how it will be aboard the *Rights*. . . . Ay, Lieutenant, you are going to take away the jewel of 'em; you are going to take away my peacemaker! . . .

"Well," said the lieutenant, who had listened with amused interest. . . . "well, blessed are the peacemakers, especially the fighting peacemakers. And such are the seventy-four beauties some of which you see poking their noses out of the portholes of yonder warship lying to for me . . ." Not only does this passage introduce Billy and his virtues, it tells us something of the world that surrounds him. It foreshadows the events that are to come, and it hints at the moral and philosophical issues that these events will raise.

A careful reader might start by analyzing how much Captain Graveling's portrait of Billy tells us about both the handsome young sailor and about the world that surrounds him. Attempting to clarify his earlier comment that Billy was his "best man . . . the jewel of 'em," Captain Graveling describes life aboard the *Rights* as a "rat-pit of quarrels" before Billy came aboard. Billy's effect upon this contentious world is striking, and Graveling begins his description with an analogy. Billy was "like a Catholic priest striking a peace in an Irish shindy." This analogy anticipates Graveling's closing comment, "you are going to take away my peacemaker." Still further, Billy's shipmates "took to him like hornets to treacle." This paragraph continues to amplify both Billy's virtues and the effects of these virtues on the contentious, "dark" world of the merchant ship. You might note the captain's use of animal imagery to describe his crew. They are like hornets, and their quarreling nature creates a "rat-pit" aboard the ship. The red-whiskered man taunts Billy because he "could hardly have the spirit of a gamecock." Attentive readers will ask why Melville embedded this abundance of animal imagery in the description of the men of the merchant ship. How does aligning these men with rats, hornets, and gamecocks help to develop and explain their characters?

Stuck aboard a ship with pugnacious sailors who clearly value and expect similar characteristics among their comrades, Billy— "to whom aught like a quarrel is hateful"—is something of an anomaly. The captain's analogy comparing the young man to a priest underlines this fact. If the others are animalistic and truculent, Billy is human and almost holy. He has a taming, soothing effect, "striking peace," and "sugaring the sour ones." Graveling connects him to sweetness, likening him to treacle and sugar, and the Red Whisker mockingly calls him "a sweet and pleasant fellow." You might consider the implications and the connotations of these descriptions. The paragraph seems to overstate Billy's sweetness. The captain's comparison of Billy to treacle is especially suggestive here. How does this reference, coupled with the repeated references to sweetness, modify or develop the positive portrait of Billy that Captain Graveling paints? Further, do these references in any way help to explain the red-whiskered man's response to Billy? Building upon these hints at a possible flaw or weakness in Billy's character, an astute reader may well notice the particular phrasing that Graveling uses as he describes Billy's pacifying effect upon the other sailors: "not that he preached to them or said or did anything in particular; but a virtue went out of him." This description is clearly meant to praise Billy and his peacemaking character. After all, no one appreciates sermonizing in a peer. Yet, this passage also indicates a lack of agency or activity on Billy's part: He does nothing "in particular." In fact, grammatically, Graveling's statement that "a virtue went out of him," removes Billy from the subject position of the sentence. Instead, his virtue is the active subject of the clause, and Billy is the passive object from which that virtue emanates. The phrasing indicates a certain unconsciousness about Billy. He seems to have little awareness and, consequently, little control over his abilities. This phrasing, of course, anticipates the later incident when, in response to the red-whiskered sailor's insult, "[q]uick as lightning Billy let fly his arm." Graveling emphasizes, "I dare say he never meant to do quite so much as he did." Once again, Billy seems to lacks both self-control and self-awareness, and a thoughtful reader cannot help but see a flaw in the character of Graveling's "peacemaker." In fact, one might wonder if Billy's lack of self-awareness and self-control do not in some way align his nature with that of his more animalistic colleagues. As Lieutenant Ratcliffe's comment about the "fighting peacemakers" makes clear, there is an irony or inconsistency in the notion of a man who makes the peace through violence. In spite of Graveling's obvious love and respect for his "jewel," his "peacemaker," a careful reader is already aware of potential flaws in Billy and recognizes a certain doubleness in Billy, the "fighting peacemaker."

At this point a careful reader also wonders about Billy's fitness for life aboard a warship, which Melville's narrator will soon refer to as "the ampler and more knowing world of a great warship." Nor will such a reader be surprised when Billy, in frustration and desperation, lashes out at Claggart and kills him. This early passage has provided sufficient information about Billy and his world and has effectively foreshadowed the forthcoming plot crisis. Similarly, Ratcliffe's ironic yoking of Christ's Sermon on the Mount ("blessed are the peacemakers") with the guns of the warship anticipates a later issue in *Billy Budd*: the relationship between war and religion. Careful readers of *Billy Budd*'s early pages will be well prepared for the issues of plot, character, and theme, and they can read the text with an eye toward issues that could form the basis of strong, thoughtful papers on *Billy Budd*.

TOPICS AND STRATEGIES

This section of the chapter provides you with broad topic ideas that should help you develop an essay on *Billy Budd*. Remember that these topics are just springboards for your own exploration; you will need to focus your analysis and develop your own specific thesis.

Themes

Melville emphasizes Billy's innocence from the very beginning of the text, clearly announcing innocence and its encounter with the fallen world as one of the major themes of *Billy Budd*. As the paragraphs above indicate, examining Billy as a study in innocence can be a complicated matter. Similarly, Melville's extensive revisions of the text developed other important themes, especially the complex issues of individual rights, state's rights, and the role of the law. Any of these themes could provide a number of ways to focus a paper. Whatever theme you find compelling, you should prepare to write a paper on that theme by deciding what points the novella makes about it. If you are writing about law and justice, you should think about why Melville writes about that theme. Why is it important? What does he say about it? What conclusions does he reach? How does he use narrative style, imagery, or character development to shape his ideas about human perception and understanding?

Sample Topics:

1. **Innocence and the Fall:** In chapter 2, rife with references marking Billy as prelapsarian, Melville makes clear that elements of *Billy Budd* echo the biblical story of the Fall. "And here be it submitted," he says, "that apparently going to corroborate the doctrine of man's Fall, a doctrine now popularly ignored, it is observable that where certain virtues pristine and unadulterated peculiarly characterize anybody in the external uniform of civilization, they will upon scrutiny seem not to be derived from custom or convention, but rather out of keeping with these, as if indeed exceptionally transmitted from a period prior to Cain's city and citified man." Can you read *Billy Budd* as a parable of the Fall? If in his portrayal of Billy and his confrontation with "the ampler and more knowing world of the great warship," Melville "corroborate[s] the doctrine of man's Fall," just what does he say about it? What elements, aspects, or interpretation of the Fall is his story corroborating?

   You might begin your treatment of this issue with a thorough analysis of Billy. Be sure to carefully consider the assessments of Billy's innocence provided by the narrator and by the other characters. Of particular relevance are Vere and Claggart's assessments. Beyond this, you might consider how Melville's allegory of the Fall plays out in the text. Do you think that one can justifiably argue that Billy falls from innocence in this text? Why or why not? If you believe that you can call Billy fallen, who and what bear the burden of responsibility? How does Billy's fall differ from the biblical fall of Adam and Eve? You should also pay particular attention to the context of the allegory here, for in the quotation cited above Melville makes it clear that the story of his Adam involves the confrontation of a prelapsarian character with the fallen world. How does the fact that Billy is like an innocent "exceptionally transmitted" into the 18th century affect the text's treatment of the Fall? In what other ways is the world that Billy is "transmitted" into exceptional or remarkable? How do all these facts help you to read *Billy Budd* as a commentary on Melville's world? Finally, you might want to consider the theory of the fortunate fall, which holds that the Fall was necessary in order for humanity to reach salvation. Can *Billy Budd* be read as a commentary on the concept of the fortunate fall?

2. **Silence, speech, and truth telling:** In chapter 2, as the narrator introduces Billy, comparing him to the Handsome Sailor, the narrator remarks that despite Billy's "masculine beauty . . . there was just one thing amiss in him. No visible blemish indeed . . . but an occasional liability to a vocal defect." The plot of *Billy Budd* hinges not only upon this "organic hesitancy" in Billy's speech, but also upon numerous other instances of speech and silence. Consider *Billy Budd* as a commentary on human speech and its capacity to express the truth.

   While this question asks you to address Billy's stutter and his inability to declare the truth of his innocence, a paper on speech and silence in *Billy Budd* should go far beyond Billy's "vocal defect." Obviously, Claggart's lie motivates the plot's crisis, and this is worth considering in some detail. You should also consider other examples of speech and silence and their relation to truth. What other instances of silence seem important? Consider, too, who is silent in these instances and why. Sometimes characters choose not to speak, and sometimes they are silenced. At other times, the narrator also falls silent, choosing not to render scenes that seem important to the plot and its resolution. Why does he choose silence over elucidation? What do these silences and gaps in the text express about the human capacity to capture and relate the truth of experience? Similarly, you should pay close attention to speech in the text. Frequently, the narrator explicitly draws attention to certain speech acts, commenting on the characters' diction and manner of speaking. Why would Melville highlight particular acts of speech in this way? How do these tactics comment on "the Art of Telling the Truth" (a phrase Melville used in "Hawthorne and His Mosses")? Finally, any thorough investigation of this issue needs to explore the proceedings of the drumhead court, since the court's job should be to reach a decision about the truth of Billy's guilt or innocence.

3. **Law and justice:** The centerpiece of *Billy Budd* is a trial, and, as a consequence, Melville focuses on the workings of law and justice. What does *Billy Budd* say about human law and its ability to administer justice?

This question asks you to explore a very complex question, and Melville's text is complicated by numerous (and apparently deliberate) ambiguities that further muddy an already difficult issue. Even a short exploration of critical commentary on the novella will show that literary scholars have profound disagreements about this text. You will need to consider your own opinion of the drumhead court's decision. Since Billy killed a superior officer, he was legally guilty of mutiny. Should Billy have been executed? Why do you believe as you do? You will need to spend a great deal of time analyzing chapter 21. In that chapter, Melville frequently alludes to differing—and apparently contradictory—codes of law. Do you agree with Vere's argument about the primacy of martial law? Is his argument just and logical? Why or why not? How is conscience related to law and justice? Even beyond the complicated arguments and issues in chapter 21, there is a great deal more to consider in the novella. Is the drumhead court the proper vehicle for justice in this instance? What do you think about the manner in which the drumhead court is conducted? You might also ask if Vere's observation in chapter 27—"with mankind . . . forms, measured forms, are everything"—has any bearing on the novella's treatment of law and justice.

4. **Democracy and class issues:** Melville often used shipboard settings to comment on larger issues. Like the *San Dominic* in *Benito Cereno* and the *Pequod* in *Moby-Dick,* the *Bellipotent* seems to present a political microcosm. How might you read Melville's portrayal of the events on the *Bellipotent* as a commentary on democracy and class relations?

Consider the names of the two ships in the novella as well as Billy's impressment from the *Rights-of-Man* to the "more ample world" of the *Bellipotent.* Similarly, examine the social structures aboard the ships. The method of "preserving order" on the latter ship, for example, should prove relevant to your analysis. As you examine the social structures, analyze the characters and their positions. Think about Captain Vere, his personal characteristics and his philosophies. The chapters leading up to Billy's trial are particularly revealing here. You might also consider the various accounts or "histories" of Billy. How might these be related to issues of class and social structure? Think about Claggart, too—his background, his role as master-at-arms, and his relationship with the crew.

5. **Revolution and revolt:** *Billy Budd* takes place in the wake of the French Revolution during the Napoleonic War, and clearly the threat of revolt underlies the whole of the narrative. Examine *Billy Budd* as a commentary on revolution.

A response to this question must consider the historical circumstances that Melville sets out in chapter 3. How do the circumstances of the Spithead and Nore mutinies inform the plot and the circumstances of *Billy Budd*? How does the treatment of mutiny reflect upon the larger issues of revolution and revolt?

6. **War:** *Billy Budd* is set on a warship during a time of war. How is the novella a comment on war?

Begin thinking about this question by exploring what the text says about peace and about war early in the novella. In chapter 1, Lieutenant Ratcliffe calls the *Bellipotent*'s guns "fighting peacemakers." How is that comment suggestive for a paper about *Billy Budd* and war? Still further, examine war's effect on many of the elements of Melville's story. How does it affect Vere and Billy? What is war's relationship with Christianity and with law? Your response should be built from careful consideration of the court-martial. In chapter 21, Vere tells his officers that the drumhead court operates under the Mutiny Act, which he calls "war's child." What does a close analysis of the court-martial and Billy's execution say about the relationship between war and justice? In the latter chapters of the novella, Melville calls readers' attention to the roles of the surgeon and the chaplain. How does his treatment of these two men and their roles develop the novella as a commentary on war?

Character

Billy, Vere, and Claggart all provide possible focal points for papers on character. A character study on any of these three could benefit from a study of Melville's revisions and the evolution of the text. Each of these characters and their situations evolved as Melville returned to the text of *Billy Budd* again and again. You might, consequently, develop a thesis about the evolution of a particular character. If you are more interested in the presentation of character only in the "final" version of the text, you still might approach your topic through the idea of evolution. Consider how your character changes as the story progresses. Do you see any change or development in that character? Still further, you should consider not only the narrator's assessments of the character, but the character's own words along with the assessments of other characters in the text. A thorough study of Billy, for instance, needs to consider his effects upon his shipmates on both the *Rights-of-Man* and the *Bellipotent.*

Sample Topics:

1. **Billy:** Melville leaves little doubt that Billy is an innocent, and in chapter 2 he presents him "as Adam presumably might have been ere the urbane Serpent wriggled himself into his company." The rest of the text repeatedly emphasizes Billy's innocence. Why does Melville seem to belabor his innocence? How is this innocence important to the larger purposes of the novella?

   Because Melville makes Billy's status as an innocent so readily apparent, any exploration of his character must do more than establish the fact of Billy's innocence. Exploring the significance of that innocence should prove both more challenging and more productive. In chapter 12, the narrator comments on "the moral phenomenon presented in Billy." You might begin to explore the significance of this through a thorough analysis of the many different ways that Melville presents his hero's innocent nature. What analogies, metaphors, and patterns of imagery does Melville use to communicate this aspect of Billy's person? Do all these methods of characterization work similarly? What does each suggest about Billy? You should also carefully analyze the other characters' responses to Billy. Claggart's, for instance, assumes the form of disdain: "to be nothing more than innocent!" While Claggart's disdain is an outgrowth of envy, you still might ask if there is any truth to his reaction. Are there ways in which Billy's innocence renders him inadequate or insufficient? You could also find it useful to consider how and why Billy's innocence throws other elements of the novella into relief. How does it reflect upon the themes of war, law and justice, or truth? Why, in other words, did Melville choose to create a character who is like Adam before the fall but place him aboard an 18th-century English man-of-war?

2. **Claggart:** In chapter 11, the narrator says of Claggart, "But for the adequate comprehending of Claggart by a normal nature these hints are insufficient. To pass from a normal nature to

him one must cross 'the deadly space between.' And this is best done by indirection." In your opinion, what best accounts for Claggart's antipathy toward Billy? How do you explain and comprehend the master-at-arms?

As the quotation cited above indicates, the narrator describes Claggart through "hints" and "indirection." Through metaphor and discussions of Claggart's background, personality, and physique he hints at various potential "reasons" for Claggart's visceral dislike of Billy. Sometimes he seems to tie the antipathy to particular emotions. Sometimes he connects his behavior to theological and philosophical musings. Consider these possibilities carefully as you assess Claggart's character and motives. What connections can you draw between Claggart and the novella's treatment of law, theology, and philosophy? Further, consider the language and imagery that Melville uses in describing the master-at-arms. How do they shed light on his portrait and his function in the novella? Finally, you should also examine Vere's feelings toward Claggart as well as his assessments of him during the trial scene.

3. **Vere:** In the years since *Billy Budd*'s publication, Captain Vere's portrayal has sparked the most critical controversy. The question at the heart of that controversy is whether Melville praises Vere or condemns him. Critical arguments have grown quite heated on both sides of this debate. Analyze Melville's portrait of Vere closely. Is there a third way of viewing the captain that is neither "pro Vere" nor "anti Vere"? If so, how can you construct this interpretation and what implications does it have for Melville's text?

This question requires that you study closely the chapters that introduce Vere. Similarly, you will need to examine the court-martial in chapter 21 in great detail. Consider, too, what the other characters think of Vere, and examine Vere's treatment of others aboard the ship. How do the interactions of Vere and the others aboard the ship help to develop the portrait of Vere provided by the narrator? Consider the private interview between Billy and Vere and the way that the narrator relates that interview to the reader. What does this incident imply about Vere and about Billy's assessment of him? Why are Billy's final words "God bless Captain Vere"? Why does Vere murmur Billy's name on his deathbed? You might also find it instructive to examine the many revisions that Melville made to Vere's character as he drafted and redrafted the novella. The edition of *Billy Budd* produced by Harrison Hayford and Merton M. Sealts, Jr., contains both the standard text and a "Genetic Text," which shows the growth of the novella as Melville revised. What does an examination of the "Genetic Text" of *Billy Budd* suggest about Melville's attitudes toward Vere?

History and Context

Given the historical setting of *Billy Budd*, you must approach the text with some awareness of its historical situation and tensions. Melville provides some of this background himself when he tells of the Spithead and Nore mutinies. You will need to know something of impressment and sailor's attitudes toward it, just as you need to be familiar with the tensions between England and France in the wake of the French Revolution. In addition to enhancing your understanding of the text, such background can help you to develop topics on *Billy Budd*. Similarly, a familiarity with Melville's life and his revisions of *Billy Budd* might provide you with numerous avenues to pursue in papers about the historical context that surround and affect the text and its meanings.

Sample Topics:

1. **Nelson:** The narrator begins chapter 4 with what he calls a "bypath" in his narrative, a discussion of the British captain Lord Nelson, and he asks the reader to forgive him for committing "a literary sin." Melville spent so much time revising *Billy Budd* that he had many opportunities to delete this chapter from the text, and yet he retained it. What relevance does Nelson have for the reader's understanding of *Billy Budd*?

Not only did Melville have the opportunity to cut the discussion of Nelson from his text, textual scholarship indicates that he actually did so for a time. A comprehensive discussion of Nelson and his relevance to the text must develop from both an understanding of Nelson and his career as well as from a thorough understanding of *Billy Budd*'s textual history. The Hayford and Sealts edition of *Billy Budd* along with Hershel Parker's *Reading* Billy Budd should provide valuable insight into Melville's revisions of the text. On one level, it seems clear that Nelson could provide a touchstone for the reader's assessment of Vere, but the textual history shows that Melville's attitudes toward Vere and toward chapter 4 were complicated.

2. **Melville's revisions of the text:** Melville probably began *Billy Budd* in 1886, when he wrote the poem "Billy in the Darbies," which appears at the end of the novella. According to Harrison Hayford and Merton M. Sealts, Jr., Melville drafted and edited the manuscript of *Billy Budd* "in nine major stages." When Melville died in 1891, he was still in the process of revision. This history has complicated the critical history of *Billy Budd.* After you have read the novella closely and thought about its ideas, explore the textual history of *Billy Budd.* How does your work as literary detective affect your understanding and interpretation of the work?

   Melville's revision process was both protracted and complicated, but by exploring what scholars have learned about the process of revision you have a rare opportunity to observe the evolution of a literary work. Many scholars believe that Melville's process of revision demonstrates just how thoroughly Melville rethought his purpose. While the Hayford and Sealts edition of *Billy Budd* along with Hershel Parker's *Reading Billy Budd* provide necessary starting places for an investigation of Melville's revisions, most of the scholarship published after the Hayford and Sealts edition considers this textual history. You may find it helpful to examine how the focus of the novella changed as Melville reworked it. Pay particular attention to his treatment of character and think about what elements of the text seem to constitute Melville's major concerns and interests in the final stages of the work. You might also want to consider whether it is possible to understand *Billy Budd* without some knowledge of its textual history.

3. **America of the 1880s:** Although *Billy Budd* takes place on a British man-of-war in the 18th century, critics have long held that Melville uses the situation aboard the *Bellipotent* to comment on America of the 1880s. How can you read *Billy Budd* as a political commentary on Melville's America?

Clearly, Billy's impressment from the *Rights-of-Man* signals the novella's concerns with the rights of the individual. Similarly, once aboard the *Bellipotent* Billy encounters a world of social hierarchy and a place where the rights of the individual are weighed against the laws and the well-being of the state. These elements provide background for any investigation into the text's commentary on Melville's America. Beyond this, you might find it both interesting and helpful to focus your investigation even further. You might, for instance, choose to explore the connections between *Billy Budd* and the rights of the working class in the 1880s. Biographical studies of Melville and his work (such as Delbanco's *Melville: His World and His Work*) could provide a good starting place for your research. Conversely, since the crisis of *Billy Budd* centers on Vere's decision to hang Billy, you could also explore attitudes toward capital punishment in Melville's America. H. Bruce Franklin's article, "Billy Budd and Capital Punishment: A Tale of Three Centuries," should prove helpful. Yet another avenue of approach would be a paper that considers American attitudes toward war in the years after the Civil War.

4. **The USS *Somers*:** Some scholars have drawn parallels to the events that happened aboard the USS *Somers* in 1842 in which several sailors were hanged after rumors of a planned mutiny were reported to the commander, Alexander Mackenzie. Conduct some research into the events that took place aboard the

Somers. How does knowledge of the events aboard the *Somers* affect or enhance a reader's understanding of *Billy Budd*?

Melville's own history at sea, along with the role played by his cousin Guert Gansevoort, make it likely that Melville knew of the alleged mutiny aboard the *Somers.* In addition to conducting some historical research into the events aboard the *Somers,* you should find biographical research about Melville helpful, too. How does Melville's own history aboard naval ships affect his attitudes toward the *Somers* affair? Do any of his other works help support your assessment? You might also consider that *Billy Budd* was begun decades after the events that occurred on the *Somers.* Is it likely that Melville's attitudes toward the event remained the same in the intervening years? Why or why not?

5. **Fathers and sons—*Billy Budd* and Melville's biography:** Like so many of Melville's characters, Billy is a foundling, and Melville seems to establish Vere as a sort of father figure for the innocent young sailor. Some literary scholars have argued for biographical readings of *Billy Budd.* Some see in the father-son relationship echoes of Melville's loss of his own father at age 12. Still others argue that in his treatment of Vere and Billy Melville was working through the trauma and the guilt associated with his son Malcolm's suicide in 1867. Do you think that such biographical and psychological interpretations of the text are valid ways to understand *Billy Budd*? Why or why not?

Clearly, biographies of Melville provide obvious starting places for a paper that addresses this question. In his introduction to *Billy Budd and other Stories*, Frederick Busch briefly introduces the possibility of reading the novella as a reflection of Melville's paternal guilt over Malcolm's suicide. Also consider the biblical echoes of Abraham sacrificing Isaac. Do these reflect on a possible biographical reading of the text?

6. **Slavery, Justice Lemuel Shaw, and the Fugitive Slave Law:** Melville's biographers as well as literary scholars often comment on

the influence that Melville's father-in-law, Justice Lemuel Shaw, had upon Melville's life and his writing. Shaw, though he was resolutely opposed to slavery, presided over the Sims case in 1851 and ruled that Thomas Sims should be returned to slavery, thereby upholding the 1850 Fugitive Slave Law. Most frequently scholars trace the influence of this decision on Melville to his treatment of slavery in *Benito Cereno.* Is it possible to draw a connection between *Billy Budd* and Shaw's decision in the Sims case?

Biographical studies such as Delbanco's and Parker's can provide a good starting place for this inquiry. These studies provide insight into the historical context. You will need to think about the legal issues involved in both the Sims case and in Billy's court-martial, so you should also consider the questions posed in the Themes section of this chapter under the topic of Law and Justice.

7. ***Billy Budd* and the critics:** Because of the ambiguity created by Melville's revisions, a number of literary scholars argue that *Billy Budd* becomes a kind of literary mirror in which scholars see their particular interests or philosophy reflected back at them. Still others have argued that the critical history of *Billy Budd* mirrors the history of the political climate in America. Explore the history of literary scholarship on *Billy Budd.* Do you agree that scholarly reactions to the text provide a mirror of the political climate of the times?

You will have to spend some time exploring the critical history of *Billy Budd* in order to answer this question. Additionally, you should know something about the political climate in the United States in the 20th and 21st centuries. More recent scholarship—especially recent collections of articles on *Billy Budd,* such as *Herman Melville: Reassessments*—gives you a good starting place for this exploration. Modern critics often contextualize their own arguments within the critical history of a work, thus providing readers with a partial overview of scholarship. As you explore 21st-century reactions to *Billy*

Budd, think about the connections between the Patriot Act and Vere's assessment of the function of the Mutiny Act. Does the political climate in the wake of the Patriot Act affect critical response to *Billy Budd* and, particularly, to Vere?

Philosophy and Ideas

When Billy is impressed from a ship named the *Rights-of-Man* onto a ship whose name translates as "war power," Melville has announced that philosophical issues of individual rights and the effects of war upon those rights underlie the action of his novella. In order to analyze questions of human rights, you should familiarize yourself with the ideas of Thomas Paine and Edmund Burke, whose philosophical differences are clearly referenced in Paine's work *Rights of Man.*

Sample Topics:

1. **Free will versus fate:** When Billy kills Claggart, Vere whispers, "fated boy." At other times, the narrator comments on the characters' free will or their lack thereof. Chapter 12, for instance, ends with an analogy between Claggart and a scorpion, claiming that "like the scorpion" the master-at-arms "act[s] out to the end the part allotted to [him]." Is *Billy Budd* an argument against human free will? Is Melville arguing that humans merely act out roles assigned to them?

   Examine the text closely for other references to characters' agency or their lack thereof. Consider what these instances say about characters' motivations. What drives Billy's actions? What motivates Claggart? As you examine Vere's facilitation of the court-martial, what role does choice play in his actions and his decisions? As you assess these characters and their situations, you should also be attentive to the imagery that Melville uses to describe them. Are the metaphors and analogies in any way relevant to the question of human free will? The philosophical question of fate versus free will is largely a theological one, and this topic certainly asks you to consider some of the same material that the theme of innocence and the Fall addresses. As an allegory of the Fall, the theological questions behind the portrayal of Billy and Claggart are quite important. Does Vere have a role if *Billy Budd* is Melville's meditation on the Fall? Similarly, does the narrative's context—the Napoleonic war, the Spithead and the Nore mutinies, the Muntiny Act—bear any relation to the allegory of the Fall that seems to play out between Billy and Claggart? Can you relate these two aspects of the text? What possible dimensions and directions do these questions suggest for an exploration of free will versus fate in *Billy Budd*?

2. **Natural rights:** Melville clearly announces one philosophical thread that is woven into the texture of *Billy Budd* in the first chapter. Billy is impressed and taken from the *Rights-of-Man* to the *Bellipotent*, and the narrator tells readers more about the first ship's name: "That was the merchant ship's name, though by her master and crew abbreviated in sailor fashion into the *Rights*. The hardheaded Dundee owner was a staunch admirer of Thomas Paine, whose book in rejoinder to Burke's arraignment of the French Revolution had then been published for some time and had gone everywhere." Indeed, *Billy Budd* takes up the philosophical questions about the balance of individual's natural rights versus the interests of the state. What does *Billy Budd* assert about the balance between the individual's natural rights and the interests of the state?

This question requires that you familiarize yourself with the arguments of Edmund Burke, who wrote *Reflections on the Revolution in France* (1790), and Thomas Paine, whose work *Rights of Man* was a rejoinder to Burke and his ideas. Clearly, assessing Melville's stance on this philosophical argument requires that you address many of the questions raised in the sections of this chapter on law and justice, democracy, and revolution. Clearly, too, you must grapple with Vere and his role in Billy's court-martial.

Form and Genre

Melville challenged and experimented with traditional narrative forms in many of his works. *Typee, Moby-Dick,* and *Benito Cereno* provide obvious examples. In *Billy Budd*, Melville experiments with form, though perhaps not so overtly as he does in a text like *Benito Cereno*. At many points in *Billy Budd*, though, the narrator speaks overtly about both narrative form and the connections between narrative and truth. This focus could provide a particularly interesting and productive topic for a paper about the novella.

Sample Topics:

1. **Forms of fiction:** One of the most frequently quoted lines from *Billy Budd* is Vere's: "With mankind . . . forms, measured forms, are everything." While Vere's statement does not comment on the form of fiction, it reflects *Billy Budd*'s preoccupation with questions of form. Just two paragraphs later, at the start of chapter 28, the narrator says, "The symmetry of form attainable in pure fiction cannot so readily be achieved in a narration essentially having less to do with fable than with fact. Truth uncompromisingly told will always have its ragged edges; hence the conclusion of such a narration is apt to be less finished than an architectural finial." How does the form of *Billy Budd* reflect the narrator's beliefs about the forms of fiction and the forms of truth?

   You might begin thinking about this question by considering *Billy Budd* and its relation to both truth and fiction. Clearly, it is a work of fiction and, thus, should be able to obtain the "symmetry of form" of which the narrator speaks. Is this the case? Why or why not? Are there places where you see "ragged edges" in Melville's novella? If so, do you believe that these edges are the result of Melville's incomplete editing process or are they purposeful? What is the significance of the novella's subtitle, "An Inside Narrative," and how is it related to issues of the form of truth and the form of fiction? You should also read the text closely to discover the many other places where the narrator comments on the narrative form and on his ability to tell his tale.

Language, Symbols, and Imagery

As the opening section of this chapter hints, *Billy Budd* incorporates a plethora of animal references. The abundance of animal imagery can provide a number of approaches for papers on the novella. How does animal imagery mark a particular character, and does Melville use that imagery in traditional or nontraditional ways? You may want to tie the abundance of animal imagery to Darwin and his theory of evolution. In order to write a paper about Melville's use of this imagery, you should reread the story and pay close attention to its language and the meanings and connotations of some of the repeated language and imagery.

Sample Topics:

1. **Animal imagery:** Even a cursory reading of *Billy Budd* should be sufficient for any reader to notice the abundance of animal imagery embedded in the text. How does this imagery function in *Billy Budd*?

Your first step toward a paper on the function of animal imagery in *Billy Budd* is to closely read and note the use of this imagery. Who and what is described through Melville's use of animal imagery? Still further, how are Melville's choices of specific animals significant? How do Melville's comparisons reflect upon the characters and their situations? Some scholars have suggested that Melville's use of animal imagery reflects his treatment of Darwin and his theories of evolution. (Darwin published *On the Origin of Species* in 1859.) Do you think that such an estimation of Melville's use of animal imagery sheds valuable light on *Billy Budd*? Why or why not?

Compare and Contrast Essays

Billy Budd should provide you with plenty of material for compare and contrast papers. As Melville's last text, the novella revisits many themes and issues that the author grappled with throughout his career, including questions of truth and truth telling. Similarly, he returns to the figure of the innocent and the orphan, both of which appear repeatedly in his fiction. Whatever your approach or topic, remember that your thesis should make a clear, specific point about the relevance or the significance of the comparisons you draw. An effective compare and contrast paper does much more than just point out similarities and differences. Remember, you need to tell your readers why your comparisons are significant.

Sample Topics:

1. **Silence and speech in *Billy Budd* and "Bartleby":** The act of speaking plays a central role in both *Billy Budd* and "Bartleby, the Scrivener." More specifically, the crisis in both works arises from a failure to speak. Compare Melville's treatment of speech and silence in these two works. What does Melville say through his treatment of the silence of Billy Budd and of Bartleby?

   Bartleby's silence and Billy's failure to speak derive from different causes. Bartleby "prefers not to" speak, and Billy, despite his passionate desire to counter Claggart's lie, cannot speak. Despite these differences, you might draw connections. Consider why Bartleby chooses not to speak. Consider what it is that Bartleby chooses not to speak about. Does it seem likely that his fate might have been different had he chosen to speak more? Is Bartleby's silence a kind of protest? If so, what is he protesting? You might also want to consider the role of speaking in both of these texts. Both also consider the role of rumors and lies. Claggart's lie engenders the crisis of *Billy Budd*, and the narrator tells readers of various speculations about Bartleby and his identity. Consider, too, the fact that the narrator's own version of Bartleby's story is an account of an "unaccountable" man. How does this fact compare to the narrator's assessments of the efficacy of fiction in *Billy Budd*? If you consider all these questions, you should have a number of directions in which to take a paper on speech and silence in these two works.

2. **Fallen innocents—Billy and Hawthorne's Donatello:** Numerous literary critics have noted the similarities between Billy Budd and Donatello of Nathaniel Hawthorne's *The Marble Faun*. Compare Hawthorne's and Melville's treatment of these two characters portrayed as prelapsarian innocents.

   Hawthorne's last novel was published in 1860, and Melville and Hawthorne knew each other and each other's work. Both Donatello and Billy are portrayed as innocents. Examine the two characters as the authors' meditations on the nature of innocence. A more interesting approach could examine the place of the prelapsarian innocent in the fallen world, since both characters seem to have been transported into the "modern" world from a time before the Fall. Finally, you might explore the fates of both these characters. How does each character and his experience tell readers something about his creator's philosophy of the Fall?

3. **The theme of truth telling:** In an 1851 letter to Hawthorne, Melville wrote: "Try to get a living by the Truth—and go to the Soup Societies. Heavens! Let any clergyman try to preach the Truth from its very stronghold, the pulpit, and they would ride him out of his church on his own pulpit banister. . . . Truth is ridiculous to men." And yet, in "Hawthorne and His Mosses," Melville indicates that both Shakespeare and Hawthorne were "masters of the great Art of Telling the Truth," and he comments on these authors' ability to tell the truth through their fiction. Compare Melville's ideas about the relationship between fiction and truth in "Hawthorne and His Mosses" and *Billy Budd*.

   You might begin an investigation into this topic through *Billy Budd*'s subtitle: "An Inside Narrative." What relationship should such an "inside narrative" bear to "the truth"? Does *Billy Budd* in any way attest to the difficulties in telling the truth that Melville describes in his letter and in "Hawthorne and His Mosses"? Similarly, you would do well to note the many places in *Billy Budd* that the narrator comments on fiction and the form of fiction. *Benito Cereno* also shares with *Billy Budd* the aim of finding and telling the truth of an incident that happened aboard a ship at sea. It, too, includes a trial as well as the proliferation of differing "accounts" of the events that occurred aboard the ship. Finally, you could examine the eighth sketch of "The Encantadas," which is filled with narrative gaps and contemplations on telling the truth of an individual's experience.

4. **Foundlings and orphans in Melville's fiction:** Billy, like so many of Melville's characters, is a foundling who is without a

father and without a past. Compare Melville's treatment of the theme of orphanage in *Billy Budd* with that in another of his works.

Foundlings and outcasts populate *Moby-Dick*. Ishamel, Ahab, and Pip all seem to be without family and without a history. Similarly, Bartleby might be another character that you could study in a paper on this topic.

5. **Innocence in Melville's fiction:** Compare the theme of innocence and Melville's treatment of characters marked as innocents in *Billy Budd* and another work of Melville.

   Early in the text, Melville compares Billy to an "upright barbarian." Such a label clearly invites comparison with the Typees in *Typee* and his treatment of Eden and innocence in that text. You might find it particularly interesting to compare the encounter between innocence and "civilized"/enlightened society in both these texts.

6. **Law:** Compare Melville's meditations on the role and the effectiveness of the law in *Billy Budd* and another of his works.

   Because *Benito Cereno* involves a slave revolt (a kind of mutiny), a trial, and accounts of both the events at sea and of the trial, it provides a particularly interesting possibility for comparison. Another productive comparison might be Starbuck and his relationship to law in *Moby-Dick*. Chapter 123, "The Musket," might prove a useful starting place for this comparison. You would also do well to consider that the narrator of "Bartleby" is a lawyer and that legal considerations play a large role in his treatment of Bartleby.

7. **Animal imagery:** Compare Melville's use of animal imagery in *Billy Budd* with that of another of his works. How does this imagery function in each of these texts?

Moby-Dick provides a particularly apt comparison here. Both texts describe humans through comparisons (both implicit and explicit) to animals. Consider whether you think Melville's purpose is the same in these two works. "The Encantadas" should also provide ample material for comparison. Much of Melville's focus seems to be on the animal life of the Galápagos Islands. Here, too, the human characters are described through animal imagery.

Bibliography and Online Resources for *Billy Budd, Sailor*

Adamson, Joseph. *Melville, Shame, and the Evil Eye: A Psychoanalytic Reading.* Albany: SUNY P, 1997.

Arvin, Newton. *Herman Melville.* New York: William Sloane, 1950.

Berthold, Dennis. "Melville, Garibaldi, and the Medusa of Revolution." *National Imaginaries, American Identities: The Cultural Work of American Iconography.* Ed. Larry Hunter Reynolds. Princeton, NJ: Princeton UP, 2000. 104–37.

Bloom, Harold. *Herman Melville's* Billy Budd, *"Benito Cereno," "Bartleby, the Scrivener," and Other Tales.* New York: Chelsea House, 1987.

Bryant, John, ed. *A Companion to Melville Studies.* New York: Greenwood, 1986.

Bryant, John, and Robert Milder, eds. *Melville's Evermoving Dawn.* Kent, OH: Kent State UP, 1997.

Busch, Frederick. Introduction. *Billy Budd and Other Stories.* By Herman Melville. New York: Penguin, 1986. vii–xxiv.

Coffler, Gail. "Clasical Iconography in the Aesthetics of *Billy Budd, Sailor.*" *Savage Eye: Melville and the Visual Arts.* Ed. Christopher Stern. Kent, OH: Ohio State UP, 1991. 257–76.

———. *Melville's Allusions to Religion: A Comprehensive Index and Glossary.* New York: Praeger, 2004.

Crain, Caleb. *American Sympathy: Men, Friendship, and Literature in the New Nation.* New Haven, CT: Yale UP, 2001.

Delbanco, Andrew. *Melville: His World and His Work.* New York: Knopf, 2005.

Dryden, Edgar. *Melville's Thematics of Form: The Great Art of Telling the Truth.* Baltimore: Johns Hopkins UP, 1968.

Franklin, H. Bruce. "*Billy Budd* and Captial Punishment: A Tale of Three Centuries." *American Literature* 69 (1997): 337–59.

Harris, W. C. *E Pluribus Unum: Nineteenth-Century Literature and the Constitutional Paradox.* Iowa City: U of Iowa P, 2005.

Johnson, Barbara. *The Critical Difference: Essays in the Contemporary Rhetoric of Reading.* Baltimore: Johns Hopkins UP, 1980.

———. "Melville's Fist: The Execution of *Billy Budd.*" *Herman Melville: A Collection of Critical Essays.* Ed. Myra Jehlen. Englewood Cliffs, NJ: Prentice Hall, 1994. 235–48.

Lawry, Robert P. "Justice in *Billy Budd.*" *Law and Literature Perspectives.* Ed. Bruce L. Kevelson and Roberta Rockwood. New York: Peter Lang, 1996. 169–91.

Lee, Robert A., ed. *Herman Melville: Reassessments.* New York: Barnes and Noble, 1984.

Lewis, R. W. B. *The American Adam: Innocence, Tragedy and Tradition in the Nineteenth Century.* Chicago: U of Chicago P, 1955.

Martin, Robert K. *Hero, Captain, and Stranger: Male Friendship, Social Critiques and Literary Form in the Novels of Herman Melville.* Chapel Hill: U of North Carolina P, 1986.

Matthiessen, F. O. *American Renaissance: Art and Expression in the Age of Emerson and Whitman.* New York: Oxford UP, 1941.

McGlamery, Thomas. *Protest and the Body in Melville, Dos Passos, and Hurston (Literary Criticism and Cultural Theory).* New York: Routledge, 2004.

McWilliams, John P., Jr. "Innocent Criminal or Criminal Innocence: The Trial in American Fiction." *Law and American Literature: A Collection of Essays.* Ed. John McWilliams, Carl Smith, and Maxwell Bloomfield. New York: Knopf, 1983. 45–124.

Melville, Herman. *Billy Budd, Sailor (an Inside Narrative).* Eds. Harrison Hayford and Merton M. Sealts, Jr. Chicago: U of Chicago P, 1962.

Milder, Robert, ed. *Critical Essays on Melville's* Billy Budd, Sailor. Boston: G. K. Hall, 1989.

Milder, Robert. *Exiled Royalties: Melville and the Life We Imagine.* New York: Oxford UP, 2006.

Parker, Hershel. "From the Plot of *Billy Budd* and the Politics of Interpreting It." *Melville's Short Novels: Authoritative Text, Contexts, Criticisms.* Ed. Dan McCall. Norton: New York, 2002. 341–42.

———. *Herman Melville.* 2 vols. Baltimore: Johns Hopkins UP, 1996, 2002.

———. *Reading Billy Budd.* Evanston, IL: Northwestern UP, 1990.

Reuben. Paul. PAL: Chapter 3: "Herman Melville. Perspectives in American Literature—A Research and Reference Guide—An Ongoing Project." Available online. URL: http://web.csustan.edu/english/reuben/pal/chap3/melville.html. Downloaded on October 25, 2007.

Ruttenburg, Nancy. *Democratic Personality: Popular Voice and the Trial of American Authorship.* Stanford, CA: Stanford UP, 1998.

Scorza, Thomas J. "An Inside Narrative." *Melville's Short Novels: Authoritative Text, Contexts, Criticisms.* Ed. Dan McCall. Norton: New York: 2002. 371–74.

Stafford, William T. *Melville's* Billy Budd *and the Critics.* San Francisco: Wadsworth, 1961.

Sten, Christopher W. "Vere's Use of the 'Forms': Means and Ends in *Billy Budd.*" *On Melville: The Best from American Literature.* Ed. Louis J. Budd and Edwin Cady. Durham, NC: Duke UP, 1988. 188–202.

Thompson, Lawrance. *Melville's Quarrel with God.* Princeton, NJ: Princeton UP, 1952.

Vincent, Howard P. *Twentieth Century Interpretations of* Billy Budd. Englewood Cliffs, NJ: Prentice Hall, 1971.

Yanella, Donald, ed. *New Essays on "Billy Budd."* Cambridge: Cambridge UP, 2002.

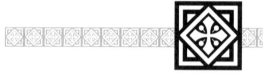

INDEX